«DAO-DE-JING-LONG-JANG»

道德經論正

THE TRUE TEACHING OF THE TIMELESS PATH OF THE HEART

The Path toward Life includes several steps of learning: On the first level you learn, but nothing comes from it, and you have a feeling that you and all others are worthless. – On the medium level you still feel worthless; you see your flaws and the flaws of the others. – On a higher level you are proud of your skills. You are lauded by the others, and complain about the inabilities of your comrades: That's when you are indeed worth something. – On the highest level however, you look as if you had no clue of what so ever.
But there is a level that still surpasses this level. This is the highest one of them all: Here you are conscious that you will never stop penetrating into The Path, and you never think you are perfect. You really know your flaws and never suppose to have attained your goal. You have no pride, but are conscious of the Path in complete humility ...
During your whole life you advance a little bit further on The Path every day, becoming more adept than the day before – more adept than today. It never ends.
(Hagakuré – The Book of the Samurai)

Lao-Dse as the ‹Blind Seer›

LAO~DSE
DAO~DE~JING
(TAO~TE~KING)
GNOSIS
IN ANCIENT CHINA

An entirely new, most faithful translation
from Chinese by M.P. Steiner,
explained on three levels of understanding
for our time

Point n'est besoin d'espérer
pour entreprendre
ni de réussir pour persévérer

EDITION ORIFLAMME
2023

Edition in English:
Lao-Dse: Dao-De-Jing (Tao-Te-King) – Gnosis in Ancient China
An entirely new, most faithful translation from Chinese by M.P. Steiner,
explained on three levels of understanding for our time. – Illustrated
Short title: Dao-De-Jing (Tao-Te-King).

Edition: in German:
Lao-Dse: Dao-De-Ging (Tao-Te-King) – Die Gnosis im Alten China:
Aus dem Chinesischen ins Deutsche gebracht, auf drei Ebenen aktuell erklärt und
mit einigen Anmerkungen versehen durch M.P. Steiner. – Illustriert.
Kurztitel: Dao-De-Ging (Tao-Te-King).
ISBN: 978-3-9523616-8-9. – © 2013 Edition Oriflamme, Basel

CIP:
Deutsche Nationalbibliothek
Central Library of Switzerland

Search terms:
Initiation, Gnosis, History of Religions
Chinese lore, Taoism, Transfiguration,

ISBN: 978-3-907103-104 – © 2023 Edition Oriflamme, Basel
edition.oriflamme@vtxmail.ch.
Produced by: Adhoc-Organisation, Basel. – Printed in Germany.

Edition Oriflamme

CONTENT

ILLUSTRATIONS

DAO AS THE EMPRESS-MOTHER WITH THE HOLY INFANT
Wall picture in the Daoist Yongle Palace (7th c.a.D.)

INTRODUCTION

DAO –Daoism as a System – is an exact spiritual science – precisely like Gnosis: a science embracing spirit, body and soul. And precisely as does Gnosis, Daoism can be considered as two interlocked halves: Firstly as the science studying the Essence of Life itself in its presence and in its attendance: This is, so to speak, *the Yin-Side* of knowledge about Dao. – Secondly, as the science of dealing with the dynamics of all its intermingling phenomena and beings: This is *the Yang-Side* and agency of Dao.

Unlike Gnosis with its almost exclusively *mystical magic*, ancient Chinese Daoism also acts through *practical magic*. However, this doesn't work like the arch-Celtic magic known in the ancient Western world: The latter was realized employing chants, conjurations and *active rituals* – often quite dramatic, and always physically performed, thus in the way of what is still known as *Wigga* : Daoism instead is a completely refined and interiorized mode of magic in the way of ancient Arian India : a way of *letting things happen through inactive concentration* – known as *«non-doing»* – or as *« doing without doing»*.

The magic tradition of the Celts (Galata, Galilee, Gaul, Galicia and so forth) relates tales about men and half-gods (e.g. Cuchullain), who from their eyes and nostrils could emit fiery flames [1], let massive rocks fly through the air, or, by means of their cry, *«flung down Pharaoh and his counsel, killing many of them»*[2]. – It also tells of women who by a word or a song – or even by a laughter – could change someone's fate. – The Magic of Dao instead consists in concentration on clarity, soberness, simplicity and meekness – and even in complete discreteness. Later chapters in the present book will explain this closer.

Dao – Daoism as a philosophy – could as well be named: the most comprehensive, deepest teaching, valid in every domain of existence throughout the world, and oriented toward *concrete practical realization in all manifestations in earthly life*: Science of state governance and warfare; – science of successful agriculture and cohabitation ; – science of healing, of high strung spirituality, and sublime spiritual achievements. – In the western world, the original Anthroposophy of Rudolf Steiner is the only philosophy comparable to pure Daoism.

The typical *gnostic philosophy*, however, is almost exclusively oriented in a mystical way. It never will mingle nor interact with worldly happenings. In fact it explicitly says that while it *stands in this world*, it does *not belong to this world.*

So, if Daoism remains oriented almost exclusively toward the physically manifested world the way the latter *is*, ‹modern›, or rather *actual Gnosis* sees itself at the turn of the new world-era, where dematerialization of the physically manifested world will be a fact, while dematerialization as part of macrocosmic evolution yet only casts forward its first lights. The individual *‹quantum leap›* of consciousness in this sense, has already begun today: Gnostic spiritual science names it the *process of purification, renewal and transformation* (*Transfiguration*). Corresponding movements in East and West all speak of a *Path*, of a *Journey* or *Pilgrimage towards the One Universal Goal or Destination*: It means unification with the All-One– the eternally unalterable Al[l]-one-Good – i.e., with God. The main criterion in order to achieve this highest of all aims is *shrinking of the Ego*: The ego-will need to step down in favor of the ‹All-Will› – while the Candidates drop their idle hustling and bustling, thus entering inner harmony where they can hear the ‹Voce of Silence›, and become aware of the divine Harmony of the Universe (despite all damages).

Now, if the beginnings of the Daoist or *‹Chinese› Gnosis* (depending of chosen criteria) goes back to the time of 1500 b.C., or even to 3000 b.C., the direct roots of actual Gnosis are at the turn of our *era of Pisces*, namely around 200 b.C. until approximately 200 a.D. This is the time when in ancient Egyptian Alexandria *Hermetism* flourished: Thence the so-called *Hermetic Tradition*, with its reference to the ‹Greek› *Hermes Trismegistos*, i.e. the Egyptian *THOT-ANUBIS (Tehuti or Djehuti)*, viz. the Babylonian *Ningishziddah*, Son of Enki, and Brother of Marduk-Re. [3]

Today, the term *Gnosis* is generally meant to signify *initiation*, viz. *self-initiation* into knowledge of the Mysteries from Antiquity until today. This is the study of all causes and effects experienced in the Universe *throughout time*: in the past, today, and at any time in the future. *Gnosis* is no academic intellectual matter, but the disclosure of awareness and consciousness through a process mentioned in many sacred scriptures as *Rebirth from Water, Spirit and Fire*, or in similar terms. Thus, if the present book uses the expressions *Dao*, *Wisdom*, and *Gnosis* as absolute equivalents, this is acceptable on the grounds of some very good reasons. – The most important differences between said terms instead have already been mentioned.

道

One of the most venerable scriptures in the spiritual evolution of Humankind is, without any doubt, the *Dao-De-Jing* –known also as *Tao-Te-King,* or *Tao-Te-Ching, Daodeging* and other names. These different transcriptions of this name already point at the basic difficulty of transferring the message of this famous Chinese ‹Classic›, or ‹Ging›, into modern languages and surroundings, ca. 2500 years after its appearance: Even this emergence itself lies hidden in the mists of several myths around the life of *Lao-Dse* (*Lao-Tse, Lao-Dzu, Lao-Tseu* and other spellings). The latter with hard consonants partially derive from Latin at the very beginning of the ‹West› exploring the vast country of China – almost a continent for itself and, at that time, culturally quite inhomogeneous as a Nation. The other descends from the Anglo-Saxon culture. The spellings with soft consonants came in use only in a more recent past, as the country, the culture and the language of China became better known in the West. The best example is ‹Peking›, today known as *Beijing* even in the most popular language – and this corresponds to actual Chinese itself.

By bibliographic reasons mainly, the present book invariably sticks to the spellings *«Lao-Dse»* and *«Dao-De-Jing».* This has the advantage also to stay closer to the *I-Jing* (today mostly named *I-Ging*, and even *Yi-Jing*). The latter is another fundamental ‹Classic› of Daoism: Published for the first time around the verge of our calendar (hence between 2066 b.C. and 220 a.D.), the *I-Jing* is the *«Book named the Classic of Transformations»*, today falsely known as *Book of Change*.[4]

Another Chinese classic is *Understanding Reality* by . Here we are confronted with Chinese Alchemy.[5] – Correspondingly, the *Dao-De-Jing* might be named *the Classic of the Path toward the Center (DAO) and toward Virtue (DE).* Even the term *DAO* has many interpretations such as *path, method, wisdom, knowledge* ... and this by right, if we consider *Gnosis* like a multilayer concept of

Lao-Dse as Philosophic Emperor (actual China)

the supra-cosmic plane of the *Godhead*, on the plane of the Universe (*macrocosms*), on the cosmic plane of *our sun system,* and lastly on the plane of each human being (*microcosmos*).[5-A] This is another reason why the Chinese *DAO* may be taken as a real equivalent to Hellenistic-Egyptian *Hermetic Gnosis*: *The latter term* surfaced approximately at the same time as *the book of I-Jing.*

But when did the *Dao-De-Jing* appear? – Of course during the lifetime of Lao-Dse (admitting him to have been a real historical person); that is – given that the *Dao-De-Jing* is valued as an *opus summæ sapientiæ* – as a *compendium of the highest wisdom* – towards the end of the latter's lifetime. However, even this time frame is doubtful: the relevant histories about the subject vary between the 6th and 4th century b.C., the 6th c. being more likely, for one of the myths indicates a definite time, mentioning the name of a historically ascertained general, while most other myths mention no name but that of *Lao-Dse.*

Thus, following these comments, *Lao-Dse* lived at the same time as *Platon* and *Buddha*, viz. as *Sokrátès*. This would imply that *Platon* – and maybe even *Buddha* – knew the Message of Lao-Dse. Voyages, pilgrimages and exchange of knowledge have always been the main activities of all Initiates in the World, from *Buddhist* missionaries in Palestine at the end of the 4th c.b.C (these leading to the gnostic movement of the *Essenes*, and thus to parts of the teachings of primitive *Christianism*) onto the *Arabian knights* and some *Christian monks* – and from there to the *Disciples of actual Gnosis* throughout the modern world.

Since the Middle-Ages, we see the worldwide presence of *itinerant scholars,* from which *itinerant preachers* differ only by their proselytism. Original texts like many of those rediscovered during our 20th c. at Qumran and Nag-Hammadi, but disqualified by The Church as ‹apocrypha›, are testimonies for such influence: ‹Gospels›, ‹Acts› and ‹Letters›, together with innumerable other hermetic scrolls and books of Greek, Syrian, Egyptian and rabbinical inspiration, more or less obviously allude to a heritage of far-Eastern Philosophies including *Daoism* and *Zen* in China, and Vedic India. From this resulted an elastic mass of teachings and traditions adapted to their original cultural and temporal environments, which in general Occultists call *Universal Tradition*, or else *Universal Doctrine*. – This ‹Universal Doctrine› is an overwhelming source of vivifying spiritual nutrition and stimulation, and is considered by all seekers of Truth as the *crown of wisdom*, into which some new gems are inserted with every era. To the established castes of priests, this always was a crown with as many thorns. Here Jesus' crown of thorns as related in the New Testament appears as the precise inversion of this image, apt to inspire the most profound contemplations.

Together with said influences from the near, the middle and far East, the *Dao-De-Jing* thus is an integral part of the wide spread roots of western spirituality – the *western Gnosis*. On the other hand, far-East traditions annexed many influences from the migrations of Celtic tribes, or from western pilgrims. Between the two stands the high culture of *Druidism*, but which has been annihilated almost completely by the Romans under Caius Julius Cæsar. The intense cultural exchange between spiritual strains world-wide were then fomented along the *Silk Street*, through the *crusades*, through the persecutions of Jews in Europe, et cetera.

道

A glance upon the *history of Ancient China* lets emerge from the prehistoric mists, and unfold before our eyes, the *Shang-Dynasty* (1765-1123 b.C.). In the latter's second half we see the

evolution of the Chinese ‹writing›. Divulgation of writing outside oft the temples however always was at the peril of oral tradition. Moreover, *written formulation* of history (myths) and maxims (*doctrines*) has ever lead to their *formalization and formatting* – and from there again to concurring, and often hostile, *dogmata* with their adherents and adversaries, along with the leaders of both, and with their well-known wrangles and blood-shed, where the *homo sapiens often* proves to be a *homo rudens ruens* – more ruthless and more ferocious indeed than any beast: No beast would force its opinion upon a whole pack, or even onto an entire race of other beasts by killing them (!); – or even to use *mass-killing (‹genocide›) as a means to achieve uniformity of teachings and opinions*: «*He calls it reason , yet uses it only to be more beastly than any beast! ...*», as says Mephistopheles in Gœthe's *Doctor Faustus*. —

‹*Written communication*› always means *pictorial communication*. That's why writing systems and symbolism always are closely linked. This is particularly well demonstrated by Chinese glyphs and Celtic runes along with Egyptian, Persian and Maya hieroglyphs, some symbols being similar or identical in all cultures of the World and throughout time – particularly regarding the Sun.

As soon as the use of writing is spread generally, there quite naturally so-called ‹erudition› leaves the temples and palaces of the privileged casts – thus reaching the surrounding populace. And this again leads to intermingling, viz. profanation, of teachings and systems: From divination in the frame of offering rituals (holocausts and hieroscopy) – in China preferably by prophesy over bones – emerged the less onerous methods using cards, bamboo sticks, pebbles, yarrow stalks, or ashes, wind, water, earth fire and stars.

Magic formulæ used by priests became prayers, then folk songs and magic again (en-chant-ments). – That's how the wheel of knowledge, beliefs and superstitions is kept whirling round and round, time and again – with all the well-known consequences.

There is an outstanding linguistic curiosity for Chinese: The pronunciation of given signs differs from one Chinese ethnic group to the other – depending on where an individual is dwelling. From this ensues that two Chinese from different provinces may have difficulties to understand each other speaking, and thus need to communicate by writing, as Chinese writing has been fixed interculturally by the State around 200 b.C. and has remained the same ever since. Therefore, its *images (pictoglyphs) are concepts*.

A critical reader may see therein a twofold instrument of stately power: This difference between languages and standardization of writing corresponds to the well-known principle *divide et impera – divide and rule* – of all centralistic and imperialistic power systems all over the World.

One tool among others in order to standardize, and thus dominate and manipulate not just writing, but also expressions in the frame of culture, science, world views – and other human soul-expression that ensues from them – was the system of *Confucianism* dominating cultural China – and this during centuries. Its representatives were in charge, among other, for the normative codification of all philo-

Tierisches Schädeldach als Wahrsage-Knochen.

sophical writings. From this, under the Manju-Reign resulted a *‹Canon of the most important writings›* – then named *Wei-De-Tang-Wu-Żung* – that is: *«Five different scriptures, out of the hall ‹Nothing but Virtue› »*. During the 15th century, this codex appeared as *Dao-Dsang-Dsi-Yao*. During the 70-ies of the 20th century, the same canon was printed anew. It contains five *Gings, or Jings,* i.e. *five Classics*: The *Dao-De-Jing*, the *I-Ging* or *Yi-Ging*, the *Sing-Ming-Xuang-Xiu-Hui-Ming-Jing*, i.e. *the Classic of orientation toward consciousness and Life*; – the *Tai-I-Żin-Hua-Dsung-Ji* (i.e. *The Principle of the golden Flower of the Great One* – since the edition by R. Wilhelm and C.G. Jung known as *The Secret of the Golden Flower*[6]) – and, fifth, *the Classic of the Eight Wise Men – Huainan-Dse Jing.*

The *Hui-Min-Jing* is ascribed to one *Liu-Ha-Yang*; the *Secret of the Golden Flower* on the other hand, to the excellent Daoist *Lü-Yen* (born. 755 b.C.), known as well by his surname *Lü-Dung-Bin* – i.e. ‹*Cave-Guest*›, or as *Lü-Dse* (i.e. *Master Lü*). The latter was one of the «*Eight Saints*», and the founder of the Daoist *esoteric Secret Society of the Golden Elixir of Life – Gin-Dan-Giau.* – This occurred around 800 a. D.

Lü-Yen – says R. Wilhelm – dated his teachings (which are said to be a reform of the traditional, but at that time degenerated, Confucianistic Daoism), back to Master *Guan Yin Hi* – the very person for whom, as one of several myths declares, Lao-Dse wrote down his *Dao-De-Jing* – hence, way back before *Lao-Dse*'s accredited ‹successor› – Master *Żuang-Dse*.[7]

The first printed editions of these teachings of wisdom were issued not earlier than our 16th century. – However, before as well as after that, and even until to-date, many commentaries were written by numerous philosophers, in order to elucidate this codex of the mentioned five sacred scriptures ordained by the State. – One of the greatest authors in this sense was *Wang-Bi*, the *‹Prodigious Infant›*: During his short life (226-249 a.D.) he authored a commentary to the *I-Jing* as well as to the *Dao-De-Jing*, and also a ‹condensed introduction› to the book *Zhou-Yi* – a complementary work to the *I-Ging*. His opus became *the* reference endorsed by all spiritual positions throughout China – not just in his time, but also during many centuries to follow, and even up-today. His textual version of the *Dao-De-Jing* is one among the three we have used for the present, *completely new and independent* translation from Chinese. Wang-Bi opposed the strongly established Confucianistic ‹School› of the *Han-Dynasty* (206 b.C. -220 a.D). – From 618 to 906 the empire underwent a new period of turmoil, which was soothed only during the Song-Dynasty (960-1279), with the help of *Neo-Confucianism*, the latter being closer to Daoism. This occurred again in favor of uniform culture as ordained by the State.

At the turn of the 18th c., Emperor *Kang-Xi* (Qing-Dynasty, 1644 - 1911) demanded another standardization of the mentioned principal texts, and had them printed in the Palace of Bei-Jing, together with neo-Confucianistic commentaries. Clearly, this standardization served the form, and not its *content.* Never the less, it is reported that this 1715 print of the *Dao-De-Jing* very faithfully reproduced its oldest known manuscript found in a tomb of 138 b.C. (Wilhelm).

Looked at it with respect to the spiritual surroundings of the time, the *Dao-De-Jing* in the form as we know it today, is not just a ‹Chinese sacred scripture›, but the syncretistic result from all influences it took between 800 b.C. and ca. 900 b.C. It is mainly characterized by original Daoism, but also leans toward other oriental religions of the time: Buddhism, Sufism, with in-between Nestorianism and Maniism, then gnostic tradition with its Hellenistic, Egyptian, Syrian, rabbinic tints, come from the West at that time, including so-called *Hermetism*. And it is important to know that all these systems – each and everyone – contain the tradition of operative Alchemy, with their symbolisms being absolutely compatible or even identical. In mystic Daoism, this was of course mystified in the same way as in mystic Christianism. The allegories of ‹Earth›, ‹Water›, ‹Air›, ‹Fire› and ‹Ether› for example are common to all – although with some individual traits.

Even the *Scala Philosophorum* of western Alchemists has got its place in the pictoglyph for *Dao* (as a combination of *head*, *Path* and *foot*). This sign is interpreted also as *consciousness, Path* (or *stair*), and as *to go, process, cycle*, a.s.f. – One can see there also the relations of Microcosmos (*siao-tien-di – small Universe*), Cosmos (*tien-di – Heaven and Earth*) and Macrocosmos (*tien-di-ji-hsing – the Law after which Heaven and Earth live*), expressed by means of the notions *‹course›* (of Man) and *‹trajectory›* (of the fixed stars' constellations), as they are indicated in verse 47 of the *Dao-De-Jing*. The condition for ultimate unification of all contraries then is *Dao*

道

– or *Tai-Ji*, the *‹One without a second one›*, from which continuously issues the pair of *Yin-Yang* as well as all the inseparable pairs of contraries: *active and passive, dark and light*; *planning versus formation*; *potent secretion versus fertile adsorption,* etc. –These contraries, or *Duals* generate all dynamics of the Universe; and only thanks to them the World can subsist and prosper. – The Jungian interpretation here sees *Animus* and *Anima.* According to this, a human being *at the moment of its conception* divides itself into *Being and Life* (*Essence* and *Dynamics*) – into *Ming* and *Sing.* Between them there stands *Sin*, the *‹Heart›* as an emotional center of consciousness.

Sing (*‹Animus›*), says Wilhelm, tends towards the *Logos*, and is the portion that in the afterlife beyond, after the decomposition of the microcosm – viz. in the next prenatal state – exists as *a supra-conscious state* of each spiritual entity and as a ‹spiritual factor›. At the spermatic union to produce a form of manifestation, Sing mates intimately with *Ming* (the ‹animal factor› – *‹Anima›*). The latter determines its being-human: that is its *individual fate* and its *supra-personal, heavenly destiny* or ‹Inner Law› (Karma or collective soul), that, following Wilhelm's view, is considered in Daoism as a *quirk.*

Ming, the ‹dull will› that, sparked by passions, drives man to *gush forth his vital forces,* is conceived as *sinking* or *falling*; *Sing* as *rising*. Thereby, the *Ego gets* into a floating status, where it is coaxed to make a choice: If it decides to gush forth its vital force, it will fall toward death. If instead it achieves to spiritualize its vital forces, so that those – through an ‹inner rotation of the Monad – are able to build up a stable, independent life-cycle (remember ‹circulation› in the Athanor) – then a *rising* movement is initiated, whereby the Ego can alight from being mixed up with the ‹10'000 things› of the World, and thus after the physical death of the person remains alive and effective. Such Entities are the sacred spiritual helpers and inspirators of humanity from the Beyond – high *‹spirits›* that in Chinese are named *‹Shen›* – a *god.* It is quite possible that the Arabian *Djinni* is derived from this expression, giving in Latin (that knows no «sh») the western *Genius* …

These genii however are still perishable personalities, and thus doomed at some point, like Heaven and Earth. The only perfectly immutable thing in the World is the *Golden Flower*, fully unfolded as a consequence of the complete liberation of the human personality from all things, persons and worlds. This is the *Golden*

Gung-Fu-Dse («Confucius»), 551-479 b.C.

Flower of ancient Daoism – the *Golden Rose* of today's *Order of the Golden Rosicross.* Such an Ego is not limited to the monad anymore: it breaks through the Universe of dichotomies, uniting with the *‹One without another›* – with *Dao.*

Now, if in *Buddhism* this unification signifies complete extinction oft the Ego (the latter as such being an illusion), in *Daoism* there remains a transfigured ego-substance as an essence of individual consciousness (Wilhelm names it «the idea behind the person»). The latter enters the *memory of the Universe*: This is the *«Light that returns to itself»*: *«ming»* also means: *to shine.* [7-A]

The course in between consists in a human life *partially directed ‹upwards›*, where-after the ‹Ego› (understood the western way) enters a phase of astral purification, where (understood the Daoist way) as a blessed spirit – a retiring Demon (Chinese *‹Gui›*) – it harvests the fruits of its good and evil deeds during its past lifetime. This however is but a powerless shadow with no ‹destiny› nor impact, able to stay in this intermediate sphere only as long as the offerings of its survivors – family, subjects, believers etc. – nourish it (see picture on p. 235. At the same time, it builds up the ‹psychic› provisions with which – after passing another maternal womb – it will commence a next physical life cycle. Whoever knows the *Universal Doctrine* will recognize the parallels.

Unlike the markedly intellectual mystic and *dogmatically stringent Western teaching* about the same item, the *Chinese concept* and its method stay much closer to physical experience and its *Inner Magic*, inasmuch as here abstract elements are not explicitly mentioned. Rather, imaginative analogies touch the supra-personal unconscious like the string of a violin, inviting it to resonate the way this corresponds to the pictorial consciousness oft Antiquity and the ancient Chinese World. The key for the Westerner to understand this train of thought is *childlike pictorial empathy.* The same goes for Chinese scripture as a means of *communication independent of spoken language* (see above) – and this also is what made possible our present translation directly from Chinese *writing.*

道

It is on the basis of this insight into the ‹Chinese soul› that we undertook the present translation of the *Dao-De-Jing* directly from Chinese, and its commentaries in a gnostic spirit, – but only after *meticulous in-depth analysis – i.e.*: committed to most faithful translation, avoiding every possible modern and western interpolation, insinuation or comment: 1° to bring the text into relation to the sociocultural frame at the time when the *Dao-De-Jing* was authored; 2° to know the philosophical era of that time; and 3° to understand the concept of the inner Path of Humankind through the millennia – but especially since the turn of the last past century – in other terms: with human necessities at the present turn from one era to the next – the second one since the emergence of the original *Dao-De-Jing*. – Our translations throughout the present book therefore had to meet three severe fundamental criteria in order to satisfy its claim for *textual and spiritual authority*:

1° The whole text of a ‹paragraph›, or ‹chapter›, must be in inner harmony, i.e.: it may not (except for the *‹Daoist parádoxon›*) contradict itself: Eventually apparent ambiguities must be in cognitive harmony with the ‹thread› of the whole. Earlier versions in all languages often contradict themselves in inconceivable ways – occasionally even in one and the same line!

2° Every ‹verse›, or ‹number›, must convey a fundamental thought, a basic mood, a main message – or all three of these.

3° Every paragraph must – besides a worldly human claim every serious ruler can satisfy – suggest an esoteric meaning, relevant and practicable on the Path of Initiation to DAO (the title, *Dao-De-Jing* itself clearly emphasizes exactly this claim).

In order to satisfy in the best possible way these three levels of understanding, a great number of western ‹translations› were studied: The German versions of one ‹Anonymus› (2005); then the famous versions by publicly accredited ‹experts› like Werner Classen (1945); O. Sumitomo (no date); Hans Knospe and Odette Brändli (1985); Asgard Gerstner (2001); Rudolf Backofen (1949); Gia-Fu Feng & Jane English (ed. in German by U. Lütjohann) ; Vincenz Hundhausen (1942) ; Bodo Kirchner (2000) ; Ernst Schwarz (1978) ; Richard Wilhelm (1911) ; – the certainly most competent French version by Stanislas Julien (no date); – the Italian version by Luciano Parinetto (1995); – the Spanish versions by Antonio Rivas (no date) and ‹Ratmachine› (no date) ; – the Dutch version by John Wilemsens (1990 /1992, ed. J.L.L. Duyvendak). – English versions by R.B. Blakney, Stephen Mitchell, Brian B. Walker, Sam Torode & Dwight Goddard, Jonathan Star, Chu Ta-Kao, Ursula K. Le Guin,

Thomas Cleary, Victor H. Mair, Gia-Fu Feng & Jane English (English); and finally: Addiss, Lombardo & Watso; Man-Ho Kwok & Martin Palmer. – All of them proved to be unsatisfactory!

All together, thus, the extensive amount of 30 western versions in 6 languages were examined. So, it soon became clear that only a self provided translation on the basis of three authentic Chinese texts – among them the one by *Wang-Bi*, see above – could satisfy mentioned strict conditions – and were made possible thanks to electronic translation machines on ‹Google›, ‹Babylon›, and the MDBG Chinese-English Dictionary – plus thanks to many, many Chinese interpretations available on Internet.[8]

Thus translated, most of Lao-Dse's texts appeared in a most different new light, and many in stark disagreement among each other, including the most famous translations by earlier authors. The footnotes to the texts explain many of these differences, and even indicate other possible variants. But basically, the present new translation faithfully reflects – pictoglyph after pictoglyph – the respective original. It is quite natural instead, that out of an often great number of possibilities, the most plausible variant with regard to history, folk-lore, spirituality, etc. has been chosen *subjectively*.

Intense studies of the Path of Gnosis through the millennia, plus some personal experience of the present author on this same Path, may legitimate our courage and perseverance to dare and undertake these translations and commentaries. How closely the result of our work reflects the endeavour and said high prerequisites of the editor – how far from them it remains and must remain because of the incompatibility of the two Worlds and the two Natures, a benevolent number of readers shall have to decide..

道

The present book is the translation of the *Dao-De-Ging* from Chinese into German, forwarded *by the same hand* from German into English, bringing for the first time all 81 Verses, or Numbers, in a truly faithful translation and with in-depth commentaries – practical, moral, and esoteric. Due to the history of this exploit, the ‹Verses› 1-33 provide just a few footnotes relative to the text and for their interpretation. Some relate to later chapters: A book entitled *Chinese Gnosis*, with esoteric comments to Verses 1 to 33, appeared already in the year of 1980. Its author, *Jan van Rijckenborgh*, and the final editor after the latter's decease, *Catharose de* Petri, both became famous because at the beginning of the 21st c. they revived the classic Gnostic tradition throughout Europe, and subsequently throughout the World. *The Rosicrucian movement* ensuing from this – *the Mystery-school of the Golden Rosicross* – represents the decisive step to elevate the strongly Indish oriented *Theosophy of H.P. Blavatsky* with its Masonic strains, out of the exclusivity of small circles and lodges, and to propagate it throughout the World. It goes without saying: This pan-human movement was founded on the basis of previous Fraternities like the *Cathars* of the 11th to 14th c., and the *classic Rosicrucians* of the 17th and 18th centuries – but also upon some very old heritage, same as the prime *Anthroposophy* of the great Rosicrucian, *Dr. Rudolf Steiner*, but whose Rosicrucian Initiative was not taken up by his spiritual disciples.

The present book continues to revive the same effort in a form adapted to our present time – but *in the service of the same ideation* – using the same successful ‹formula›, but this time – at the beginning of a new world period – aiming at both general public and Initiates. It is conceived so as to open *an unpretentious entry to the Dao-De-Jing for all readers of today* – and at the same time offers *an insight to the principles and views of actual Gnosis*.[8-A]

At any rate, the present work cannot, and wishes not to be, conclusive in any way: Rather it wishes to drill new openings into partly crystallized opinions formed during the past 19th and 20th c. by a combination of self-content of the intellect with mystical dreams and magical insecurity of the soul. – For, in this domain, there is nothing stable or fix for us humans: All is floating, including the immobile One that eternally keeps changing – and which in its continuous motion always reposes in it self: ‹Brahma› – ‹Dao› – ‹Gnosis›; – Light, Truth and Life!

Our thanks go to the young Chinese scholar, Ms. Dr. *Tao Wang*, who approved of our translation, by the by contributing some useful suggestions, which have now been integrated into the present amended and enlarged edition.

The commentaries shed a light not only upon purely spiritual aspects, but also upon some parallels and interactions between a serious gnostic *Quest*, the stormy sea of actual world history of today, and the cultural history of Ancient China. Therefore, the present edition of the *Dao-De-Jing* addresses itself also to such people as don't aspire to follow a genuine *spiritual Path* as such, but are just willing to enjoy the often *poetic beauty* of this unique collection of texts, and to read an actual but undogmatic interpretation to them, easy to understand and to accept. – May all readers find here what they are seeking: for – that is our most intimate wish!

The esoteric commentaries to ‹Verses› 34 through 37 of *Part I – DAO-GING* – form like a bridge to the semantic world of the book – another reason to open its *Part II – DE-GING* – with its Verses 38 through 81, with another (authentic!) sub-title leaf.

Our whole book would like – as does the *Dao-De-Jing* itself – animate *three stages at a time*: A first, moral and ethic level for everyday's life of everybody; a second level regarding the ‹high virtues› of a father or a ruler (DE) – and a third, top-level, dedicated to the true aim, the essential objective and *inner destination of all life*: the *Sacred Marriage* between the *solitary* ones (humans of this World) with the *‹One without an Other› the Al(-l-)one-Good*, the *All-in-All*: This is the marriage of the perishable human-born soul under the stigma of the Nature of Death, with the *‹fundamentally Other› – New Heavenly Man himself.*

The inconceivable beauty of this prospect is indicated by the hopeful verse taken from the *Hui-Min- Ging*:

Clouds vanish into cerulean Space —
the mountains blazingly shine.
Conscience into free vision melts —
the Moon's disk lonely lounges ...

小人而大心 *

* *«Trifle is Man, yet great is his determination»*

PART I:

«DAO-JING»

道 經

THE INALTERABLE PATH

Plausible translation of the red line:

Of The Famous Golden Verses, of The Blossoms Of Inner Teachings, The First Part.[*]

錦繡中華之一頁

第一章

道可道，非常道。名可名，非常名。
無名天地之始；有名萬物之母。
故常無，欲以觀其妙；常有，欲以觀其徼。
此兩者，同出而異名，同謂之玄。玄之又玄，眾妙之門。

[*] Translated precisely, the first *two glyphs together* mean *famous, glorious, and wonderful*. – Each read as a single one, means: *golden, magnificent*, resp. *broideries, ornaments.* – The second pair of glyphs, one by one, means: *Inner teaching, conveying*, resp. *superb, flowery*.

Combined instead they signify, since millennia, *China* (the Empire of the Middle). The three last glyphs may be read as: *Their one, or first, part [of (the) two, Dao-Ging* and *De-Ging]*. In combination this gives (for the justification of this lecture, see later examples): *The famous gold-broideries of esoteric teachings of China, first part.* Our version here means to allude to the *Golden Verses of Pythagoras,* the latter maybe having lived as a contemporary to *Lao-Dse*.

01.

DAO as a Path one can follow
is not the eternal DAO. —*
No name we might find
will ever be the name of the Eternal One. —

No name has the origin of Heaven and Earth —
The existing name means the Mother of the 10'000 things.

Therefore:
Few are those longing to see IT's wonders —
Many are those who study IT's outside —**

Thus there are the two kinds:
Similar are the motivations of both, and the secretive name —
Similarly they invoke the Mysteries:
Mysterious, very secret and manifold wondrous are their entrances.

* As *solitary glyphs*, the two 非常 could be read as: *is not the eternal way* or *path.* – This would be wrong in reality; for, *this is*, as taught since ‹eternal times›, the ‹sempiternal› way. As *a pair of* glyphs, 非常 means: *extraordinary, immeasurable, infinite, immense, enormous, inconceivable, extremely precious.* – For a simple lecture thus: *an unspeakable way.* – The very few who follow this Way, or Path, with all its consequences, experience how *unspeakable* this voyage really is. The entire *Dao-De-Ging* is about sidestepping the impossibility of articulating, the heavenly nature and practical reality of DAO, which in fact *it both is as well.* Understood in this truly esoteric sense, the *Path of DAO* can be glossed the same way as the Path of operative Alchemy: *«Out of 1000, hardly one has brought IT to its blissful End».* –

Correspondingly read as a ‹ combined version›, the *name one can pronounce – DAO – « ... is not really the name of the Absolute»*: A name is but a sign – is just a symbol. – Unspeakable content is everything!

The more rudimentary the texts of the *Dao-De-Ging* appear, the more layers of significance they reveal (or unveil) – and the larger are *freedom and dilemma* of the reader seeking for *his own* «true» inner significance: So even the modern Chinese versions differ – sometimes even dramatically. A definitely correct understanding is possible neither here nor elsewhere. At most, one can exclude what yields no sensible message – what obviously violates the intent oft the text, or, finally, what is completely at odds with the usages in China at the time of *Lao-Dse*, as emphasized for some examples in later chapters. This *play with glyphs – sign-language* as a play with *pictoglyphs* – is typical throughout the entire *Dao-De-Ging.*

第二章

天下皆知美之為美，斯惡已。皆知善之為善，斯不善已。
有無相生，難易相成，長短相形，高下相傾，音聲相和，前后相隨。
是以聖人處無為之事，行不言之教；萬物作而弗始，
生而弗有，為而弗恃，功成而不居。夫唯弗居，是以不去。

02.

This is common knowledge: Good follows Good,
as long as Evil is suspended.
Everybody knows: propriety follows propriety,
as long as decency does not cease.

Thence follows : [*]
The reality of opposed pairs emerges:
Problems and success alternate —
Wealth and Scarcity appear in turns —
Excellence and lowness chase each other —
Harmony and noise are intertwined —
Earlier and later prevail over each other.

That's the way it goes, unendingly. [**]

The true Initiate choses non-doing as his goal
and applies non-talking as his schooling.
All the 10'000 things attack him – but he does not give up.
Evolving, not being —
Acting, but relying on nothing —
Achieving great deeds, but not resting —
Lonesome as a human, and without a home —
Doing what is right, unceasingly.

[*] All *parts in blue* throughout this book are taken from the text of *Wang-Bi.*

[**] All *parts in red* throughout this book come from a third original text version by an unknown source (see comments beginning with N° 34).

第三章

不尚賢，使民不爭；不貴難得之貨，使民不為盜；不見可欲
使民心不亂。
是以聖人之治，虛其心，實其腹，弱其志，強其骨。常使民
知無欲。使夫智者不敢為也。為無為，則無不治。

03.

[Bestow] no awards for high performance,
so people won't fight for them.
[Show] no precious goods hard to attain,
so people won't be thieves.
Indulge in fewer cravings,
*so the masses won't plot any upheaval**
The truly wise [ruler] rules like this:
Void [of cravings and arguments] is his heart —
Full [of frugality] is his belly.
Subdued is his will —
Forceful are his intent, spirit and soul. **

*Always he endeavors to keep the People ignorant and disinterested —****
He achieves that humans are sensible subjects,
not daring to do too much.

Acting through non-doing, he rules without any calamity.

* By *people*, or *masses*, the esoteric meaning must always be understood to be *parts or all of the Candidate's own personality* (see commentary in later chapters, from N° 34 on).

** The *polyvalence* of Chinese ideograms like 心 – *heart*, and 志 – *will, aspiration, craving* (containing the glyph for heart), can be translated on our side only by *several expressions in parallel* (see commentary in later chapters, from N° 34 on).

*** Compare text N° 65 and commentary.

※ … meaning: without being overthrown or assassinated.

第四章

道沖，而用之或不盈。淵兮，似萬物之宗；挫其銳，解其紛

和其光，同其塵。湛兮，似或存。吾不知誰之子，象帝之先

04.

Dao is an Ocean nobody can ever drink out.
Oh you Unfathomable One!
The 10'000 things are allegories after your example! *
To overcome ones fierceness —
To clarify ones confusion —
To harmonize ones lights —
To become one with ones dust — **

Oh Deepness! *** ***– That anything like this really can exist!***

* Both creations as a whole and every creature they contain are images and metaphors of the Arch-Mother who birthed them – DAO. This corresponds to the statement by the *Corpus Hermeticum*: *«As are the small things, so are the big ones»*. – Universes, ‹milky way systems› (macrocosms), solar systems (Cosmoi), each creature (microcosms) and every tiny cell down to the atom correspond to each other – despite their different individual natures – on the fundamental basis of the common, universal, and entirely spiritual energy of Divine Love that drives everything – compare the ‹Platonic Bodies› and their being built up from one common primary element – the *tetrahedron* that in turn corresponds to the *Pythagorean Tetraktys* …

** These four lines are identical on the dot with those in the second paragraph of N° 56. (see there, and the in-depth commentary thereto).

*** The Valentinian Gnostics as well named the primitive, fundamental origin, from which all and everything originates (Bœhme's ‹Ungrund›), *«the Depth»* (and *«Silence»* among other) – and maybe even invoked it so. – Modern Physics calls this *space-time energy*.

第五章

天地不仁，以萬物為芻狗；聖人不仁，以百姓為芻狗。
天地之間，其猶橐籥乎？虛而不屈，動而愈出。
多言數窮，不如守中。

05.

Heaven and Earth are of unmoved severity —
To them, the 10'000 things are like straw-dogs.
Wise men are of unmoved severity —
To them even the 100 families are like straw-dogs*

The space between Heaven and Earth – is it not like a bagpipe?**
[Nothing but] emptiness, and immobility —
[But] move (play) it, and it becomes increasingly expressive.***

Loquacity, says a proverb, is promptly at an end —
Better indeed is the moderacy of discretion.

* Sacrificial dogs made of straw. – For an explanation of this, see comment to N° 71. – The literally *‹100 names›* here probably mean the noble families – as opposed to ordinary ‹10'000 things› of any sort.

** Glyph by glyph: ... *they/ correspond / bag / flute / interrogative particle* 乎. – The interpretation as *bellows* (as writes another translator) is logically unfounded in every respect, and stands in no relation to the respective glyphs: 橐籥.

The bag-pipe instead is a ‹literal translation›. – Bag-pipes are mentioned already in the Old Testament (Daniel 3:5, 10 and 15, in connection with Nebuchadnezzar). Moreover, there were bag-pipes found in Nineveh and Assyria; and also in archeological sites of Ancient Egypt, where they were dated back to the time of 1500 b.C. In Ancient India and China, the tradition of bag-pipes was traced back even until almost 2600 b.C.!

*** This ‹verse› is apparently built up on a play with the words *moved* and *unmoved, or motionless* – as well as with *reservation* and *expressivity*. Instead of *unmoved* in the sense of unyielding one might as well speak about *inner force* – as the yet *unmoved* bag-pipe contains (as *inner force* and potential *expressivity*) all sounds that one might produce by moving it – i.e. playing it. – Thus also the transition of the text to *loquacity* and reservation becomes quite understandable as a metaphor.

第六章

谷神不死，是謂玄牝。玄牝之門，是謂天地根。綿綿若存
用之不勤。

06.

What lies below is divine and everlasting — [*]
it is a feminine Mystery.
Mysteriously feminine is its aperture. — [**]
Indeed, Heaven and Earth are named the prime fountain:
They seem to last eternally —
Their survival is not to be feared for. [***]

[*] Literally also: *the valley, the lowlands, the deeply divine* – as such to be understood like in N° 66. But we also may understand, like in the *Tabula Smaragdina*: *what is above and what is below* – or Yang and Yin. The same can be understood from the rest of this text. The significance of the whole ‹verse› can rather just be assumed than truly translated.

[**] Variant: *By right one names the Mystery a female. – [For,] mysterious is the woman's abdomen.* A *Great Mystery is* DAO; – from DAO, the Arch-Mother, come forth the ‹10'000 things›, i.e. all creatures. The woman as well (as a metaphor for DAO) is – as a mother – *«the big one like the small one»* of the *Tabula Smaragdina.* Here is the link between this line and the first and fourth lines of this text.

[***] Equally well one can read: *«Their utility [however] is not continuous …»* – This is to be understood in view of alternative periodical flooding and scorching of both hemispheres, with the subsequent inhospitability (the ‹stone age› of the ‹Golden Age). The Westerner is amazed by this obvious contradiction in one and the same glyph 勤 – a typical *«Taoist paradoxon».*

第七章

天長地久。天地所以能長且久者，以其不自生，故能長生
是以聖人后其身而身先；外其身而身存。非以其無私邪？
故能成其私。

07.

***Heavenly things are eternal, earthly things are long-lasting* (久).**
Therefore, the Universe is capable to prosper eternally,
now and forever: —
Same as it never emerged, [*]
it is capable also to last forever. (久)
The true sage lives like this:
He puts his* 身 *behind – and yet his* 身 *stands in the first place —
***he lets go of his* 身, *and so he will preserve his* 身.** [**]
Does not his impersonal detachment cause damage? [‡]
[No —]
That's why he is able to reach perfection, personally. [※]

[*] One modern Chinese interpreter formulates (here transferred into readable English): *«Because (if, in case, as) they (Heaven and Earth) don't worry about their own survival, nor about the natural course of things».*

[**] If the precedent N° contained a pun with words, the present one makes its puns with the glyph 身 (*shēn*) with its many significations: *«conditions of living, duration of life, life, person, body, corps, place, grade, position, status, main-thing*, etc. – Equivalent expressions for *«and yet»*, are *«and so»*, and *«at the same time»*. – A typical case of Chinese polyvalence …

All this gives, e.g., *«if he sets behind the duration of his life, he will live long»;« if he lets go of his status, his post will be assured for him»*. – Or, as the Gospel says: *«The last ones will be the first ones ... »* (Mt 20:16) – and: *«He who loves his present life shall lose it, and he who hates his life in this world, shall beware it into eternal life … »* (Jo 12:25). —

[‡] In two original versions used for the present book, this same line ends with the interrogative particle (‹question mark›) 乎, meaning the unarticulated answer: *«No»*). —

In *Wang-Bi*'s text, the same line ends with an exclamation mark. – Hence, (because oft the polyvalence of the glyph 邪, which also may be translated as *«absurdity», «irrationality», «disgrace», «evil»*, etc.) we get: *«Never his unselfishness* (or *his impersonal attitude*) *will cause any evil!»*

[※] A variant just as valid would be: ... *to transform his innermost core.*

第八章

上善若水。水善利萬物而不爭，處眾人之所惡，故几于道。
居善地，心善淵，與善仁，言善信，政善治，事善能，動善時
夫唯不爭，故無尤。

08.

An excellent ruler likens a stream:
A peaceful river transports innumerous things and living beings —
and this without a fight.*
If he acts so that the People hates him —
what will be his profit with regard to DAO?**
If instead he kindly cares fort his land —
if his demeanor is sincerely benevolent and virtuous —
if his speech is well put and trustworthy —
if he is a just and proficient ruler —
then he is well suited for his task,
and he will use his time in office flawlessly.***
A person only needs not to quarrel —
in order to encounter no incidents.※

* The glyph 爭 stands for whatever is connected to forced will: *fighting, arguing, railing, bump against obstacles* – as opposed to *well measured adaptability* (‹softness of water); – see also later chapters.

** *Wang-Bi* writes without a ‹question mark›: *« ... then this is hardly in harmony with DAO ».*

*** The same pictoglyphs also allow for the following reading (as opposed to the second line of the second paragraph): *«Thus he uses well his time* (the lapse of time given to him). – The meaning: Only a ruler striving for DAO is a good ruler; – only the time used with regard to one's aspiration towards DAO, is lifetime well used.

※ This glyph rendered exactly means: *nothing odd.* In later chapters, the expression *odd things* always appears in the sense of agitations, revolts and (mostly bloody) crime.– With respect to Daoist strategy and tactics following SUN-DSE, the term means *‹formlessness›* and *‹invisibility›* – see commentaries to chapters 36, 40, 49, 68, and others). We also might read: *one single man who does not fight, attracts no attention.* – Or, finally, see N° 22.

第九章

持而盈之，不如其已；揣而銳之，不可長保。
金玉滿堂，莫之能守；富貴而驕，自遺其咎。
功遂身退，天之道。

09.

Stockpiling of what you already have plenty —
this does not suit you.
To guess around where resoluteness is demanded —
such a one is not [even] fit to command a detail of guardians.*
Gold and precious stones careless at home —
Nothing and no-one can protect such a one.**
Rich, noble, and at the same time arrogant —
without effort one looses this vice !***
Who accomplishes great deeds and then withdraws — ⊗
To Heaven his trail will lead!‡

* The nouns used here by previous translators, like bow, vessel, sword etc. don't exist in any text known to us. Also, there is no question of bad habits here, but of fundamental flaws, as opposed to bravery and to the Path of DAO, which is not even mentioned explicitly, but only hinted at in the last glyph: The *profoundest meaning* of these texts is never found at their surface, and almost always relates to a ruler, and to conditions in China during the 5th c.b.C.

** The glyph 之 can mean *him*, the owner, and also *them*, the treasures; in the *mentality* of Chinese writing: *them* – both of them.

*** Another precise version would be: *surely* – or *certainly* – *such flaws* – or *this shame* – *will be lost*, or *abandoned* ...

⊗ One might as well say: « ... *and refuse a place of honor* (or *a pension for life*) ...». At any rate, this is about virtue, true nobleness, and modesty, as opposed to carelessness and plain ambition. Earlier translations render but three of the four glyphs of the same sequence.

‡ The glyph 天 can mean Heaven, God and Emperor (on different planes at the same time): Such a one is (contrary to line 3) *capable to be Emperor* – or, so to speak, *is already* an Emperor, like the one in the *Chymical Wedding of Christian Rosencreutz.*

第十章

載營魄抱一，能無離乎？
專氣致柔，能如嬰兒乎？
滌除玄鑒，能如疵乎？
愛國治民，能無為乎？
天門開闔，能為雌乎？
明白四達，能無知乎？
生之，畜之，
生而不有；為而不恃；
長而不宰，是謂玄德。

10.

[He who] commands an army, directing his heart toward the One —
can he really allow himself to disregard separation?*
[Who] feels how the Prana of Life tenderly expands —**
can [he] really behave like a little boy?
[Who] controls extirpation of filth and secrecies —
Is [he] really allowed to overlook any flaws?
[Who] rules the People with love for the land of his ancestors —
is [he] really allowed to go idle?
The human who opens and closes the doors of Heaven —
may[he] really behave playfully like a little girl?
[Who] has clearly understood the four main subjects —
may [he] really neglect his knowledge?***
[Be he] highly erudite, or a peasant:
When he was born, he neither had nor was anything —
He makes experiences, but does not rely on them —
[He] grows learning, but never dominates anything —

By right DE is named a Mystery.

* The kernel of this series of rhetorical questions is the repeated 能 … 乎 – (*can/may he/one really ...?*). The whole thing thus is about consciousness and differentiation. – The main tone of this text is (like elsewhere): The Path of DAO involves knowledge, self-knowledge, and self-discipline; the substance of DE consists of practical elements of behavior (‹way of life›, ‹tenure›) providing a number of visible signs on the recommended Path toward perfection. *«Separation»* here means everything from simple *«parting»* to *«decamp»*. – The question thus is an ambiguous one.

** The glyph 氣 means *Breath of Life*, *Spirit – ‹Qi›* (see N° 15). – Some Chinese today interpret it as *Prana*.

*** Most earlier translations of this verse are fixed too much on personal relations and exoterically philosophical commandments, so that they had to be sustained by invented things and relations. The interpretation given here is strictly following the text – except the parts in brackets, and hesitating at the fourth question: Does 四達 stand for the ‹4 corners of the World›? – the 4 cardinal virtues? – one of the proverbial meanings of 四 (comp. p. 151)? Or does it rather mean: *«One [who] has achieved radiant knowledge oft the 4 main goals* (of 達 – main qualities) – *can he really ...?》 – Not one earlier translations* has an *equivalent for* 四 at all. The challenge for the translator here is to understand the basic tenor of seemingly contradictory glyphs. An example: The glyph 玄 stands for things like: *Dirt, black, secret, Mystery*. – The basic tenor thus is: *«dark»*.

第十一章

三十輻，共一轂，當其無，有車之用。
埏埴以為器，當其無，有器之用。
鑿户牖以為室，當其無，有室之用。
故有之以為利，無之以為用。

11.

Thirty spokes – one wheel-hub —
Precisely from where there is nothing,
the wheel gets its usefulness.*
A limitation made of clay serves as a vessel —
What looks like nothing, gives to the vessel its usefulness.**
Chisels, with doors and windows as the results —
What is considered to be nothing, gives to the space its usefulness.
Therefore:
Something physical prompts the purpose of a thing —
Something immaterial achieves its usefulness.***

* This sole useful ‹nothingness› is not the arbitrary space between the spokes, but the hole in the hub, which alone gives the whole wheel its usefulness.

** This phrase has no verb like *knead*, *shape*, or similar things as invented by many previous translators – but only expressions for *rim*, *limitation,* a.s.f., thus depriving the text of any poetic charm, but adding considerably to its philosophical depth and precision: Man too is a vessel made of clay!

*** Simple repetition in English of one and the same Chinese glyph would miss the frugal polyvalence oft the text: What to Westerners looks like simple synonyma, to the Chinese is multilayered versatility, offering him nuances that to the former go completely unnoticed. This exactly is what makes the linguistic wealth and the philosophical precision of the original. These finesses are well worth meditating! – What, for example, is *‹something ... ›*? – And *not every* unsubstantial thing is useful!

第十二章

五色令人目盲；五音令人耳聾；五味令人口爽；馳騁畋獵，令人心發狂；難得之貨，令人行妨。是以聖人為腹不為目，故去彼取此。

12.

Five tints of color [together] cause the view to be blurred. —
Five commands [at the same time] cause the ear to be stoppered. —
Five spices [together] cause the mouth to remain cool. — *
To race and to run, to chase and to shove, causes
itching pain of the heart, and complete madness. **
Loss and gain with money and goods
cause good manners to decay. ***

The truly persistent sage cares [just] for nourishing assets —
he does not live from speculations. ‡

Therefore he drops the latter, adopting the former. ※

* One might as well translate: … that *the mouth is not heated up* – or, that it *remains open* (in the sense of undecided).

** And this already in the 5th c. b.C!

*** A different, somewhat more liberal lecture would be: *Oversized efforts to conquer money and possessions result in that advancement is hindered.*

‡ All variants of all lines put together: *The sage who really turns to account his advantage, serves the stomach, not the eye: he does nothing just for the sake of a good name.* – But by true nourishment we prefer to understand spiritual nutrients rather than physical ones: The sage is not *worried* about his daily bread, which he knows to be *due to him* by his destiny; that is why he bewares of speculations.

※ This final sequence of glyphs is exactly identical with the last sequence of N° 38. Even the inner signification of the whole last paragraph is similar, resp. verbally the same as the latter; – akin to the proverb: *«No-one is satiated just by the looks!».*

第十三章

寵辱若驚，貴大患若身。
何謂寵辱若驚？寵，為下，得之若驚，失之若驚，是謂寵辱若驚
何謂貴大患若身？吾所以有大患者，為吾有身，及吾無身，
吾有何患？
故貴以身為天下，若可寄天下；愛以身為天下，若可托天下。

13.

Distinction and disgrace appear as a shock —
Magnificence and great sorrow appear to be the main issue.* *
How can one say, distinction and disgrace appear as a shock?
Distinction [will become] the cause for disgrace —
to receive it, is a surprise; to loose it, is a shock.

How can one say, wealth and great sorrows are the main issue?
My working place and relative income are
a subject of great concern.
Therefore my income is the main issue.
If my income was not the main issue —
how could my existence be of great concern?** **
The consequence is:
Wealth and personal reputation are the aim of the whole world.
This seems to approve of, and to believe, the whole world.
Enamored in personal reputation is the whole world —
and of this, as it seems, is content and confident the whole world …

* The term *sorrows* (the corresponding glyph contains the element *heart:* 心) simply means the opposite of *welfare, magnificence*, *gain* and *good hope*.

** The *first person* has not been introduced by the translator: it repeatedly appears in the text, as 吾 – i.e. *I*, *my*. the whole thus is no direct admonition, nor a mystical conclusion, but a direct social criticism – relevant already in the 5th c. b.C. – see N° 12!

The materialistic main issues here are even underlined by the similitude of the glyphs regarding these main conceptions: 所 for post, working place, ‹job›; 身for personally, existence, life, status, vital; 者for subject, argument, person, intimate; 有for income, subsistence, to be, to have, to need to, to receive. – All these interpretations are picked from a great multitude of possibilities – and inside this bandbreadth they obviously are subjective …

第十四章

視之不見，名曰夷；聽之不聞，名曰希；搏之不得，名曰微。
此三者不可致詰，故混而為一。其上不皦，其下不昧。
繩繩不可名，復歸于物。是謂無狀之狀，無物之象，是謂惚恍
迎之不見其首，隨之不見其后。
執古之道，以御今之有。能知古始，是謂道紀。

VERSION BY WANG-BI FOR THE THIRD LINE OF ABOVE TEXT:

繩繩不可名，復歸於無物。
是謂無狀之狀，無物之象，是謂惚恍。

VERSION OF THE SAME TEXT BY THE UNKNOWN SOURCE:

绳绳兮不可名，复归于物。
是谓无状之状，无物之象，是谓惚恍。

14.

Study IT – it will recede —
they name IT uncouth.
Listening to IT – one turns up one's nose —
They name IT an oddity.
Grabbing for IT, one will seize nothing —
They name IT futile.
These three facts you cannot study for a long time —
they cause perplexity, but will have the same effect.
IT's highs are not pronounced — IT's lows are not withheld.* *
Excessive discretion is unsuitable for high esteem.
Complexity leads to puzzlement about what one should do.**
By right they say: Nothing is like IT – No shape resembles IT —
By right one names IT vague and bewildering.
If you go to encounter IT, it hides it's head —
If you follow IT, it hides its behind.
Comprehend and seize IT like in the past:
as a guideline and a method —
Refuse the modern ways:***
Who gets to know the ancient onset,
will by right name the Path of DAO schooling for discipline.

* Main text and Wang-Bi both have: 不皦 – *not glittering,* thus *not ‹bright›* (see N° 10); the ‹third text› has the clearer 不□ of the translation.

** Main text and Wang-Bi both have the repeated glyph for reservation: 繩繩 + 不可名 - *not may be pronounced [aloud]*; – thus, *double caution,* and therefore follows the sequence: 復歸於無物 – i.e.: *this complexity effects that one does nothing at all.* The ‹text of unknown origin› has one repeated, pus one additional glyph: 绳绳兮 representing a reinforcing *«oh!»* – followed by 复归于物 – i.e.: *this complication leads one to refrain relative to acting* – thus rather: *one knows not what to do.*

*** From the great number of significations oft the expressions throughout the two last lines two and two were combined so that the translation should better suggest their ‹basic vibration›. – For *path*, *rail*, *method* etc. the original of course always gives 道, resp. a more complex glyph than that, for DAO. Moreover, at this point the difference between Chinese and English syntax appears particularly great, and provokes speculations as for the correct meaning: Earlier translations prove this to be the case.

※Variant: an apprenticeship. – In fact we may, today as ever, name DAO ‹by right› the ‹long way of self-knowledge and self-discipline›.

第十五章

古之善為道者，微妙玄通，深不可識。夫唯不可識，故強為之容

豫兮若冬涉川；　viz.　渙兮若冰之將釋

猶兮若畏四鄰；

儼兮其若客；

渙兮其若凌釋；　viz.　飂兮若無止　viz.　蹎馊粑拗埂

敦兮其若朴；

曠兮其若谷；

混兮其若濁；

孰能濁以，靜之徐清．孰能安久，以動之徐生．

保此道者不欲盈。夫唯不盈，故能蔽不新成。

15.

Once upon a time, those who followed DAO [*]
were connoisseurs of the most subtle finesses of the Mysteries,
whose profundity one could not measure:
Not a single human can describe them —
Therefore one is forced to use figurative speech:
Precisely like someone stomping through a snowed-up plane —
Exactly as someone who has to respect four adjoining owners,
Exceedingly noble as a guest —
Most deeply relieving, like when a calumny is clarified — [**]
As outrageously sincere as the fools — [***]
As unconceivably lavish as a field of wheat — [∴]
Quite as unfathomable as muddy water —
As exceedingly still as a lake —
The Now seems to be without an end! [※]
Error and stupidity doggedly clog the canal [⊗]
Who is able to gradually clear what has been stirred up?
Who is able to gradually let emerge movement in what is immobile?
Considering this, a disciple of DAO won't desire what is superfluous.
Only humans shunning what is unessential [‡]
are capable to cover themselves, and to achieve The Renewal.

[*] Instead of 道者 – *Disciple of Dao* –Wang-Bi has the expression 士者 – *a knight*. This corresponds rather to the earliest Arabian, and then European (Frankish) knight guardians of the Grail; – said without any frame of time and space: the *Disciples of Gnosis.*

[**] The usual translation: *«like a thick sheet of ice melting»* is less plausible, for Wang Bi has, somewhat more comprehensively: 渙兮若冰之將釋; i.e., e.g.,: *«… like when a threat of chess-mate is averted».*

[***] The common version: *«raw as an uncarved block»* cannot be endorsed. – The glyph for reinforcement (兮) is here always replaced by a word.

[∴] Meaning: *generous.* – Another coherent interpretation would be: *Wild like a ravine*: Adepts are soft like water, but also hard like a rock.

[※] Only Wang-Bi has this line. Instead of *«now»* for the glyph 飂, only the term *«wind on the summit of a mountain»* could be found. – Maybe this is meant as a hint at the Universal Spirit who *«hovers above all»*?

[⊗] Only the text by an unknown source has this line. – *Canal*: the same glyph as for an *irrigation canal in a rice field* – here the plenitude of cognizance.

[‡] Only the text presented here has, in its last sequence, a 不 – *«not, without to ... »*, absent in the other originals. Our edition therefore prefers the positive idiom. – *Covered* then here means: *unrecognized.*

第十六章

致虛極，守靜篤。
萬物并作，吾以觀復。
夫物芸芸，各復歸其根。歸根曰靜，靜曰復命。
復命曰常，知常曰明。不知常，妄作凶。
知常容，容乃公，公乃王，王乃天，天乃道，道乃久，
沒身不殆。

16.

To have achieved complete emptiness, brings into being
true immovability.
The 10'000 things are involved in much bustle —
I observe their [eternal] return.
Humans and things are active — and being active
each one continuously reiterates the return to its origin.* *
To return to ones origin, is called «to rest»:
In fact it means a return to the Wheel of Destiny.* **
To return to the Wheel of Destiny is called «eternity» —
Knowledge regarding eternity is called «lucidity» —
Ignorance regarding eternity: «ridiculous bustle».* ***
To admit knowledge regarding eternity —
to admit it, and thus becoming patient —
to be patient, and thus becoming whole —
to be whole, and thus becoming unearthly —
to be unearthly, and thus becoming one with DAO —
to be one with DAO, and thus living long —
in this way, the dying off of the personality is no threat.

* The synonyma for this glyph specify this origin as *individual nature*, as *source* of everyone's character, and as their *Universe*. – This would be DAO as *«Mother of all things»* – the womb of Nature.

** Rendered more precisely: *natural law, fate, lot, life according to Nature*.

*** In order to well understand this verse, we need the *knowledge about the Wheel of lives and deaths,* and about the temporal *Netherworld a.k.a. ‹Kamaloka›* – what ordinary humans without knowledge name *«enter Eternity»*. In reality this is the *«endless return of the same»* (Nietzsche), following Nature's wheel of destiny. This is now confronted with real knowledge of *Divine Eternity*, into which true Disciples gain entry – those who through self-initiation have *freed themselves from the Wheel*.

第十七章

太上，不知有之；其次，親而譽之；其次，畏之；其次，侮之。
信不足焉，有不信焉。
悠兮其貴言。功成事遂，百姓皆謂：「我自然」。

17.

Outstanding rulers: their subjects knew them personally. *
Their successors: [their subjects] loved and revered them. —
Their successors in turn: [their subjects] feared them. —
and their successors : [their subjects] dethroned them. **
«Where the foot cannot be trusted,
there you must distrust the [whole] man!» ***
Oh, how very considerate did the nobility speak!
Achieving great deeds they served their mission.
Among the 100 families each of them said:
[I did it myself!] ※

* The sequence 下知有之 appears only in Wang-Bi's script; all other versions have 不知有之: *people knew them not.* – A mistake in transscript? – Wang Bi's version is more plausible in our present context; it corresponds to the image of an ideal ruler as servant and benefactor of the People: the image of a «king of the People», like Friedrich-Wilhelm II of Prussia, or Bismarck, or Haakon VII of Norway; or Rome's *Pater Patriæ*). – The ‹bath in the rabble› of today's top-politicians aims at the same sympathy of the plebs, but rarely the former merit it any more.

** Precisely, glyph by glyph: *disgrace, insult.*

*** It may be too daring to use the glyph 足 in this rare significance; but understood as a proverb, the image is quite adequate for a ruler whom the People distrust, thus becoming dishonest themselves – and vice-versa: Where the ruler is honest, there the people are so as well (see the N[os] 08, 15, 39, especially 57, and again 41, 45 and 81). – And is not the ruler the foot on which the whole empire stands – or falls?

※ By the *100 families* we preferably understand the upper-class nobility – Today we say: *persons of title and name*. – However, the last sequence (which by its brackets in the original is characterized as being an insert) does not fit the tone of the whole text at all. We should rather expect the logically correct way:

Achieving great deeds they served their mission./ Among the 100 families none of them said : /[I myself did it!] –unless it is meant to discharge the ruler of some mistake. – But here we cannot but speculate in favour of what we know of Chinese culture.

第十八章

大道廢，有仁義；智慧出，有大偽；六親不和，有孝慈；國家昏亂，有忠臣。

18.

The noble path of DAO has gone to ruin —
there remain [only] kindness and correctness. *
Spirituality and wisdom have disappeared —
there reigns a general make-believe
In the families there reigns disagreement —
education of children is softish. **
People and government are dulled down and chaotic —
[at present] there are servants and masters. ***

* Compare with N° 38, where these graduations are enumerated in detail.

** Remember that Ancient China was a patriarchal society: The Eldest also was the wisest the most severe, and the most lenient.

*** The two last expressions, 忠臣, are inspiring by their graphic: The first one contains the element *«heart»* (someone holds up a board or banner); the second rather likens a mural inscription (decree). – For 忠臣, most translators have *«devote minister»*. A possible variant would be: *«now there are confidential persons and courtiers.* – Today though, both Chinese glyphs carry the meaning of *«loyalist»*. Another variant for this line could be: *«Now there are courtiers loyal to the court [and others]* – in short: *Now there are political parties.* With this, this verse would come even closer to relations in our era than what it already is … —

第十九章

絕聖棄智，民利百倍；絕仁棄義，民復孝慈；絕巧棄利，盜賊無有
此三者以為文，不足。故令有所屬：見素抱樸，少思寡欲.

19.

If all the wises would renounce their teachings of wisdom,
people would find a hundred advantages.
If all the righteous would abandon their lessons of good behaviour,
people should return to simple-minded togetherness. ※
If every sly-boot would renounce his or her advantage,
then thieves and robbers would not steel anything anymore. *
Thus, three things show that words [alone] are not enough:
Through dogmata one gets in a state of dependence. **
Who ever beheld purity and allows for simplicity,
looses his personal sorrows, and becomes unselfish — ***
he renounces all imitations, and knows no grieves anymore. ‡

* This mixture of direct teaching and a Daoistic Paradoxon can be understood only with the help of *numerous modern Chinese comments*. The latter's tenor is: Glory and influence of intellectual experts and their skill should be destroyed. The applause for social virtues and pietistic charity should give way to natural, child-like awareness; and where no special possessions are accumulated, there is nothing to steal.

** Two *modern Chinese interpretations* for this second part are found: One confirms our present translation. The other says: «*Education alone is not sufficient; there must be rules. One shall keep an eye on simple living, and live accordingly in a perfect way: The smaller egotism is, the smaller desires and problems [will be]*».

*** Maybe even *self denial* is meant here.

‡ This line exists only in the text of unknown origin. It shows however that this whole ‹verse› is connected directly to the previous one.

第二十章

絕學無憂。唯之與阿，相去几何？美之與惡，相去若何？人之所畏，不可不畏。
荒兮，其未央哉！
眾人熙熙，如享太牢，如春登台。
我獨泊兮，其未兆；
沌沌兮，如嬰兒之未孩；
累累兮，若無所歸。
眾人皆有餘，而我獨若遺。我愚人之心也哉！
俗人昭昭，我獨昏昏。
俗人察察，我獨悶悶。
眾人皆有以，而我獨頑似鄙。
我獨異于人，而貴食母。

20.

Stop learning assiduously, and don't worry:
How far from each other are sympathy and flattery?
How far from each other are Good and Evil?
People are anxious not to lose their position —
they are unable not to be anxious.
How insane really are their endless lamentations and complaints!
Te mass of people lives completely happily,
as if they did exceedingly enjoy their prison — *
as if life were an outing in springtime. **
I alone am – alas! so lazy —
without the myriad of their activities — ***
like a child that has no proper name yet — ♣
being – alas! – as tired as someone who
has no house, whereto he might return home.
The mass of people lives in abundance —
I alone live in embarrassment.
I alone am a dull individual – and moreover
one with a heart!
Las! how very embarrassed am I! ⊗
Ordinary people live without a doubt, and in clearness —
I alone am doubtful and unclear.
Ordinary people are keen and fascinated —
I alone feel oppressed and unconcerned. ⋇
The mass of people is calculable and useful —
I alone am problematic and stubborn —
and moreover excluded and contempted, too. —
I alone am – alas! – different from people —
but precious is the nutrient of the Mother. ‡

(For the remarks to this verse, please see next page.

REMARKS TO N° 20 ON PREVIOUS PAGE:

* Variant: … *as enjoying an oversized sacrifice.* – Rather than a specific ritual (spring-time) sacrificial celebration as many translators want it, we suggest this to be *the sacrifice of themselves* (as a fee for the conservation of heir status or position, and of their welfare). In so far this would be a continuation to verse N° 13.

** Translated glyph by glyph, following the MDBG Chinese-English Dictionnary (there named *an old variant*, as fits well our present text): … *as if they all went joyously to the threshing floor* (to thresh, or to be themselves ‹threshed› by life?). – Or: … *as if they had entered the stage of a theater*. – Or again, as many translators propose: « … *as if at the beginning of springtime they would climb a look-out terrace …* » and similar.

*** A variant would be: «… *don't have their myriads {sorrows or things?}*»; – however, immaterial ‹things› seem to be meant, rather – e.g.: «… *don't have their destiny*» (the glyphs say precisely : their *Omen*).

□ Variant: … *like a child that is no child yet* – hence *an unborn child*. The most encountered version « ... *who does not smile yet*» is philologically and physiologically untenable: It is known that even a fetus can ‹smile›; but a conscious smile is possible only for someone with an Ego.

⊗ This sequence occurs only in Wang-Bi's text.

※ Instead of a reinforcement sign, repetition of glyphs is here ‹translated› by two complementary interpretations of the same glyph. Correspondingly, in the subsequent lines the polyvalence (certainly present for Ancient Chinese) has been translated by two variants.

‡ Here *all translators* struggle while seeking for a coherent phrase. They seek for another idiom, like a proverb, or a hint at another (material, moral or spiritual) signification. Some Chinese interpreters defend the idea that *the* Mother is DAO; others think that *nutrient* might be the deep understanding of ordinary realities. Others again (Chinese ones) interpret *nutrition plus Mother*= m*other milk*. – Many other inspirational ideas have come up on Chinese internet pages.
Instead it seems quite clear that the author of these lines wants to point out that a Disciple of DAO is badly situated *in this World*, while not really being *of this World* – albeit *lost completely in it*; however the nutrition (wisdom and philosophical clearness as provided by The Mother (DAO) more than compensate him for all the adversities encountered on the Path of DAO!

DE AS A COURT LADY – PAINTING ON SILK AT THE YONGLE-PALACE.

第二十一章

孔德之容，惟道是從。
道之為物，惟恍惟惚。惚兮恍兮，其中有象；恍兮惚兮，其中有物
窈兮冥兮，其中有精；其精甚眞，其中有信。
自今及古，其名不去，以閱眾甫。吾何以知眾甫之狀哉？以此。

21.

The appearance of DE is like a dwelling cave —
DAO instead is a narrow path!* [*]
DAO is the aim – but unclear; – but blurred.
Oh! so blurred! — Oh! so unclear!
Partly IT is a [gigantic] appearance —
Oh! so unclear — oh so blurred!
Partly IT is a [ridiculous] thing —
Oh, the profundity! — Oh the darkness!
Partly IT is the Essence of Life [**] ***—***
and this Life is extremely real. —
Partly IT is a matter of faith.
I myself have since long and until today never stopped
to exactly explain IT's significance in many ways.
And how is my way to explain IT clearly to the masses? [***]
The way I'm doing it right now! [‡]

[*] As shown on the title leafs and explained elsewhere (see N°'s 38, 51, and 55), we need to differentiate between 道 – DAO (as *Path, teaching, and method*), and 德 – DE (*moral and ethic virtue*). Earlier translators have combined the two half-lines originally clearly separated by 惟 (*«but, instead, yet»*) into only one muddled phrase. – Indeed possible variants would be: *«like a cave, estuary, tunnel etc., DE receives him; but the Path of DAO is true apprenticeship».*– Or as well: *« ... demands a decision»* – or « ... *is a way of life»* – and all combinations thereof.

[**] The approx. 60 meanings of the glyph 精 revolve around concepts like *«appearance, mind, soul, spirit, demon, life force, seed, essence ... »* – in short: around *subtly physical ‹virtue›*, as opposed to 物 – *materially manifest substance like ‹things›, stuff, gear, matter ...* – and also as opposed to 象 – *giant appearance, elephant* (see the ‹invisible› e*lephant* in N° 41).

[***] The glyph 眾 includes *and* the *great number* of methods, *and* the great number of spectators – hence, the *folks*, or *crowd.*

[‡] Colorful and high strung are all well-known translations here – but what do they say, really? Our present translations instead always remain not just *close to*, but really *identical with*, some of the original meaning(s), and, as closely as linguistically permitted, bringing repetitions in their original order. – All consulted means of translation confirm our versions; and the latter confirm the typical style of the author throughout the book, namely: sober clarity of facts, combined with poetical empathy, in the present instance enhanced by the repeated exclamation *«oh! so foggy! – oh! so fuzzy! – oh! so fuzzy! – oh! so foggy!»* in lines 3, 4 and 7.—

第二十二章

曲則全，枉則直，窪則盈，敝則新，少則多，多則惑。
是以聖人抱一為天下式。不自見，故明；不自是，故彰
不自伐，故有功；不自矜，故長。
夫唯不爭，故天下莫能與之爭。古之所謂「曲則全」者
豈虛言哉！誠全而歸之。

22.

What is flexible, usually remains unharmed:
What is bent can redress itself —
What has been deepened will one day be lifted up —
What looks disdained and silly becomes precious and influential —
What was prized and influential will be disdained —
The true sage holds fast the One, and sets an example to the world:
Not to go and see personally, but to discern — [*]
Not to judge personally, but to be acquiesced —
Not to attack personally, but to obtain victory — [**]
Not to be arrogantly aloof, but to grow as a leader. [***]
When a man just does not seek to fight,
nobody in the whole world can strive to fight him.
Formerly there were places where a person said: [‡]
« What has been bent can redress itself ... »
How could that be wrong [today]? —
Absolutely correct it is, and this time and again.

[*] This is an element from *Sun-Dse*'s book about the *Art of Daoistic warfare*; – one edition is entitled *Truly overcomes who does not fight*. This book will be quoted from repeatedly (N°'s. 34, 40, 49, 68, 69, 71, 73, 79, et passim – plus note 44).

[**] See previous note.

[***] A combination of innumerous meanings of glyphs one by one translates still better the *common basic vibration* in a somewhat sloppy variant like: ... *not to keep standing in the background with a compassionate smile, but to ‹keep going›*. – The glyph 矜 thus does not mean *modest reservation* as many translators wanted in good faith, but in the contrary the arrogance of *‹splendid isolation›* – as opposed to *«attack, unite with the* dust, like in N° 57. – N° 22 stands, so to speak, in opposition to N° 24.

[‡] Thus the absolutely precise translation. – Maybe we might as well say: *Formerly one used to say* ... (comp. the French *il y avait lieu de dire* ...). – The repeated falling and redressing of the serious Candidate is contained in this phrase as well.

第二十三章

希言自然。
故飄風不終朝，驟雨不終日。孰為此者？天地。天地尚不能久
而況于人乎？故從事于道者，同于道；德者，同于德；
失者，同于失。同于道者，道亦樂得之；同于德者，
德亦樂得之；同于失者，失亦樂得之。
信不足焉，有不信焉。

23.

An unusual proverb stunningly [says]:
«A long lasting wind does not cease in the morning —
A cloud-burst does not persist a whole day». *
And what makes that this is so? — The Universe. **
The grandiose Universe [even] cannot persist for a long time —
and what is the situation of Humanity?
Since the Beginning of time, Disciples regarding the aim of DAO
follow the path of DAO —
Humans of virtue [follow] the path of DE — ***
Lost humans [follow] the path of perdition.
Humans of the path of DAO usually gain the delights of DAO —
Humans of the path of DE usually gain the delights of DE —
Humans of the path of perdition —
Perdition regarding delights is what they gain. ※
Where faith has a flaw, there is no faith [at all]. ‡

* *«Natura non facit saltūs»* – Here we remind the typical regional wind in Europe called ‹*Mistral*›, or ‹*tramontane*› that usually blows during three days (or a multiple of three), and that indeed never stops in the morning.

** The glyph really says: *Heaven and Earth.* This is the classical pair of *above* and *below*, that appears in many verses of the book. The ancient Chinese keeps living consciously in the power-play of *Yin and Yang*, meaning at the same time the *eternal harmony of naturally opposed Duals*: DE.

*** Taking sign by sign: DE-people the way of DE (virtue; see N° 38).

※ Only Wang-Bi has this variant oft *the text with* 失於樂得之. All other lines here are in perfect analogy. The difference: The ones live on happily (in the Beyond); the others live their perdition amidst all ‹joys›. – Thus, they finally are without joy – and this not *«usually»*, because there are many delights, but only one perdition: This is Dr. Faustus' *«amidst all delights I pine away with languish!»*

‡ All known translations here are based on reciprocity: Who is not sufficiently trustful, *is not trusted either*. The corresponding statement of the Hermetical literature however aims at the Candidate: Who's faith is not flawless, has no faith at all. Quite literally, the text says: *«Where faith/sincerity /confidentiality is not flawless, there is no faith/confidentiality/sincerity at all»* – with the pairs: *where/there, why/because,* same as: *«the way you treat me, I shall treat you [in return … ».*

第二十四章

企者不立；跨者不行；自見者不明；自是者不彰；自伐者無功自矜者不長。
其在道也，曰：餘食贅形。物或惡之，故有道者不處。

24.

Who walks on toe-tips, does not stand fast —
Who walks with spread legs, will not go far —
Who goes to see for himself, will make no new cognition — [*]
Who justifies himself, is not without a flaw — [**]
Who attacks first, will not prevail — [***]
Who arrogantly holds back himself, will not expand — [‡]
Moreover, [if this occurs] on the path of DAO, [then] we say:
«To eat excessively weighs up on one's figure». [※]
[Those] things he finds sickening and contemptible —
Therefore a Disciple of DAO does not do any of this.

[*] Here understood in the sense of the teachings by *Sun-Dse*: *To know without needing to experience*, viz. *to cognize without needing to see.* (comp. N° 47 and 67 and their commentary). – One rather doubtful variant would be: *Who exposes himself remains unknown.* – 不明 stands for both.

[**] Also : «*Who is self-righteous ...* »

[***] Another hint at the teachings of *Sun-Dse*; –compare N°s 22, 40, 68 and 69 as well as note 44.

[‡] Contrarily to N° 22, and in accordance with N° 59: *To expand* means to grow inwardly *and* outwardly, in the domains of both DE and DAO .

[※] Defendable variants: *«Excessive fees encumber the existence»*. – Or, *«Who pays too much, seems to be possessive»* – and similar combinations. Here *several* translators bring into play *kitchen garbage*; but for this, one more glyph would be required – 廚 , but that is lacking *as well as the glyph* for *ulcer*, *sarcoma*, etc. as invented by the same translators – probably due to a choice including the correct additional variant: *«Excessive nutrition overstrains the body ».*

第二十五章

有物混成，先天地生。寂兮寥兮，獨立而不改，周行而不殆
可以為天地母。吾不知其名，強字之曰道，強為之名曰大。
大曰逝，逝曰遠，遠曰反。
故道大，天大，地大，人亦大。域中有四大，而人居其一焉
人法地，地法天，天法道，道法自然。

25.

There was something perfectly mixed up
before Heaven and Earth were generated
— Oh, that calm! – Oh, that silence! —
As the only thing existing and immutable —
a womb in labour, completely unconceivable, *
able to bring into existence Heaven and Earth, as a Mother. **
I do not know its name.
«Power» and «Word» I name it, and «DAO».—
Power does it work, and it is revered, and named: the Greatest.
As something big it is named ephemeral —
As something ephemeral it is named evanescent —
as something evanescent it is named ambiguous.
Therefore DAO is named the eldest,
Heaven is named the highest, Earth the huge one —
and even humans [are (named)] great. ***
Four big main regions there are —
but Humanity is the first of them. ※
Such as Man is – such is Earth —
Such as Earth is – such is Heaven —
Such as Heaven is – such is DAO —
But DAO is only such as it is itself.

* Literally, the text says *improbable.* – Synonym for probable is *conceivable – therefore → inconceivable.* Another interpretation would be *«quite harmless»*; – philosophically said: *«without any evil in it».* – This would correspond to the All-One-Good (Alone-Good) of the *Corpus Hermeticum.*

** Literally: *think out, lay out, and generate!*

*** Without a doubt this is meant as a play with the glyph 大 – *high, big* etc. – with it's many meanings and *with its comparative and superlative.* To an ancient Chinese, all these meanings were present and ‹active› at the same time.

※ Equally precise: ... *and Man is one of them.* – However, we think that here the *four reigns of Creation* are hinted at: mineral, vegetal, animal, and human, the first of which is the primary divine *idea of spiritual Man.* To those reigns we add the elemental, the *world of spirits* and the *world of gods* (神, *Elohim, Æons, Anunnaki*), and beyond all those the *reign of DAO.* This does not contradict the text, *but rather is silently confirmed* by the latter. The whole verse, and especially the analogy of the *four reigns* (a.k.a *kingdoms*, or *worlds*), corresponds to the *Corpus Hermeticum* (e.g. I, 21-25 ; II, 26 ss.; IV, 79-94; the whole book XVI) – and finally also to the *Tabula Smaragdina* (*«as above, so below»,* etc.).

第二十六章

重為輕根，靜為躁君。
是以君子終日行不離輜重。雖有榮觀，燕處超然。
奈何萬乘之主，而以身輕天下？
輕則失根，躁則失君。

26.

Self-control is the basis of indulgence —
Indulgence is the ruler of rashness.
Righteously rules therefore a Prince who is capable
not to lose – the whole day long* –
indulgence and self-control.
However, there are some [people] who,
looking for renown, exaggerate calm expectance**.
How can we help the one who owns ten thousand quadrigæ**
to rule powerfully –
and in the same time to rule leniently, during all his life?
Who is too lenient, usually looses his foundation —
Who is too impetuous, usually looses his supremacy. ※

* Variants: *Therefore, righteously governs a king who from morning to night, keeps his distance from portentous and lowly persons alike.* – Or else: *Righteously governs the ruler from sunrise to sunset ....* – Or: *A king [shall] from childhood until his death ...*; – and combinations from all these. The expression *«the Wise»*, used by other translators, is not contained in this text. Instead, the *ruler from sunrise to sunset – i.e. from East to West – could also* mean *the Emperor himself* (see note ***).

** Uncertain: *Nobody today* can give a definite expression for the glyph 燕.

*** The owner of 10'000 quadrigæ is the Emperor himself (see N° 62).

※ Unfortunately, it is impossible to render the *wondrous harmony* of this text including its symmetry of the *first and last lines*. In the first two sequences: A *effects* D *of* C (twice); and in the last two sequences: C *usually looses* D (twice). – In between, see the play with the terms *ruler* and *self- control*. Add to this the multitude of synonyma for C_1 (轻) – *lenient, soft, low, light, light-minded*, a.s.f. – as well as for D_2 (君) – *to rule, royal*, etc. – Instead of *foundation* one might as well say *foothold, basis* etc.

第二十七章

善行無轍跡，善言無瑕謫；善數不用籌策；善閉無關楗而不可開，
善結無繩約而不可解。
是以聖人常善救人，故無棄人；常善救物，故無棄物。是謂襲明。
故善人者，不善人之師；不善人者，善人之資。不貴其師，
不愛其資，雖智大迷，是謂要妙。

27.

Good deed needs not hide its tracks — [*]
Good speech can disparage a high public officer,
without one of them loosing his face. — [**]
Good calculation needs neither paper nor marker. —
Good closure needs no turning of a key— and yet nobody can open.
Good binding needs neither strap nor contract —
and yet nobody can unbind it. [***]
A wise ruler [is] always in a favorable mood to absolve people —
and so he forsakes no-one.
Always kindly inclined to preserve things,
he lets nothing go to ruin. [‡]
By right one says: «He inherits a shining robe!» [※]
Therefore:
If he is a benefactor, needy humans are his example.
If he is a needy man, some benefactors will help him. [⊗]
His models are not dear to him —
His benefactors he does not revere —
For, although great cleverness is highly appreciated,
one says by right:
«What foremost matters, is probity.!» [†]

[*] The pair 善行 means: *good deed*. – 行 *alone* means to go, to travel, a.s.f. – 辙 means *remove*, NOT *leave behind*. – Maybe that the Pythagorean *Symbola* contain the first misinterpretation of this phrase (*«When you get up, whipe out your imprint in the straw»*)?

[**] Precisely: 无瑕 = *makes no mistake*, 謫 = *disgrace* (from *blame* onto *banish*). – Above interpretation helps the western comprehension.

[***] Not just objects, also humans, contracts and messages are meant here: The fifth term of the second line (约) among other means *Arrangement, consent, clutch*; the last (解) e.g. means *point at, deliver, separate*.

[‡] The text uses the polyvalent glyph 棄 – *give up, push away, let go of, discard, squander,* etc.

[※] *The Chinese dictionary MDGB specifies: «*襲 means *‹to receive a (funeral) robe›*. Esoterically, we understand the famous *golden wedding robe.*

[⊗] Precise signification: *good person* vs. *non-good,* but (not necessarily *bad*), *person*. – See N° 62, and. commentary to it.

[†] The synonyma for 妙 reach from *cleverness* and *acuteness* over *sharpness* and *excellence* on to *mysteriously* (Sun-Dse!).

第二十八章

知其雄，守其雌，為天下溪。為天下溪，常德不離，復歸于嬰兒
知其白，守其辱，為天下谷。為天下谷，常德乃足，復歸于樸。
知其白，守其黑，為天下式。為天下式，常德不忒，復歸于無極
樸散則為器，聖人用之，則為官長，故大智不割。

28.

Who knows his male [energy], and cultivates his female [energy],*
impacts the world like a small river:
Influencing the world like a small river
he never leaves the Path of DE,
and he gains back the youthfulness of a child. —
Who shows his clarity, and retains his darkness,
serves the world as an example:—
Serving the world as an example
DE is always his support,
and he gains back the boundless undivided [One]. ** —
Who knows his merits, and stashes his humiliations,
stands in the world like a stalk of millet.***
Standing in the World like a stalk of millet, he never exaggerates DE,
and he gains back his simplicity. —
Who is simple, is delivered of being
dominated by [natural] laws like a pot:‡
As a sage he is called to
serve the Law as a responsible associate. —
Therefore he never abandons the highest order.※

* This *«cultivation»* means to enhance inwardly *and* to protect outwardly, including everything from personal shame to universal *Mysteries.* This is part of the invisibility as taught by SUN-DSE. Like in the expression for *male power* (two meanings of the same glyph), we might as well say *female adaptation*; but that is not what the text explicitly says.

** The pair of glyphs: 無極 means, quite precisely, *unlimited and free of all dualities* (of masculine poles and feminine anti-poles).

‡ 器 *Pot = vessel, vehicle,* and a (blind) *tool* – i.e. *without any soul-consciousness* (compare this 器 to the expression of 器長 in N° 67).

※ This 官 (= *partner),* among other, means *tool* as well. – The present phrase lives on three planes: 1° as a *passive tool* of the *Law of causes and effects*, 2° in the active service (*a tool*) to the *Cosmic Law of DE,* and, 3° through spirituality (*a fully conscious tool*) in the union with *DAO* – the *highest, all-embracing law in the Universe*.

将欲取天下而为之，吾见其不得已。
天下神器，不可为也，不可执也。为者败之，执者失之。
是以圣人无为，故无败；无执，故无失。
夫物或行或随；或嘘或吹；或强或羸；或载或隳。
是以圣人 去甚，去奢，去泰。

第二十九章

將欲取天下而為之，吾見其不得已。天下神器，不可為也。
為者敗之，執者失之。
故物或行或隨；或噓或吹；或強或羸；或載或隳。
是以聖人去甚，去奢，去泰。

29.

If someone's desire wanted to achieve
that everything under the sky went after his craving —
to my opinion he would fail with this:
The World is the tool of the gods —
one really must not do this —
one really may not force anything. [*]
If one did anything [of the kind] – one would spoil it — [**]
If one forced it – one would loose it.
The true sage does nothing [of the kind],
therefore he doesn't spoil anything —
he doesn't force anything, therefore he doesn't loose anything. [***]
The [profane] human gives place to things, or he adapts them —
either he whispers [in their presence] – or he roars [at them] —
either they are stronger than he – or he destroys them —
either they are useful – or he annihilates them.
The truly sage discards the extremes,
dispensing with what is exaggerated,
and leaving behind all magnificence. ※

[*] The *not possible* as well as the *not permitted* (for 不可) can also be understood as: *To us humans it is not given to ... —*

[**] *it = the World.*

[***] The text printed in red can be found only in the text from an unknown source. See the similar statement by WANG-BI, in N° 64.

※ 去 *as a verb* includes these and many other, similar meanings: If the oriental style likes the *repetition* of a polyvalent term, the Western style instead prefers *variation* with specific terms of the same thing ...

第三十章

以道佐人主者，不以兵強天下。其事好遠。師之所處，荊棘生焉
大軍之后，必有凶年。
善有果而已，不敢以取強。果而勿矜，果而勿伐，果而勿驕。
果而不得已，果而勿強。
物壯則老，是謂不道，不道早已。

30.

When the ruler uses a Disciple of DAO as a teacher — *
not with the violence of arms is it that he conquers the World.
His aim is rather, to avoid [this].
His post as a commander is an honorary office to him:
Thorn-bushes grow where a great army has passed —
and there follow cumbersome years. **
A good man conquers, then stops —
he does not dare to torture prisoners — ***
He conquers without mercy —
He is a victor, but does not attack [by himself] — ※
He is a victor, but not conceited —
He is a victor, for: so must it be —
He is a victor, but not cruel.
[Even] the greatest things must grow old —
This precisely is what one names [the Law of] DAO. ‡
[For] what is not in DAO,
will shortly end.

* This is a typical example for the multiple use of a glyph for different expressions: 道人– *a Daoist*; 道佐 – *a Disciple of DAO*; 道佐人 – a Master, or *teacher of DAO*. – 佐 = *to help*, a *collaborator*, an *assistant*; and finally: 佐人 – a *counselor*. – Possible inversion of the syntax with the same sign 以 at the beginning of the sentence: *If a ... serves a king as ...*

** This is a verbal quote from SUN-DSE's book about Daoist warfare (see N°68 plus comment, and note 44).

*** Sequence printed in blue: 敢 – only in WANG-BI.

※ Another fundamental teaching by SUN-DSE (loc. cit.).

‡ This is the universal Law of birth, blooming, aging and ‹death› …

第三十一章

夫唯兵者，不祥之器，物或惡之，故有道者不處。
君子居則貴左，用兵則貴右。兵者不祥之器，非君子之器，
不得已而用之，恬淡為上。勝而不美，而美之者，是樂殺人。
夫樂殺人者，則不可得志于天下矣。
吉事尚左，凶事尚右。偏將軍居左，上將軍居右，言以喪禮處之
殺人之眾，以悲哀泣之，戰勝以喪禮處之。

31.

Man's most beautiful weapons are harmful tools —
objects one should avoid.
Therefore, humans who live in DAO, don't use them. [*]
The Prince usually has his place of honour on the Left —
but in the array for battle his place of honour is on the Right.

Weapons are harmful tools – nothing for the use of a Prince;
Only when he has no other choice, he uses them.
Silent and solemn is then a nobleman:
If he triumphs, he is for all that not proud of himself. —
A man who is proud of himself when he prevails
is someone wo enjoys killing humans —
and someone who enjoys killing humans,
will certainly have no good name throughout the empire.
The aide-de-champ is located at the left wing of the array — [**]
the Lord commander in chief is located at the right wing.
One then says: «He stands at the funeral place» —
[For,] if many of [his] men are killed,
he mourns grieving and lamenting. —
If [instead] he battles victoriously,
he dons a mourning robe and performs a ritual [for the dead].

[*] This line as well is a quotation from a Daoist Classic – the *Yin-Fu-Jing* – *Codex of the Union Of The Yin* (see text and commentary of N° 57 and 68). – About the *Yin-Fu-Jing*, see Introduction to the present book.

[**] *Translated accurately: ...stands on the left – resp. ... the right of the array.*

第三十二章

道常無名.樸雖小，天下莫能臣。侯王若能守之，萬物將自賓

天地相合，以降甘露，民莫之令而自均。

始制有名，名亦既有，夫亦將知止，知止可以不殆。

譬道之在天下，猶川谷之于江海。

32.

DAO is eternally nameless and simple. [*]
Although clear, it is disdained never the less [**] —
[but]Heaven and Earth submit themselves to no Lord but to IT.
If noblemen and kings were able to maintain IT —
all creatures would rush toward them —
Heaven and Earth would unite so that sweet thaw would rain down,
and all nations would agree among each other,
without any further command. [***]

In the Beginning [all things] were given [their] names — [※]
[Many] names came up since then, moreover,
and humans also wanted to find out limits:
To recognize the limits, makes it possible to avoid dangers.

An allegory: DAO is for Heaven and Earth what a river is for the bottom of the valley — what the gulf is for the ocean.

[*] The red part exists only in the ‹text of unknown source›.

[**] *Clear as opposed to dark* (see N° 28). – the blue part is only in WANG-BI's text; – without it, it might read: *in spite of being disdained. ...*

[***] At the same time this is a clear hint towards the 2nd Work of operative Alchemy.

[※] The glyph 制 is composed of three elements: 失, (*let go, forget, loose*) above 而 (*«but, more-over, and, despite»* and others), besides 則 (*«prescription, law, rule, must ...»*). – The single glyph 制, thus, conveys the complete statement: *To name means to loose the sense of union and togetherness, i.e., to loose oneness, to separate* (‹right› and ‹wrong›, ‹good› and ‹evil›, ‹true› and ‹false›) – *thus creating the Law of causes and effects*). This was indeed the crucial factor for «loosing» the biblical ‹Paradise› – and therefore: abolishment of all judgments is required in order to reconquer it!

第三十三章

知人者智，自知者明。
勝人者有力，自勝者強。
知足者富。
強行者有志。
不失其所者久。
死而不亡者壽。

33.

Someone who knows human [nature], is a Wise —
Someone who knows himself is an Illuminated one.
Someone who overcomes humans, has power —
Someone who overcomes himself is strong.
Who is content with his life is rich.
Who forcefully presses forward, will enter the annals. *
Who on his post does not fail, has endurance. **
Someone who dies without decaying
is like one who [as an old person] has his birthday. ***

* Possible precise variants: *an unwavering pilgrim possesses will-power.* – Or also: *Who forces [his way] is ambitious.*

** Variant: *Who does not loose his post ...*– maybe also: *Who does not give up his post.* – The glyph 久 – *«long in time» – can also mean forbearance*. Many translators have: ... *lives long.* – *To live long*, in the view of Ancient Chinese, besides a long life also means to earn great posthumous fame – and thus, to be ‹kept alive› with sacrifices (public, or/and by his family) for a long time after his physical death.

*** The very common translation of this line – *«... lives eternally»* – is *logically correct* (especially together with the previous couplet), yet it is *philologically inaccurate* (the latter demanding for the writing 无量寿 – *wúliàngshóu – immeasurably long life*). – An old significance of 壽 instead – besides whatever means *«a long life»* – also is: *«birthday of an old person»*. Therefore the solution proposed here is not only *logically correct*, but also *philologically accurate and philosophically suggestive* – in short: *«... like someone who at a high age is born anew»*).

Physical death as the beginning of a new incarnation cycle (it starts the process of physical renewal), is at the same time a *metaphysical hour of birth.* – According to the *doctrine of Transfigurism*, however, the *«gradual metaphysical death»* (during physical lifetime of the Candidate) is followed by *«an all-embracing renewal with a gradual spiritual New Birth to eternal life»*: This is the so-called *«Rebirth from Water, Spirit and Fire »*. –

So much in order to explain our somewhat extravagant transfiguristic translation of the present ‹verse›.

大道氾兮，其可左右。
萬物恃之以生而不辭，功成而不名有。
衣養萬物而不為主，常無欲可名於小。
萬物歸焉，而不為主，可名為大。
以其終不自為大，故能成其大。

第三十四章

大道泛兮，其可左右。萬物恃之以生而不辭，功成而不有
衣養萬物而不為主，常無欲,可名于小；萬物歸焉而不為主
可名為大。以其終不自為大，故能成其大。

34.

Oh great, overflowing DAO,
you are everywhere!
In you all creatures trust; for:
You bring them forth, but you don't abandon them.
Glorious things you achieve, but not for your own glory.
Clothing and sustaining all creatures,
— but not to rule [them] — *ever selfless!*
Justly glorified are you by the lowliest.
All creatures return hither, as long as they are not divine,
justly glorifying the greatest.
Therefore ends their inability to achieve great things themselves —
Thus they become qualified to be transformed into their highest.

Having clarified the essential terms and relations in our *Introduction*, it is possible to offer an in-depth interpretation to this 34th verse, or chapter, still valid for our time. It is a very special text in so far as it makes not a single reference to ordinary earthly existence, expressing but the intimate veneration and gratitude of all creatures towards the One-and-All, the Al(l)-One-Good. In fact, here DAO is invoked directly as the macrocosmic creative force who, as the Scriptures say, *«never abandons the work of his hands»*. The whole is a poetic veneration of soul-stirring beauty, and like the end of N° 62 it recalls the central Christian prayer – the *«Lord's Prayer»*.

With good reason DAO is called upon here as *overflowing*. Under the cabalistic name *Mother of all things, DAO* generates, and receives back, every little being – animated or not; and so one can state by right that every creature – each one of the ‹10'000 things› – is safeguarded in DAO – in its uprising as well as in its recession, – in its ‹life› as well as in its ‹death›. – In the meantime, DAO is, as it were, the Law of the Universe – *Karma* in its largest sense.

Today's Christian Gnosis as well is speaking of the overflowing *River of Living Water*, which is filling the whole Universe, every being, large or small – imbuing, vivifying, and simultaneously pressing forward everything, on an immeasurable helix of ascension – an evolution not of the physical *form* of creatures, but of their spiritual *essence* – of their consciousness!

How can this *«stream of Living Water»* – this *«Divine Stream»* – be experienced? – How can it be recognized and ‹made use of›, practically? – That is what a ‹rationally› thinking human would like to know; – for, if one be a ‹believer› or not: every human, and also non-human creatures *feel* this presence, even if only vaguely, unconsciously and unable to articulate it. That is, as we know, what the very first verse of the *Dao-De-Jing* says, too.

Now, during the lifetime of a human (as this whole book is about *consciousness*, we address only Man here) a moment can arise – we also name it the *psychological* moment – where this human in a more or less physical manner *realizes* the impulse coming forth from said divine stream – often at the occasion of some dramatic, life-changing experience. Some are seeking for this impulse, for this stream, like for a very old remembrance; – very few persons even are seekers since their earliest childhood!

When a human, deeply touched in hat way, "stops in his tracks" and lets himself be *flooded* by the Living Water, so to speak, then he resembles a tired, thirsty wanderer who on his trail encounters a waterfall, spontaneously steps under it, and lets himself be flooded completely by it: Till into his innermost core he feels his being thus inundated and submerged; – never will he or she forget this magic moment!

The critical question is now: Will his clothes be dry long before he arrives «at home»? – Will his soul have completely dried up and be thirsty again – or will a first ray of sprouting life – a trace of the gnostic ‹radical humidity› be able to keep alive in his heart? – If not: The described unforeseen hunch can, during a human lifetime, arise two or three times – or only during a next one, but in that case under more difficult conditions, because there is so much to ‹make up for›. – But, if yes, the person thus consciously or unconsciously tinged by the Spirit will, knowingly or unknowingly call for a possibility to repeat said experience, in order to reinforce it, and develop it further. Already then the wondrous effect of *DAO* will set in, obeying to how the cosmic *Law of Causes and Effects* needs must work: This Law, which applies to every creature – big or small, from a little grain of sand up to a complete galaxy – this all-directing Law ‹takes care› of the seeker and ‹sees to it› that the silent echo of the call he half-consciously received, keeps resounding in him. Thus, he or her is «born from God». This is a magic renewal, by which he or she will be attracted, and led to the next contact with said stream of living water – with the Spirit: At that point indeed a ray of the Gnosis – of the *universal DAO* – has impregnated the microcosmic kernel – the spiritual seed in the seekers heart, awakening him or her to *real Life*. Even if such an individual does not yet know it: this is the germ from which his or her *individual DAO* can and will sprout, and the spark of New Life will grow …

In this or a similar way begins the voyage of a new seeker – of a new Candidate of the Gnosis; and so he or she set out on their path. In doing so, there begins to awaken their *awareness*, their *discernment* for the spiritual world – for the world of *Light, Truth and Life.* And because now also progressively wakes up their *insight* for spiritual interactions and intertwinements in the Universe, their *yearning* as well begins to grow, and the question arises: *«What shall I do? – What can I do, in order to advance on this trail of which I know as good as nothing?»*

Answers arrive; –help arrives; – *progress* shows up; – and while all this develops, the first *obstacles* arrive as well. – How will the new Candidate *react*?

If he or she remain firm and strong. they will soon recognize that they *are guided*. This is the famous *«lamp before my foot»* the Scriptures talk about. – But it is just a lamp, no compelling authority: From the very begin of this process of spiritual Rebirth, the Neophyte marches under the lawfulness of his *autonomous free will*, and of his *auto-responsibility*!

The first phase of this path consists in absorbing the basics of the so-called *Universal Doctrine*: Cosmogony and Anthropogony. This is his gnostic breast-milk (the Mother being SOPHIA herself). Absorbing these elements of what is a tradition rather than a teaching he sees a new physical reality, and gains his own experience: This is his first knowledge from first hand, his first gnosis proper – the sprout of his intimately individual *DAO.* – But for that he has not become *a Gnostic* yet – *far from it*! This denomination he earns only by incessantly seeking and learning and putting into practice – until he really *cannot live otherwise* but widening, and in auto-responsibly deepening his knowledge *from first hand* – when his heart beats uniquely for *The Path – for DAO – day and night.*

As this knowledge augments, there grows the seekers *insight*, and grows his yearning to attain his goal that he begins to discern in a distance: it is the goal of auto-liberation, which begins to shine up at the end of the course of all worlds – like a star that wants to help him finding his way. Simultaneously grows his gratitude towards Gnosis, grows his joy to be allowed and fit to follow this path – and so grows, finally, his confidence in the Gnosis who accompanies every step of his. More and more courageous and determined he sets out *«in the new morning, to meet the raising sun – with an open heart, barefoot and his head uncovered»* – as says the *Confessio Fraternitatis RC.*[9]

The more the Candidate advances that way, the more he will find reasons to be amazed, to wonder, to be grateful and glad; and so is doubled his *awe through insight*, and is strengthened his *determination* to remain faithful to The Path *«until his last breath, and beyond»*. For, even if his lifetime should not suffice to reach the sublime goal: nothing essential will be lost on the way; Everything is for the profit of *the One Divine Plan*, according to which every creature will – ‹one day› – reach its divine destination.

The ‹apocryphal›, entirely gnostic *Gospel of Thomas* says:[10]

«He who seeks shall not stop seeking, until he has found. – And when he will have found he will be astonished. And when he will have been astonished he will rule as a king. And when he will have ruled as a king he will find rest.»

This is a rest and stillness *«not of this World»* – the rest of the first biblical Sabbath: Six painful steps of discernment and deepening contemplation lie behind him, from the *discernment of Light and Darkness* through the awakening oft the ‹New Soul› forgetting any *scission into Yin and Yang*, and finally achieving definitive union as a *Spirit-Soul-Man* within the *divinely harmonious Yin-Yang*. – this is the *seventh step* – the humanly divine *Step of Perfection.*

This *intermediate* rest necessarily gives way to the complete renewal in the course of Transfiguration. It is, in fact, the *first step* for a new, much higher level of the helix of evolution: Wandering across *«a New Heaven and a New Earth»*, the *children of God* – members of the Brotherhood of truly living Humans – rise from strength to strength, and from magnificence to magnificence:

As a consequence,
ends their inability to achieve great things themselves —
and so they become able to transform themselves
into their greatest.

Emperor Hong-Wu I. — founder oft the Ming-Dynasty.

第三十五章

執大象，天下往。往而不害，安平泰。
樂與餌，過客止。道之出口，淡乎其無味，視之不足見，聽之不足聞，用之不足既。

35.

He who realizes the Great Ideal
stands in opposition to the world —
in opposition, but without hate:
content — stolid — still.
Where there music, conviviality and delicious food entice him,
the passing voyager tarries. —
DAO [instead] offers him a view without enticement:
It does not emanate a precious scent —
looking at it, it lacks a sight —
listening to it, it lacks a sound —
applying it, it lacks both.

Many are the forms in which DAO can be lived, experienced, realized or turned down. Many are those humans who like to taste it – be it in order to take a sip from its nectar while passing by, or be it in order to find real nutrition for their mind.

However, and alas, it is not as simple as that! – And why not? Is not everybody allowed to participate in it, without restriction by and for anybody? – The latter is indeed correct; and in so far it is really very simple. But with that, nothing is gained – yes, with that it cannot even begin!

If we look at *the form* of this text we notice that it contains two parts, but does not explain their essence. The wording of this essence sounds alike for both, but their meaning makes them quite divergent. Resolving this divergence we detect the comprehension of the 35th verse of the *Dao-De-Jing*:

«Voyagers» – this does not mean some random sightseer, explorer or commercial traveler. This here is a survey regarding Initiation, and LAO-DSE – as far as his teachings are concerned –might hardly have addressed himself to some fancy tourist. Outside his teaching yes, for he recommends on another occasion to *«mingle oneself to the dust»* (N° 56), *«to make the heart of everybody one's own heart»* (N° 49), a.s.f. –

In the present instant however, we need to understand the term of *‹voyager›* as being a seeker on the quest for *spiritual gold,* for *spiritual food* and for *spiritual* harmony. The expression of *‹voy-*

ager› in a spiritual sense is used in the Orient (Persia and Arabia) since many centuries. These *«voyagers»* thus are humans on a *spiritual path* – or on the *quest* for a spiritual teaching that might bring them closer to the knowledge about God, the World, and Man: A teaching that might promise, and even procure indeed, *Liberation.* Many of them ignore what they are seeking for; yes, most of them even ignore completely *that* they are seeking: Sleep-walkers on the way to spiritual perfection. This is the walk of Humanity as a whole – and, as it were, the way of all creatures in the Universe. True *«voyagers»* in the meaning of the Sacred Language, thus, are persons *consciously seeking* for a trail toward *DAO* – for a path toward *‹heavenly bliss›.*

What is ‹DAO›? – What is ‹bliss›? – It is when a being is in perfect harmony with its surroundings – physically, mentally and spiritually – thus as well, and in the present instance quite particularly so – when it is in *conscious union with God*, in the harmony of the whole Universe, and with *kosmos* – that means, in Greek, *order, beauty, and adornment.* – Is not universal Creation the adornment, the crown of the Deity?

The crown jewel however is Man, this *‹compendium›* of universal Creation. Not Humanity in its present degenerated, half-beastly appearance of course, but ‹HEAVENLY ADAM›: Man, as it was *«in the Beginning»*, as a divine *arch-image* or archetype issued from the *divine prime idea* of the truly thinking creature MAN – MANAS – who was one with the divine primitive Monad. And to return to this divine arch-image, is the *«great ideal».* – That is what the present N° 35 is talking about. Who vivifies this divine spiritual image in his or her reborn soul, becomes a voyager, an *example* for the other inhabitants of the Universe: an embodiment of the promise that The Path – that the attainment of DAO – is indeed possible – a *reality*!

Can ordinary voyagers find this path in our world? LAO DSE says: NO! – unless this voyager has encountered DAO earlier already, has been touched by IT already, and has also already entered the path of Dao: Who *grasps, holds fast and realizes* DAO (all this is indeed contained in the first glyph of the present ‹verse›!) already stands in opposition to this world – albeit without any bad feeling against it. He or she, then, is already a wanderer or voyager as explained above – and therefore also possesses other sensual organs and ideals than ordinary people.

By *music* and *delicious food* a Disciple of the inner knowledge, of DAO understands neither daring songs nor tasty tidbits or exuberant company, such as more than 200 translators of the *Dao-De-Jing* want it. A Disciple is not attracted by mellow *esoteric sentences and teachings*, and even less by the false harmony of the numberless more or less well-meant (‹bona-fide›) companies for the promotion of humanistic moral, culture and religiosity.

For China at the time of LAO-DSE, there might be included here also some sacrificial meals for the *guy's* – spirits of defunct family members – or also some temple-dances, religious celebrations and offering rituals – even some kind of ‹orgies›: processions and ecstatic dances, as we know them from traditions of the ancient Mysteries (Isis-cult), from David of the Ancient Testament, or from the ritual dances of the Indians of North America – and of course from shamanic rituals and feasts of so-called ‹primitive› nations on old continents like Asia, Australia and Africa – revived as they are by the frenzy of today's night-clubs.

The Greek word *Org-y*, by the way, comes from *very organized sacred celebrations and rituals* at the occasion of great sacrifices or consecrations. Their innermost signification was known and understandable only to the highest Initiates (like today) – but what the participating folks like best, were the scent of roast meat, lots of wine, music and dances – including exuberance of every kind, as they are still the custom during great fairs during our ‹enlightened times›, and which even today attract tourists and vagrants from near and far, as is well known to everybody. – Lao Dse in his text may have aimed at such ritualistic pleasures as well, when he used such expressions as are mostly translated as «tasty meals and music»; – in full analogy with what today we may call ‹esoteric's tourism›, and in order to emphasize that initiation is indeed no pleasure trip, *no fun-fair* in a spiritual ‹Cockaigne›, *no jumping from one tidbit to another, from one dancer to another.*

Not that Initiation should be a saddening and painful life of renunciation – not at all! Typical for the true Initiate is his supple serenity: His abdication – where it really occurs – is no suffering, but *reasonable* moderation, *reasonable* renouncement.

Moderation in olden times was one of the four cardinal virtues: *wisdom (prudence), courage, justice and moderation*. But today (besides mediocrity and foul compromises) quite different ‹virtues› have taken their place: Since the time of so-called Enlightenment during the 18th century, these four are named *bravery, liberty, goodness, justice.* But courage, justice and freedom are naught, when they are not moderated by *wisdom*! How often must we see today ‹justice› perverted into injustice, rules turned into ‹justice› without kindness nor wisdom; – and the demand for ‹freedom› without prudence in today's humanity has fostered selfishness and often even tyranny: The famous law-suit of the two women quarreling before SALOMON, about which one was the mother of that child, is often solved today – alas! – by cutting the child in two ... –

The temperance of the Initiate instead is subdued to his *prudence*: What cannot be accomplished in good-hearted serenity should be left alone. What is not based on sober reason and inner knowledge, is alien to the true path of DAO. And still, destiny will offer to the authentic voyager on the path of DAO so many unexpected «delicate meals», which then he will enjoy with even more gratitude – and many a thought received in silent meditation, many a word found through one of his companions will fill his ear and soul, like a wondrous music!

For ordinary people – the ‹tourists› in this world – they who not yet have seized the spiritual aim of life, the path of DAO is colourless, odourless, tasteless ... – in short: without attraction. Therefore, who applies he path of DAO and realizes it, lives contrarily to the rest of the World, and outside of it, so to speak. Thanks to his insight he sees through the Great Play, that generates, moves, and lets disappear again all things and beings of tis World. He sees the dichotomy of this World: On one side, divinely inspired, animated and enlivened, full of divine beauty and harmony. Flawed on the other, perishable in all, full of contradictions and opposing duals. – That is the realistic view, dogmatists of this World call *Dualism*.

But even to the authentic wanderers – those seekers for the Spirit who ‹tarry› at the discrete table of DAO – the juicy tidbits are not just put into their mouth: They needs must *prepare them themselves* by their own effort. Also, they must learn to chew and digest everything well, should this nutrition for soul, spirit and body bring the best possible profit, namely some advancement on the Path of DAO. Well prepared, it is a daily pleasure to nourish oneself from this inexhaustible provision, and to grow, renewing ones cells and organs in «silent *maturation*», as the translation by Bachofen has it – and finally, to step higher up on the immense coil of spiritual evolution as a *New Divine Man*: *«per aspera ad astra»!*

It therefore is necessary to see and to hear what the ordinary eye cannot see, and what an ordinary ear cannot hear, following Paul in his 1. Cor 2:9 – *«What no eye has seen and no ear has heard, and what has come in no human heart; – what God has prepared for those who love Him»*.

When he or she achieves this, they will meet, on a higher plane, with other seekers, pilgrims, voyagers and finders – *‹Trobadors›* –like in the second phrase of the 35th ‹verse› of the *Dao-De-Jing*: They have *anew enlivened* in themselves *the Great Ideal*; and as they will prove faithful to it, they are immersed in the inexhaustible plenitude of *spiritual nutrition and music of DAO* – and thus have become One: *«No strangers anymore, but fellow lodgers of God»* – as His children, brothers and sisters.

The thing is, to *pierce* the outer ‹clothing› of the inner teaching, to cast aside the veil, and to *penetrate* the inner significance of the salutary message and its core philosophy. This means: To *learn* and to *understand*; – to *dissolve* obvious contradictions and ‹mistakes›, and thus to find the truth oneself there where no words can explain it, and where no sign can make them visible. And it becomes necessary to pass on from study and absorption to application and multiplication: to realization in ones own ‹inside› first, to practice as a living example, and finally to the transmission of the same teaching out of love for all other creatures, and out of compassion for those who find no taste in the dishes at the table of Gnosis yet.

This proves once more that it is not enough to study with great appetite and tenacity the *Good Tidings* of Gnosis – to read it aloud, and to preserve their ‹nectar› inside of large libraries or in a admirable memory, like bees who store their honey in large honeycombs: The unavoidable postulate is to translate into action all this, in a daily attitude of life that gives a *silent testimony* for the communion of the pilgrim with The Spirit.

Not that a library were superfluous, nor that an impressing memory were but an idle show: Not a single high Initiate ever lived without speaking several languages, without studying several philosophical systems, without knowing and even exercising at least one art: Thence issue the *Seven Arts* of Antiquity, with their Muses, whose Lord is Apollon, the god of the Sun himself!

Yet all *learning* is not yet the *knowledge* of DAO, and even *daily realization* is but an important set of instruments that facilitates many things. Nothing on The Path occurs ‹automatically›; – everything is Grace – reward for one's own efforts. Effort and grace are like right hand and left hand. ‹Humanistic› erudition and skill are a great help for the digestion oft the dishes offered on the table of Dao: They help understand the real significance of myths, rituals, symbols, and of sacred scriptures.

«Firstly aspire to the reign of God and to His justice, and all the rest will be added to this!» – said the Master.

This *«all the rest»* is explained by the tradition of operative Alchemy, where we read about the *three gifts* that the *Philosophers Stone* bestows on its Adept: welfare, health, and a long life. – In Ancient China the wish for a long life was one of the most important ones: not for the sake of enjoying as long as possible *«the scent of roast meat, and music»*, but in order to be able to progress as far as possible on the path of DAO, before the curtain falls once more, and in order to both *apply* a maximum of the Good Teaching, *and multiply it in the World.*

With this, our voyager has become a *guardian, witness and teacher or even preacher* in the revival of the Great Ideal – for his own sake as well as for that of the Universe: for the small as well as for the big, for his surroundings like inside himself! Thus, the original divine Monad, whose light was almost completely extinct, has regained *Truth, Light and Life* – thanks to *continuous conscious nourishment* through incessant efforts *and divine grace.* – Now our Pilgrim stands amidst the plenitude of DAO – amidst the spiritual treasure that can never ever be exhausted.

Who in his way has turned away from ‹the World› and all its noise, living in the stillness of DAO, and knowing that sufficient is enough – to him *«all the rest will fall to, freely».* He will lack nothing, have all he needs, and live in perfect inner harmony:

content without hate – stolid – still.

道

Candidates waiting to enter the exam for public officials. – Ming-Dynasty.

第三十六章

將欲歙之，必故張之；將欲弱之，必故強之；將欲廢之，必故興之；將欲取之，必故與之。是謂微明。
柔弱勝剛強。魚不可脫于淵，國之利器不可以示人。

36.

What one wishes to limit quickly,
one needs to let entirely unfold first. —
What one wants to weaken definitely,
needs to be overwhelmingly strong first. —
What shall be annihilated without effort,
one needs to let fully blossom out first. —
In order to take easily,
one needs to give first.

This really is called true knowledge:
Flexible and weak overcome hard and portentous.
The wells catfish must not ascend to the surface —
Advantages and possibilities of a nation
must not be shown to the people.

This chapter is an instruction for princes and generals, so that they should rule, viz. command, with success.

The mentioned *«true knowledge»* may equally well be translated as *detailed knowledge*, and the whole behaviour described throughout this verse clearly hints at the teachings of SUN-DSE regarding Daoist warfare: The latter will be explained more in-depth later on, under the slogan : *Truly overcomes who does not fight*. Verse N° 22 of the *Dao-De-Jing* as well explained this behaviour in pairs of contradictory duals, which are based entirely on SUN-DSE's teachings about *‹plenitude›* and *‹deficiency›*. –

N° 26 moreover shows how these contradictory pairs even produce each other reciprocally (like in N° 2 and some others): Too much power weakens itself by itself. The last example, though, says almost ‹verbally›: *«a prosperous nation must be discreet»*!

All this is about entirely developing things – better still: letting them fully unfold by themselves until reaching their climax, where by themselves they begin to develop the tendency to weaken, according to the cosmic Law of generation, blossom time, maturity and decay, following which everything in the world sooner or later will convert itself into its contrary and perish, because it needs must do so, following the Law of Nature. – At that point, however, the ruler or strategist *must act*, resolutely and with firmness.

With this, one of the most fundamental principles in the Universe is evoked – namely, the phenomenon oft the innumerous opposed ‹duals› – material or immaterial, visible or invisible. These phenomena in every manifestation of the Universe make the irritation for whoever has no spiritual understanding:

«How is it possible that so much injustice exists in this World?» – «How is it possible that a God who is named the All-Good, also allows for so much evil in this World?» – Many similar questions are uttered by ordinary people; and the answers found on this low level are very seldom satisfactory. Mephisto in Gœthe's Faust comments it in his short and enigmatic way: «Well, there you see these things the way ordinary people use to see these things … !»

The spiritually conscious ‹Disciple› or ‹voyager› instead «sees these things» *differently*: He knows that every experience we make here is a move on the Path of *DAO* – following the laws of Nature known to us. The first Law according to which the Universe lives, says: *Whatever has a beginning, must also have an end.* From this follows that this Law cannot but produce ‹things› already pregnant with their contrary – and forces that carry their opposite forces with them, since the first moment of Time: This is the Wheel of Nature, the Wheel of births and ‹death›. Contemplated on this plane, our present N° 36 is «easy to understand». Therefore everybody can apply this verse on everybody's life – be he a business man, a farmer or a King. – On a higher level instead, things prove to be somewhat more complex: The four couplets of two lines on *cause and effects* (*«actio = reactio»*) at the beginning of the text, read on the level of the *Law of DAO*, articulate already some higher wisdom.

First of all, it is obvious that said eight lines do not all mean the same thing, and the most obvious case is the one about *give* and *take*: What one gives is not always the same as what one receives, and not always a *quid pro quo* either. – And the same goes for the other pairs. Here we remember two things: One is that all martial arts teach not to bluntly overpower an adversary, but to let him weaken himself, possibly without fight. The other is the word of Jesus: *«Do not fight evil!»* (see later).

What is meant with the *give* and *take* however is not just the direct ‹payment› or ‹compensation› known from *ordinary material life*: Spiritual life as well knows the proverbial *«no pain – no gain»*. – On the all- comprising plane of spiritual science we see again and again: Nothing is experienced undeservedly – neither pain nor joy, neither gain nor loss. Here we talk about the *Law of Karma*, which in its wondrous and entirely incomprehensible precision compensates even the smallest inequity – somehow, some time or other, and often in absolutely incomprehensible ways: The smallest effort gets its reward; the smallest fault is retaliated by the universal law of this «equalizing justice» of causes and effects – of wrong-doing and correction – of effort and grace.

Matthew in his Gospel says it like this (Mt 10:29-30): «*Are not two sparrows sold for a farthing, and not one of them shall fall on the ground without your Father; – but the very hairs of your head are all numbered*» (King James version).

N° 73 of the *Dao-De-Jing* calls this unfailing Law an *unescapable net*. From here comes the motive for the fatalism of many people, and their objection out of fear of existence: *«If really everything is predestined anyway, nothing can be done about it, and there is no use in any personal effort at all, !»* –

This is a gross objection out of ordinary low reasoning and of plane ignorance regarding the fact that even Karma must follow its own law, as it is opposed to its *counter-force*: the law of *free will*, according to which people following the attractions of Karma undergo (or escape) a certain situation with the precision of a second's time or a millimeter, but still have the possibility and the responsibility of making their own choice.

The *postulate of free will* is a dilemma challenging religious leaders of all strains since many centuries, for it reduces their power to normalize or dictate their *«correct teaching»* – their *orthodoxy* which, besides of fundamentally different creeds, and due to the tragic of general human half-wittedness, again and again undergoes changes, disputes, and even wars. —

But let us return to our N° 36 with its four direct pairs of actions and their effects:

The pilgrim on the Gnostic Path receives here some important recommendations and teachings – and in the meantime an equally important warning. – In order to consciously let fade away and neutralize undue energies, it is necessary to well observe one's impulses, and to unmask more and more clearly ones motivations; – for, how should a Candidate drop ‹wrong habits›, avoid failures, and *change flaws into strengths* if he does not acknowledge them? Growing awareness is what is demanded here: an ever sharp eye for one's behaviour and motives, an ever sharp ear for one's own words, and an ever wake consciousness for one's own thoughts … – Yes, the concrete daily life of a Candidate striving towards the highest wisdom and sanctity gets more and more critical, his path still narrower, and the demand for clarity, purity, and truthfulness becomes more and more stringent!

That's when it gets more and more crucial that he follow the indirect recommendation of verse 36. of the *Dao-De-Jing*: not to eschew any possible experience, but to let unfold all energies under the scope of self-control, in love and comprehension of the Disciple for himself: He is his own observer and mentor for his own gnostic self-initiation – he alone can and must be the one! – Jesus descended down to Hades before ascending to the Heavens!

True, all traditions – from Buddha unto modern Gnosis – speak of the *«mortification of desires»*; but none of these teachings understand this as a violent ‹killing› of any impulsion, what so ever. All of them understand it as a mental and emotional *letting go*, the conscious neutralization and the dynamic *decay* of old desires, habits, thought-images, and fixed ideas. *That is* the inner process of purification – and it concentrates on heart and head – on thinking, willing and feeling!

Before a ‹false› habit, a strong impeding desire can decay as just mentioned, it needs must become consciously *experienced* and, as people say, *«fully lived»*. The measure of this full experience is very individual for every single human on this hell-bound trip, this deep *catharsis* – this *rinsing* 同其塵，是謂玄同 through innermost experience. Some need to make it a series of intense physical sensations, until actual nausea. – To others, becoming conscious through intense empathy into astral and etheric processes suffices to experience a mental satiety as intense as if it had been undergone physically. Thus the ‹thirst› can die out – especially when it is taken under progressing conscious control, until becoming so weak that even the first impulse can be dismissed.
Paulus (Ro. 7:19) says it like this: «… for, the good I want, that I don't do – but the evil I don't want, that I do».

In utter clarity these facts present themselves before the eyes of the conscientious Candidate – and this may in the beginning appear discouraging; – but as he practices again and again not to judge anybody and nothing, he neither judges himself too harshly. He sees, he understands, maybe he shakes his head with a smile, and pursues his path. But slowly heart and head learn to naturally abdict and overcome his ancient personality.

The warning contained in this verse N° 36 thus says: *«Do not avoid any experience – neither by force nor by fear – for every piece of experience is also a piece of learning. What has been eschewed out of best intentions, may pop up in the worst of moments – maybe even on an otherwise very high level of evolution – and the consequences might be disastrous!»*. –

Yes indeed, neither by forcible ascetics nor by painful exercises the desired self-education can be achieved, but only as in «flexible reservation» the Candidate observes and *in free will* choses his path. – Thus, here as well, *flexibility will prove to be stronger than firmness, and smoothness more powerful than rigidity* – as is the way of Daoism.

Remains the last paragraph of the 36th verse of the *Dao-De-Jing*, where there is question of some fish, and of the *«ease»* of a nation. Entangling is this verse – and entangled were a great many translators of this passage: What about this *«fish in dark depth»* – this *«sharpest sword in the view oft the people»*, may we ask? – Really: What is the reader to think about *Lao-Dse the Great Sage,* if the latter erupts in the cranky observation, as another translator insinuates: *«Fish belong into the water, the sword belongs into the sheath »*?

True: *ease* and *advantages* of a nation may be translated also as *sharp tools* (meaning *talents and opportunities!*); – but *formlessness* and *invisibility* as emphasized in *Sun-Dse*'s book about strategies are closer to the real meaning, no doubt:

Just as the wells-catfish digs into his muddy pond, in order to better surprise its victim and become even fatter, so a ‹nation› shall neither provoke its neighbors by its strength, nor attract them by its commodities. –

On a spiritual level though, we may understand that one issue of said discretion is *to protect the Mysteries*, same as we read in one of the *Rosicrucian Manifesto*'s of the 17th century: *«Neither throw pearls to the pigs, nor roses to the asses!»* –

This really is what one names farsighted action!

第三十七章

道常無為而無不為。侯王若能守之，萬物將自化。
化而欲作，吾將鎮之以無名之樸。無名之樸，夫亦將不欲
不欲以靜，天下將自正。

37.

DAO is continuous non-doing –
but nothing remains undone.

Princes and kings appear to preserve themselves —
but all things themselves ask for changes —
for changes and for activity.

To cool down my desires, I use the unspeakable, and am simple:
When they cool down using the unspeakable and are simple,
all humans are without desires. —
Without desires – and therefore calm and still
the whole World will arrange itself, by itself.

The *Dao-De-Jing* has dedicated several chapters to what it calls «non-doing»: five of them specifically, and in general at least ten more. This not only emphasizes the importance of *‹non-doing›* when it comes to following the Path, but it also shows the multiplicity of possible standpoints for contemplation. There are so many different ways to influence the course of events, in the outside world as well as within oneself, without recurring to direct action, or even to active violence: Even thoughts, including thoughtless feelings, are equal to acting! This shows once more how important it is to know precisely one's own motives and desires, to acknowledge them every time and – very often – to *unmask* them as some action obnoxious to the Path.

Why is that so? – The Universe, and indeed each single atom of it, is constantly, in every second, undergoing changes. – Change is movement, and movement is *Life!* – Without changes, the World should have to die! But all these changes are not chaotic nor incoherent; they don't occur by incident, but in every second, in every atom follow the one universal Law – the universal Divine Plan. And every creature in the Universe has an innate consciousness of these movements – with the sole exception of average Man!

Man today – instead of universal cosmic consciousness – has what we call an individual self-consciousness. Through this self-consciousness he accumulates, in the course of his lifespan in this world, numberless images, impressions, and experiences. – And he equally develops an uncountable mass of ideas, wishes, plans, aims, anguishes and strategies in order to achieve or avoid this or that. It is only in some rare instances that he sets priorities for his life as a whole: clear aims, chosen *by free will.* But these aims hardly once further the lively advancement of the Universe, but again serve egocentric short-term interests – aims that are meant to fasten the personal *status quo.* – And this is true, most of all really, for many modern kings, and for most politicians.

Routines of apperception and behavior are turned into norms for a general attitude of life as a whole (if anything at all); – but this norm of life remains more or less unknown to the individual. – Yes, even if a person were capable to specify examples for such a ‹norm of life›, his or her enumeration would be incomplete, or inadequate – or both.

From there, the timeless encouragement of all Initiates to get to know oneself: *Γνωϑι σεαυτόν – gnothi seautón* was the slogan in Greek that served as a basis for Initiation in Antiquity. It even became the title for a book oft the first Theosophist at the beginning of our modern times: VALENTIN WEIGEL, a Lutheran pastor who was connected to the first little circle of 17th century Rosicrucians – the so-called *Circle of Tubingue* around VALENTIN ANDREÆ – wrote this precious philosophical book around 1570.[58]

This *«get to know thyself»* is complicated by the structure oft the thinking, sensing, willing and acting human character globally named the *personality.* The latter's usual ruler is its Ego. This Ego differs in no way of any other ruler or king, but moreover is dominated by the so-called *Auric Being* – the *Super-Ego.* In the previous chapter we hinted at the importance and impenetrability of motives and motivations for the human existence. Here now, we want to give two definitions:

Motivations are meant to be – in a positive sense – ideals and aims of a general, or dominant nature; a *motive* is meat to animate the instantaneous dynamic of feelings, thoughts or will-impulses (if they go as far as that). Thus, these are mostly spontaneous mechanisms, triggering some act *without control by conscious reasoning.* Thus, the outer drive of an action itself is no motive, but only an impulse that principally might be enacted – translated into some action – by every person in a different way, where – let us emphasize it once more – the term *action* explicitly includes all thoughts and emotions related to it: These are, as it were, only differently densified correspondences of what a ‹subject› sets in motion objectively.

Looked at it under this auspice, the present text acquires an unimaginably large impact and high importance for the ‹voyager› on the Path of Dao – for the Disciple of Gnosis.

Supposed the pilgrim has already made a few steps on *The Path*, and thus has even acquired already a general overview of what *The Path* is composed of, then he also has understood that each step of *new knowledge* must be preceded by a step of *new insight*: Insight into the significance of the world, of the Universe and of Humanity – insight into the significance of *The Path*, and insight into what we need to understand about the many, and even uncountable, concepts regarding the Divinity.

But has he – has she also obtained a deep insight into his or her own being? – an insight into his or her own Ego – an insight deeper than that of an average ordinary human?

We presume that this is the case, for, as this apprentice is no actual beginner any more, he has learnt about the basics of Hermetism; and therefore he also knows the correspondences between Above and Below – of Large and Small – of Inside and Outside. And if he has indeed studied his own personality to some extent, he also has found out that, the deeper his understanding for God, World and Humanity has become, the deeper his assessment of his own personality has gotten as well. Since long he then has got used to accompany every observation outside of himself with the question: «*And what does this mean for my own Self? – How about it in and for myself (my own Ego)?* – Am I conscious of this element, this dynamic, this attribute with regard of my own character – it being but a mirror of what I can see and understand outside of myself – and vice-versa?»

Now the fundamental thought behind the 37th verse oft the *Dao-De-Jing* appears to be the *harmony of non-doing*. – What is the main idea behind this?

It is the *dominance of quietude and peace* that becomes the second nature of who in DAO has found his refuge and his help. Where there is calmness and peace, there is harmony – there finally also reigns DAO. This is, as the text suggests, true for every private individual as well as for kings and their kingdoms – in other words, for the microcosmic «king» (the Ego), and for his peers and subjects in the microcosmos (traits of character, and possessive spirits).

The *highest ruler of a human personality* (its Super-Ego) is indeed an imperious king, a power-mad tyrant who exploits his people, manipulating them by all possible means. And this he does in such a cunning way that the regent of the personality – the person's ego-consciousness – is very slow to only *perceive* this system – and even much slower to detect and block it. If the precedent chapter looked at training awareness, the present one is about actual self-control – and that not only when an action has already occurred or can't be stopped anymore, but bye and bye already before, and even without effort. – The issue is to refute all uncontrolled impulses, wherever it is possible – to *limit them* and to *«cool down»* the heat of flashing reactions, as says the text.

The text does not say *«suppress»*, for this would correspond to an act of violence, and violence cannot but call for more violence (counter-violence). And it has been said already: Where the *subjects* – i.e. impulses, habits and inclinations – are suppressed through *too much* self-control, there they will sooner or later revolt – and *King Ego* will emerge from this trial of strength as the winner – each time, and inevitably!

The concept of *ascetics* is best explained by a quotation from the preface to the book of AL-GHAZALĪ – *Letter to the Disciple – Ayuha-'l Walad*:

«The expression ασκέω, askéo *– exercise, endeavour – originally meant no forcible abstinence, but an exercise or practice – through insight – of a pure, priestly attitude where earthly desires and impulsions are minimized, without constraint, to the biological minimum, and as a natural consequence: to a pure orientation on the Path. This concept of deliberate abstinence in favor of inner purification, has been alienated until culminating in Jesuit and ‹pagan› flagellantism, and has become a heavy burden for the psyche of the people. Even the mass of teachers were unable to understand the background of this very reasonable concept – and this even less as it was, and still is today, abused by established institutions to cultivate a psychosis of sinful unworthiness, and complexes of ‹mortal sin› – an ideal basis for unscrupulous manipulation and domination of the masses ... – During Antiquity, such painful exercises were intended to let early humans develop a kind of ego-consciousness. For the mystic Path of ego-renouncement ... and for the mystical union with the sublime All-One however, this kind of techniques of negative ego-cultivation are not just a superstitious exaggeration, but also a gruesome, absolutely condemnable obstacle.»*[14]

There must be no forcible struggle, wherein the Ego would try to *subjugate* itself – thereby really *reinforcing* itself.

What can be done here? Our text gives us a clear answer – even thrice on a few lines: The trick is to undertake nothing at all, save to concentrate on Gnosis as the one and only highest priority, i.e. to let oneself be determined exclusively by Gnosis. From this strong link or even solid union with the Gnosis, everyone may scoop *simplicity, stillness, and peace*: So all the rest will arrange itself, melting into the harmony of the All-One, and re-become one with IT, «as it was in the Beginning». If the ego-will thus submits entirely to DAO, the «King» will again, like in Antiquity, be *the most noble servant of the* Empire – the servant on the Path toward DAO. –

And who are the «king»'s peers and nobility? They too are required to be purified, and put in the service of the One Unspeakable! – These are: The heart (the inner Self), the soul (the highest longing for the Light), sober devotion (highest humble aspiration), faith (pure knowledge by experience), intelligence (the capability to perceive and to discriminate), self-consciousness (opinions by third parties, pre-judgements, ideas, conceptions, and anxiety) and the Marsian will resulting from all these.

The Candidate thus needs to gain growing control oft his personal Ego: the latter exists, it cannot, and for said reasons must not, be denied, but in the light of Gnosis increasingly submits to the control of the Candidate's exclusive devotion to DAO and to growing insight and self-control: *«To cool down my desires, I use the unspeakable, and am simple».* – Since the «State's Government» has been arranged as explained, since all perceptions are refined in the pure orientation toward TAO, the Candidate needs to acquire simplicity and confidence, and to turn himself completely to the Center: to the still and unmoving epicenter of the Wheel – to the *«Pearl in the Lotus» or, as modern Rosicrucians say, to the primary divine spark in the most-inner kernel of the kernel of the microcosmos.»* Here, and only here, stillness and peace are inalterable. From here everything can happen in harmony with DAO – thus teaches us *Lao-Dse*.

Not *do* must the Candidate on The Path, but just *let happen* that DAO performs IT in the Candidate: *«Not I – but the Christos within myself»*, or, as *Lao-Dse* says in his unsurpassable sharpness:

DAO is continuous non-doing – but nothing remains undone.

PART II:

«DE-GING»

德經

CONSTANT VIRTUE

第三十八章

上德不德，是以有德；下德不失德，是以無德。
上德無為而無以為；下德為之而有以為。
上仁為之而無以為；上義為之而有以為。
上禮為之而莫之應，則攘臂而扔之。
故失道而后德，失德而后仁，失仁而后義，失義而后禮。
夫禮者，忠信之薄，而亂之首。
前識者，道之華，而愚之始。
是以大丈夫處其厚，不居其薄；處其實，不居其華。故去彼取此

38.

Highest DE is without ambition for DE —
this exactly is the essence of DE.
Low DE is: not to let go of DE —
that exactly is not in keeping with DE.
The highest DE is, to be unmoved without thinking about it —
Low DE is, to be unmoved, and in the same time to think.
Highest goodness is, to serve without thinking [about it] —
Highest righteousness is, to serve and to think something
while doing it.
Highest morality is, to do something and, when nobody agrees,
to throw up one's arms, and disdain it.

Therefore:

Where DAO is neglected, there rules DE —
Where DE is neglected, there rules goodness —
Where goodness is neglected, there rules righteousness —
Where righteousness is neglected, there rules morality.

A well-bred person is humble, candid and modest —
but his thinking is without an aim.

In ancient times, this was common knowledge:
DAO is wonderful; – but dull is its begin. —
Therefore, a person who is firmly committed
lives in rich deepness rather than in measly insignificance —
in true Life rather than in sweet-scented exclusiveness. —
And so he quits [all] that, and choses This [One]. [14-A]

The vast differences between the numerous translations for this chapter of the *Dao-De-Jing* are amazing – including modern Chinese comments, and including even our own variants. But this is quite understandable: What *is* the Path – what is it *not*? – What *does* the ‹finder of wisdom› *do*, and what does he *not do*? Whoever during a certain time has toiled on the Path, has learnt that finding often begins just there where the search ends – that progress on the path must lie just there where the thought of advancement has been abandoned. Such a one will understand the contradictions and vagueness of the text, and be able to integrate them into the philosophy of *actual Gnosis*. – The trouble then lies with the insistence of modern humans, to fully equip every sentence with all the elements modern syntax includes and demands: pronomina, conjunctions, interjections – and of course judgement-like *qualifications*. Because of this however, a polyvalent text is fixed onto one sole ‹track›, and its interpretative wealth goes lost.

So, the interested lector may encounter a host of in-part truly tangled variants of ‹translation›: Knowing The Path only from mystical theories, they labour to find some tasty formulations using modern language and logic. The results often are nice to read, but lack the elaborate mistiness as is characteristic for the speech of the Mysteries since eons; and with that, *the inner – the esoteric content* is lost.

This is particularly what makes the difference between modern ‹civilized› language and the old Chinese texts. The latter gives just the sober facts: *Or* something *is* there, visibly, effective, present (all this being expressed by the same glyph) – *or* it is *absent, lacking, forgotten or left out* (all this again being indicated by one single sign), and all this without moral or sentimental critics: *Or «he» is* a human on the Path, a *‹wise man›, a warrior, or even already entirely united with DAO – or* he *is not*.

The challenge consists in that *one glyph* can stand for so many things – likely following esthetical, rhythmical or musical linguistic sentiment, and no rational logic. This versatile Chinese language renders an absolutely accurate translation quite impossible, but it helps understand the significance of a verse.

Certainly it also was the intention of the author, to use in his book a maximum of *soul-oriented word-signs* using a minimum of logical conceptions. Who knows the Path of DAO may easily understand all this; but the editor of a book who wrestles to achieve a valuable translation finds himself confronted to a very complex task!

Why do these remarks appear here, and not in the main preface to this book? They stand there as well, but here they are part of the commentary to N° 38. Also, it must be said that the original book (as opposed to other translations) mentions DAO only in its second part – and even there just by the by. The first part mentions but DE – roughly translatable as *aspiration for virtue*. But virtue is by far not wisdom yet. The text rightfully says that aspiration for virtue includes being able to let go of aspiration for virtue!

Equally, one is tempted to say, in the style of the *Dao-De-Jing*: «Who really wants to talk about *DAO* does *not speak of* DAO!» – and in this sense, extremely to the point, even: «Who in the highest manner aims at DAO, using DE, does not think of *DE as a method*, nor of *DAO as a result* of his endeavours: He, or she, strives without thinking about it! This means (again!) *complete dedication* to the Path, in joyful *self-forgetfulness*, also named *self-sacrifice.*

Lao-Dse repeats it: The Path of DAO is the path of forgetting, or of loosing, but not of forcible deadening of the Ego. The ruler of the ego-personality and its Ego must die, but neither the Ego nor the personality as such: they both are needed as servants for as long as possible, not just in order to follow the Path while living, but also to make it known to as many humans as possible! The Ego destined to die is not the personality's *natural carnal Self* – even less the *inner-most spiritual Self*, but the focus of centripetal flurry, whence spring the sparks of astral impulses, thought by vulgar people to be their Ego.

The formal *‹deadening of the Ego›* issues from an ascetic misunderstanding about the modern Gnosis of the last past century. and the reason for that is as follows: At the beginning oft the last past century, when it was *impossible yet* to openly speak about Gnosis, and during the decennia after that, when it was *forbidden* to speak of it, the ascetic understanding was the only possible way to officially follow some gnostic practice – be it as a finder or as a witness of the Gnosis in then actual ways and forms. This is illustrated by the fact that the foundation of a proper Rosicrucian Mystery School by Dr. Rudolf Steiner during the early twenties of the 20-eth century was exclusively mentioned by all as a *High-School*, albeit R.St. announced right from the beginning the aims and characteristics of a *Mystery-School*. However, his ‹followers› disavowed his innermost ideal, and the Nazi-regime sought to kill him. – On the other side, it is as obvious as it is wondrous: Precisely when R.St. had to abandon his project of a Mystery School, consequently falling ill and dying, a real Rosicrucian Mystery School was indeed founded in Holland. This new organization proposed a more modest goal for its existence: Reanimation of the teachings and endeavors of the Rosicrucians of the 17th century, with their (and R. Steiner's) *Father-Brother Christian Rosencreutz*, along with the ‹education› of humans who would gain a newly born *‹Living Soul›* –i.e., who following the words of the Lord's *Sermon on the Mountain*, would have mystically experienced an inner *«Baptism With Water»*. This immediately indicates a *process of inner purification, renewal and transformation*; – a helicoïdal evolution, the first turn of which produces the ‹New-born Soul›, as said before. The second turn consequently is the *«Baptism with Spirit»*, and the third, then, is the fiery, ‹structural transformation› into real *New Divine Man* – thus, the actual *Transfiguration regarding* soul, spirit and body.

With that however the spiral path of evolution is not finished. Just a higher level – a higher dimension – is attained, from where then a truly high engagement for God, Universe and Humanity can begin.

On the grounds of this and earlier remarks one cannot speak of *truly high aspiration toward virtue – thus toward DE* – as long as this aspiration and the conditions thereto still fill the thoughts and wants oft the Candidate – i.e. as long as the latter holds thoughts like: *«I must – I want – I wish to transfigure»*. – No, it is precisely *not I* who transfigures (resp. *might get to be transfigured*); – and there is *no must* either – otherwise: where would there be the free will? – where maturation of the soul? – *Wanting* too has no place here; for, who is it who *«wants»*, if not old *centripetal Ego*? And *«I wish»*, besides egocentricity, also shows a lack of *fundamental faith*. But an unshakable faith is the absolute precondition (and refuge) of all transfiguristic endeavours, and thus of the whole voyage toward DAO – and it is indispensable to the Candidate as air is for breathing!

Whatever is not in accord with all this, may be considered as *less high* ambition – e.g. purely religious strife for virtue; – as goodliness – or as often hypocritical mysticism or ‹good moral›, like in the way of the Ancient Testament. But where both moral and ancient customs (rituals) are missing, the doors are wide open for *«all kind of disorder and turmoil»*. – With this is translated the polyvalence of a Chinese expression in just one glyph that our translation simply renders with «aimless». And that is what the first lines of verse N° 38 mean to convey regarding both *exertion* and *non-exertion* as well as regarding *doing*, *non*-doing, and *non-doing while doing* – the well-known *‹Wu-Wei›*.

Earlier renditions indulge in terms like: *«Lawfulness is ... the begin of disorder»* (Kirchner); – «*Rituals spoiled loyalty and fidelity, and confusion lifted her head» (Schwarz); – «l'urbanité* (meaning: *civilité*) … est la source du *désordre* (Julien); – *«La religión es el fin de la virtud y [de] la honestidad»* (Rivas); – «*Zedelijkheid* is … de begin van de *wanorde*» (Wilemsens). – What are we to think about such profane deliveries in the most famous *philosophical œuvre* promoting the *path toward highest wisdom* on every plane of our daily life: The ‹Emperor›, his ‹peers›, stately ‹clerks› and all their ‹subjects›? — Really !!

Thus, verse 38, the first of the *Second Part* of the *Dao-De-Jing* presents in a nut-shell, in the most concise and at the same time the most pertinent way possible, the central elements composing the kernel of the teachings regarding DAO and DE. –

Renown Theologist and philosopher *Karl Barth* in his major work comments this terseness like this: *«The actual absence of any intent, that in its simplicity solves the riddle, has, maybe, never throughout all philosophy, so decisively been made the fundament of all truth of agency, as is the case with Lao-Dse».*[11] –

The mention of *«aimlessness»*, by the way, appears almost as a pre-phase immediately before the ‹outbreak› of the Chinese *«Era of the fighting nations»* (403-256 b.C.).

The last part of this N° 38 answers some typical questions regarding *The* Path: *«What is the practical essence of all this? – What are these essentials' criteria? – What are the possible guidelines, and how can one assess ones own ‹progress›? – What is the difference between what is called here the «lower virtues», and the «highest virtue» of the Path of DAO? »* –

The answer is: The (philosophic) level of the goal must be *kept in mind incessantly*: This, and this alone, makes the difference between the worldly king and the ‹philosophical king›, who also appears in the very old language of medieval *operative Alchemy* – and in modern times again in that of the *Chymical Wedding of Christian Rosencreutz. – The beginning of ignorance* consists in that one quits said full attention for *DAO and DE*. Its end is marked by the *re-assessment of Gnosis. This is «that great success», «that real Glory»*. All the rest is *«mediocre survival in this beguiling and narcotizing dwelling»* – in this world of embezzlement: As soon as one turns away from *this*, one will acquire *that*!

The *«trail back»* is marked by scientific precision, and by the royal capability to differentiate at any moment between what is important and what is not – between speculation and fools-play on one side, and solid certitude on the other. On one hand, we are asked to let go of, forget and forgive what, from a transfiguristic standpoint, has become obsolete– and on the other, to grasp and hold fast what is new, genuine, authentic, and actual. — Now!

And so he quits [all] that, and choses this [One].

昔之得一者。
天得一以清。地得一以寧。神得一以靈。
谷得一以盈。萬物得一以生。侯王得一以為天下貞。
其致之。
天無以清將恐裂。地無以寧將恐廢。神無以靈將恐歇。
谷無以盈將恐竭。萬物無以生將恐滅。
侯王無以貞將恐蹶。
故貴以賤為本，高以下為基。
是以侯王自稱孤、寡、不穀。
此非以賤為本邪
非乎?
至譽無譽。
不欲琭琭如玉
珞珞如石。

第三十九章

昔之得一者：天得一以清；地得一以寧；神得一以靈；
谷得一以生；侯王得一以為天下貞。
其致之也，天無以清將恐裂；地無以寧，將恐發；神無以靈，
將恐歇；谷無以盈，將恐竭；萬物無以生，將恐滅；
侯王無以高貴，將恐蹶。
故貴以賤為本，高以下為基。是以侯王自稱孤、寡、不穀。
此非以賤為本邪？非乎？故致輿無輿。
是故不欲□□如玉，珞珞如石。

39.

Formerly, each thing had its One destination:
The One destination of Heaven was its clarity —
The One destination of Earth was its continuity —
The One destination of the World of Spirits was its watchfulness —
The One destination of the corn-fields was their abundance —
The One destination of the 10'000 things was their vitality —
The One destination of noblemen and kings was
to serve the Empire in flawless perfection. —
As is the one, so also is the other. –

Thus says tradition – and moreover it says:
If Heaven lacks clarity,
we must verily fear that it might burst.
If Earth lacks continuity,
we must verily fear that it might explode.
If the World of Spirits lacks watchfulness,
we must verily fear that it might go down.
If the corn-fields lack abundance,
we must verily fear that they consume themselves.
If the 10'000 things lack vitality,
we must verily fear that they die out.

If kings and noblemen lack perfection,
we must verily fear that they will be deposed.
Premeditated splendor creates causes for indigence —
Arrogance creates causes for humiliation. —
Certain princes and kings feign themselves to be
lonely, little and indigent.
What a sordid way to not create indigence —
is it not?

Highest honor does not glorify itself.
To acquire calculated glory is no glory.
That an honest man ***thus*** *desire* ***not*** *⌊to sound⌉* ***like little jade*** *⌊bells⌉***:**
stone against stone *[sounds]* ***like stone.***

This chapter presents itself as another lesson for a prince or king. It does not stand in a direct relation to the Path of DAO, but it shows a moral frame of conduct wherein DAO can develop itself. What this chapter is about, therefore, is the consciousness that every creature has – *ab origine* – its very specific task and position attributed to it by the Creator, and that *the world* can prosper only if *every cell of every organ* keeps following its *One destination.* To understand this fact is also one of the fundaments allowing us to consciously experience the *Union of All – ‹things› and beings* throughout the Universe. This is the first step of gaining consciousness and virtue: *What is low is the footboard for what is high*, as several translators suggest, inverting the glyphs of the text.

Now, a harmonious translation that follows the rhythm and the main statement of this text is possible only as long as one does lose sight neither of the intention of the *Dao-De-Jing* nor of its being embedded in the feudalism of Ancient China, with the Emperor as *heavenly ruler* of the *earthly World* – son of Heaven, and a god himself. Now, in Chinese, World and Heaven being designated by the same glyph, *Heaven and Earth* of this text designate both *the Emperor and his subjects.* This said, we understand even better that if the various *Reigns of Creation* stop fulfilling their *One* destination, the *order of the whole Creation* (Greek *kosmos*) is more or less seriously severed, and inevitably the fall of the ruler – the Emperor in one case, and Mother Nature in the other, is imminent.

The second part of this text is the admonition to the ruler to be honest and modest: He is not to despise lowliness because of his own excellency, nor to provoke the people – but he is to be aware that highness needs lowliness from which it has come forth (as several translations explicitly say). With this goes along the final warning not to strive for honor (even less by shady means): Dishonest behavior will always betray itself, or be discovered and punished. Other translators underline that a good ruler cannot be loved by all: *Praise by all is praise by none*.

In some cases the variations in differing translations come from differing originals. The present variant combines our ‹basic text› and the text by *Wang-Bi* (text in blue stands in *Wang-Bi* only, text in red only in the ‹basic text›).

The end of the text is particularly interesting, as it appears in the robe of epigrammatic wisdom. But in order to firstly understand the remarks around «jade» and «stone», and secondly to apply them to our present example as we should, we need to delve into the cultural surroundings of Ancient China. This effort is well awarded, even if the result partly remains subject to doubts because of the terms put into ⌊a kind of brackets⌉ : The segments at the end can also be interpreted as *necklace of jade,* resp. *necklace of* stone, whereas jade is a stone as well, but a very noble one. This doesn't really change the inner meaning of the text, yet it is interesting to dig deeper into the cultural history of China, and this short excursion is most self-rewarding:

That in China jade is more precious and more *ominous* than all other stones is well known. But translations speaking straight out of *precious stones* are certainly on a wrong track: Not the *material value* counts here as the plutocratic Westerners of today would be inclined to expect, but the *magic sound – the increment to the harmony as an ensemble* – thus again the fulfillment of *the One destination* (but not of the *purpose*!) of the whole. Even such obsolete insets as: *«the parts of a wagon are not the wagon» and suchlike* turns that cannot be found in any of the Chinese texts we studied, have the same *signification.* At any rate, it is quite worth while to meditate the conceptions of *value*, *destination*, and *purpose*, in order to well understand the text.

To come back to *jade* and *stone*: A *lithophone* is a musical instrument composed of carved or uncarved stones of any size and form – from raw natural rock formations (*‹rock-gongs»*) over carved stalactites (*‹stalac-pipes»*) onto African, north-American, north-European, Indian and Asian lithophones (stone chains or rows of stones in the way of a xylophone) composed of appropriate material – also named *phonoliths. Carl Orf,* a German composer of our times mentions in some of his compositions the use of a lithophone as well. The oldest discoveries of lithophones in China are dated back to the time of 2400 b.C., but their use is alleged to have been much prior to that.

The Chinese *bian-qing*, consists of L-shaped *stone wedges* suspended in a frame of wood or bronze that can be played melodiously. This instrument partly still plays an important role in folk music, at the court, and in rituals, along with the little *bronze bells* (Chinese *Bian-zhong*) known in Buddhism as well. A special variant of this are the *qing*'s made from small *jade balls* (some piriforme as little bells). These were mainly used in the most solemn rituals and ceremonies of the Emperor, and for those oft the nobility. Another very special occasion to use these instruments were the ceremonial sacrifices for Heaven, Earth and ancestors.

From this, the last line is quite self-explaining in connection with praise, self-praise and humility: The issue is not to present and behave oneself as being more precious and noble than what one really is; for, the real value of a person will sooner or later prove itself. The little jade bells at the ceremonies of the nobility make a delicate melodious sound; the simple stone slabs of the lowly folk in their rural dances sound coarse and dry.

«Don't try to appear as if you were of a higher grade of nobility than what you really are, for your true value will show itself by the *sound of your soul*: So, don't you try to sound like some chimes of jade, while you cannot sound better than lime or black stone, least we must *verily fear that you will burst* and be thrown away!». That is what the text means to convey; – but the literal meaning of these glyphs in brackets (viz. the lacuna they were filled in for) remains impenetrable. – As for the significance of the term ‹necklace› we regret to have been unable to find an adequate picture proving what we were expecting to find: In Ancient China honorary jade necklaces were presented as decorations the way we know it from Ancient Egypt (Egyptologist's ‹honorary collars›).

However: We cannot ascertain our translation to be absolutely ‹water-proof›, I spite of having combined the available elements as best we could – even less so as the three originals we used for our traditions end in different ways. At any rate, ours is less fantastic and less queer, but more coherent than all others. – By the way, neck-laces are honorary attributes in old civilizations since millennia and millennia. – Most of all: our version is in harmony with itself, with the surroundings of the 39th Verse, with historically established conditions, and – finally – with the global frame of the *Dao-De-Jing* as a gnostic scripture for education and initiation.

How ever that may be now: Many of the existing variants have some interesting appeal; but even the large number of modern Chinese interpretations does not allow for one of them to be ‹crowned› as the ultimately correct and best one:

Deliberate splendor creates causes for indigence —
Haughtiness creates causes for abasement!

德

Chinese Chime – Piang-zhong

Small Chinese lithophone – Piang-Qing.

第四十章

反者道之動；弱者道之用。
天下萬物生于有，有生于無。

40.

Recurrence is DAO'S presence —
Compliance is DAO's essence.
The vitality of the 10'000 things beneath Heaven
surges from [their] presence —
The vitality of existence is rooted in non-being.

This chapter of the *Dao-De-Jing* is like a casual definition of *Dao*, the term *essence* here meaning *the inner way and force of being*. But DAO *is itself* the essence – essence of existence – its center as well as its setting. DAO is the focal point of the circle, and at the same time its periphery. Dao is both the path and the goal; it is meaning, origin and bye-law; it is measure and immeasurability, it's cloud, source and ocean, is spark, fire and ashes (the latter being fire as well); is change amidst continuity of the «I» in *I-GING* – Spirit – and one with the latter.

Spirit – *Spirit divine* – is itself absolute entirety of being, as the sum total of all being, and in the meantime the essence of all existence – and vice-versa: All existentiality of the 10'000 things, with all that surrounds them and triggers them – is nothing else but an expression of one or more aspects – ‹facets› – of this incessantly changing, ever unchanged same spiritual entirety of being; – is repose and movement in one.

From «Spirit» everything comes forth; «Spirit» is everything; into «Spirit» everything returns. Spirit is *force, heat* and *movement* all together – infinitely recurrent movement: the Wheel that sets in motion the cycles of *Life*, of *existence* and of *essentiality*. That is the *active aspect* of Spirit. *DAO as spirituality* is *the axis*, too, around which all ‹things› keep rotating. This is the passive aspect of DAO – the aspect of essential conservation, of ‹breeding›, of enabling and of expectation. It comes as no coincidence that biblical Genesis says: «And the Spirit of God was *brooding* over the surface of the Waters»!

The *I-Ging* expresses this duality of Spirit by the pair of Yang and Yin: ▬▬ means the active or ‹male› aspect of Spirit, ▬ ▬ means the passive or ‹feminine› one. Let us say: The male aspect of Spirit is its *existence* (its continuity); its female aspect is its essence (continuous change).

Now humans of all times were and are conscious that Spirit – that DAO – cannot as such be known, nor named, nor as such experienced, but only trough its *agencies*, its numberless ways and *forms of manifestation.*

Whatever is an expression of Spirit, cannot *exist* without manifest dynamics; cannot *be-there* without some kind of *movement* – that is *how things are* – their *essence.* While now Spirit is *«eternal»*, ‹things› instead are *«perishable»* – but only within a conception of *space-time*. For, as Spirit is constantly changing, so are the 10'000 things – embedded as they are in a cycle of continuous renewal. The *«eternal recurrence of the same»* in a new shape and energetic *essence* (*way of being*) is for itself an expression of *statics*: Who of us is permanently conscious of the fact that our continuous respiration is a process – a *cycle of continuous change* – a counteraction and interaction of aging (decay) and renewal? And yet: So it really is! But because this occurs *quite unconsciously*, respiration is no cycle of conscious *renewal* anymore, but works as a *combustion process*. – What exceeds human reasoning in this process is the fact that every renewal in *essence* – hence primarily of *the soul* – demands for a phase of disintegration of the *manifested form*.

Now, it is a privilege of Man to consciously experience his existence, and so he is also conscious of his passing on – his decrepitude and ‹mortality›. Therefore he also is conscious of the difference between ‹living› and ‹dying› existence – including what today is named *death.* A second privilege of Man is the (relatively) conscious perception of his surroundings – physical and non-physical. From this relative consciousness follows, quite naturally, a third exclusively human ‹privilege›: the privilege of *questioning.*

In the eyes of average humans, consciousness stops when they pass away physically. Spiritually informed persons instead can ‹see› that consciousness is bound to no material form, not even to a subtly physical one; – hence his fourth ‹privilege› (that surpasses ordinary human faculties): the *possibility* to become conscious of the continuity and everlasting essence of every creature – and moreover of the fact that everything is embedded into the *One-And-All.* From the *namelessness* of any individual in its actual phase of renewal Man can deduce the microcosmic equivalent of the namelessness of DAO, and thence the way the Monad is rooted in, and united with, DAO, the Arch-Monad as source, medium and end of all existence. Thus the spiritually Initiate also experiences the physical death of things and beings as an expression of *Life* – as an expression of the eternal life-sphere of DAO – of Spirit. And he understands: *Essence* as an expression of this life is at the same time *‹meekness›*, or *‹compliance›* in the sense of Daoism – i.e. *‹flexibility›* – *adaptability* to continual recurrences and life cycles throughout al reigns of the Universe. Therefore, DAO is also *dynamic life* – translated in the present book as *vitality*, in most of earlier translations however as *«being born»*; and this includes, following the laws of the Worlds Nature, growth, flowering, bearing fruit, aging and passing off.

Thus: In so far as DAO represents the core essence of all existence, it is unmovable, inalterable, firm – the Archimedic focal point in the Universe, the universal One, the **I**. But in so far as DAO brings forth the ‹10'000 things› (who or what else should bring them forth?), it is in perpetual movement and in incessant transformation – and thus *‹volatile›*, in spite of its continuous *existence*.

Thus, in so far as DAO is the *moving force* of everything, DAO is the *existence in itself*. And in so far as DAO is the *Mother of all existence*, it is the *essence of non-being in itself*. In so far as it is Yang, then, ⚊, it is *strength*. In so far as it is Yin instead, ⚋, it is, following the glyphs of the *Dao-De-Jing*, *‹weakness›*. But this is no *lack of strength*, but *meekness – reserve of strength* – in Daoism equivalent to *concentration of strength*. Such is the *essence – way of being* of DAO, i.e. its inner dynamic.

This conception of reserved and outwardly invisible continuity of dynamics and strength is the fundament of the whole Daoist teaching regarding the *counter-play of forces* as well as about the *harmony* of all processes in the *Universe*, in every *cosmos* and – given the harmonious transposition of these forces by conscious humans – also within the latter's individual *microcosmoi*.

The book by *Sun-Dse* about *Daoist warfare* that we have mentioned earlier and will mention again, connects the reservation of strength (physical, mental, strategic) with the conception of *plenitude* – but rushing ahead (and attacking) instead with that of *depletion* and subsequent *exhaustion*. The strategy of a good general (strategist) is therefore, to simulate himself and his army to be *weak*, thereby provoking the adversary to become active and thus *debilitate himself* – i.e. to let him [the adversary] empty himself of strength, while [the good strategist] preserves his own means and forces, *concentrating* them without fighting – and thus himself remaining in the *plenitude* of forces: *«One should let the adversary come* (let him deplete himself of strength), and *not advance oneself first* (i.e. remain full [of strength])», says *Sun-Dse*. –

Thus, if verse 38 emphasizes the *essence of the Path*, verse 40 instead illustrates what DAO *really is* – and in so doing defines the kernel of recognition of DAO: DAO is universal dynamic circulation; its *essence* is concentration of *strength*; – strength is *life*; and *life is consciousness*.

Verse 39 already hints at this relational concept when it makes the difference between Gnosis and earthly humanity – between order and disorder. Therefore, if the present translation of verse 40 uses the term: *«Life-force issues from existence – viz. from non-being»*, we might as well add: *Life-force issues from* the *existence, or presence,* [of DAO] – and at the same time of the latter's *non-being* – hence from DAO's *essence in its non-being* – but not of its *absence*! – And that is how it really is, but what modern agnostics cannot see, being incapable to recognize and acknowledge any agency, the cause of which they cannot measure with the undersized yardstick of human intellectuality.

So Daoism clearly points out that the innumerable opposed duals, visible and invisible – in the physical as well as in the spiritual worlds – represent *no emergency order*, as some occultists use to say: These duals are an absolute necessity, in order to successfully dynamize the Universe – a *necessary order* Man needs to become aware of. Those duals really are but the manifest expression of the creative duality of Spirit (Yang and Yin: movement and rest, construction and destruction) – and along with this the unalterable basis for the whole creation to emerge and to develop its flowers and fruits, until it passes its maturity and returns to its original chaos whence it came from – and whence it will surge again … —

Pure divine Spirit – DAO, the *Word*, *Gnosis* – the LOGOS – is eternal. Its existential presence is the cycle and circulation of everything – microcosmoi, cosmoi, macrocosmoi or Universe. – Their *essence – their way of being* – however is the flow of their changes, of their transformations and transmutations, *adapted* to the flow of circumstances and life conditions (*adaptatione*, as says the Tabula Smaragdina), in wise reservation of their plenitude of strength: in *non-being*.

Recurrence is DAO's existence —
The vitality of existence is rooted in non-being.

第四十一章

上士聞道，勤而行之；中士聞道，若存若亡；
下士聞道，大笑之。不笑不足以為道。故建言有之：
明道若昧；　　進道若退；
夷道若□；　　上德若谷；
廣德若不足；　建德若偷；
質眞若渝；　　大白若辱；
大方無隅；　　大器晚成；
大音希聲；　　大象無形；　　道隱無名。
夫唯道，善貸且成。

41.

Highly educated persons learn about DAO – and invert their life.
People of second-rate education learn about DAO – and partly apply it, partly ignore it. —
Uneducated people learn about DAO – and laugh out loud.

Without laughter there is no reason to seriously look at DAO.
Therefore old proverbial wisdom says:
The light of DAO seems to be obscured —
The entrance to DAO seems to be blocked —
The smoothness of DAO seems deceptive —

Great amiability is looked upon as self-complacency —
Magnanimity passes for deficiency —
Well-founded education is deemed to be indecency —
Honesty of character passes for perfidy —
Great purity is reputed as ignominy —

The largest street has no corners —
A large vessel takes much time to reach perfection —
A very big voice has an unfamiliar sound —
The biggest elephant cannot be compared to anything. —

DAO is mysterious and nameless.
Whoever believes in it will be capable to accept it —
and, moreover, to achieve it.

First of all, an inevitable misunderstanding needs explanation:

A *«highly educated person»* is, translated precisely, a *«clerk»*. However, for the Chinese world at the time of *Dao-De-Jing's appearance*, this was one and the same: At that time a high formal education was mandatory, in order to be eligible as a clerk. In order to be a private teacher, a consultant or a hedge lawyer, a person (like today) needed no special formation nor experience. But to become an accredited imperial clerk, one had to pass an imperial exam for clerks. An image from the Ming era (see p. 111) shows hundreds of candidates: Some of them have come on horse back. Most of them are clothed in white, many in blue (indigo: scribes, teachers), one in black (lawyers) and two in gray (physicians). Servants and some of the candidates are clothed in brown (see N° 35 and N° 70). The movie film *A Touch of Zen* depicts these conditions in Ancient China in quite impressive a way (see note 35).

If we admit that many chapters of the *Dao-De*-Jing are addressed to the ruler of a province («a nation») or of the Empire («the World»), then our N° 41 implies a veiled incentive for such a prince to prove that he is *«highly educated»*, by *«entering the Path of DAO without hesitation»*. This said, it becomes clear that *«entering the Path of Dao»* is no minor matter – no whim one can follow now and neglect again (*«following a twisted trail»*, as N° 53 puts it). – No, who is serious about the Path of DAO needs to be *«highly educated»* i.e. *conditioned for DAO.* He and she must *«invert their life»* – with all the consequences this entails!

This *new orientation* and consequent *rearrangement* of life seems to have been rather exceptional already at the time of *Lao-D*se, and looked at askance, as suggests our text. The diverse rhythmic proverbs give a very clear picture. They remember the melancholic ‹prophesies› of Ancient Egyptian *Ipw-Wr* – a name meaning as much as *«that really great one»*[12], who already around 1500 b.C. criticized what our present text is deploring, and what applies increasingly from every century to the next:

Education, formation and high talents are looked at with suspicion or dismissal. Virtue is censured as weakness, openness to learn rates as conformity or as arrogance; Purity of the heart and generosity are looked at as naiveté – as detrimental to the successful pursuit for perishable ‹happiness›, and therefore an embarrassment. – This depreciation is quite justified, for, who dedicates oneself to the *Path of DAO* – the *Path of Gnosis* – depreciates precisely what the ‹soldiers of fortune› in this World regard as the main issue in life – and reveres exactly those virtues and talents the hunters for ‹happiness› and ‹success› despise (see N° 13):

The Great Path brings no honor. One needs rather to be grateful that today (and for how long?) the Disciples of DAO are not persecuted, but allowed to follow and openly propagate the old gnostic Traditions and Doctrine.

Lao Dse does not only criticize the modern way of life, however: He also manifests his understanding for this having to be as it is, given that ordinary people's views about life, the Universe and God neither inwardly nor outwardly surpass the optics of a small domestic animal: A lice knows nothing of the tree on which it sits – a little krill animal cannot see the whale who is swallowing it. – The same way, most humans during their whole lifetime never recognize in the least the spiritual world always surrounding them … —

Compared to the smallness of worldly sorrows and occupations DAO appears as something exceedingly big, and as so extraordinary that it can be described only through unusual images (see N° 15). One remembers the film *Gulliver's Travels* (Paramount pictures, Max & Dave Fleischer, 1939: The Lilliputians climb up and about the giant body quite for a while before becoming aware of it.

The images *Lao Dse* uses for the N° 41 of his *Dao-De Jing* need no further explanation: they are self-explaining. Yet it may be useful still to mention two out of the numerous modern Chinese commentaries: There the image of the *elephant* is so popular that two of the comments are right a way titled *«The Invisible Elephant»*!

Also, there the *«big sound»* is linked to the harmony of the Universe. – The sequence of glyphs used for the comparison of *sound* and *voice* however might as well be inverted, making a *«big sound»* to become a *very deep* or *very high pitched* one, that therefore would *«hardly be audible»*: Indeed, as we know, both are inaudible for the ordinary human ear – and this is true also for the ‹sound› of DAO – the *«Voice of Silence»*.

Many other translations are possible – particularly for the most dubious last line of this text; and they can be found *en masse* throughout the well known versions mentioned along the introduction to the present book. Of these, many use multiple abstract terms – even terms that are boldly invented and far off what the glyphs may indicate. The present version instead is sure to come really close to the Daoist way of thinking and its way of life. At any rate, it conveys to the text a realistic interpretation, life and warmth. The *Very Big Vessel* might as well *be «filled»* instead of *«reaching perfection»*. Probably it is with no intention that this vessel reminds the *«Maha-Yana»* of Buddhist esotericism, but it is most adequate.

Another variant to the last line must not be neglected: Instead of using the expression *«to achieve it»* one might very well use the wording: *«to transform oneself»*: The *Path of Gnosis* is, as is well known, longer than a physical human's lifespan, even if it can be achieved only during a human's physical life-span:

Whoever believes in it will be capable to accept it —
and moreover to achieve it.

第四十二章

道生一，一生二，二生三，三生萬物。
萬物負陰而抱陽，沖氣以爲和。
人之所惡，唯孤、寡、不谷，而王公以爲稱。
故物或損之而益，或益之而損。
人之所教，我亦教之。強梁者不得其死，吾將以爲教父。

42.

DAO brings forth the One. – The One brings forth the Two.
The Two bring forth the Three. – The Three bring forth
the 10'000 things.
The 10'000 things leave the Shadow and embrace the Sun. —
In the ocean of Spirit they enjoy an existence of full tranquility.
The position of Man is precarious: lonely, forlorn, needy … —
Even kings and princes assert this [regarding themselves].
Mayhap one loses something, and still gains thereby —
Or one gains something, and still loses thereby —
The position of Man teaches, and I myself teach it:
A man as mighty as a ridge rafter must not be unbending.
On this basis, my resolution is to serve as a priest and teacher.

This chapter appears to be a brainteaser even for today's Chinese: Even in their materialistic communist circles it is widely discussed. More than a hundred interpretations are offered in the Internet already for the last line alone; the rest of the text is partly interpreted in the way of classic Daoism.

The first paragraph is very close to the gnostical Pythagorean philosophy; and in fact *Pythagoras* (6th c.b.C.), or *Platon* (4th c.b.C.) may partially have lived at the same time as *Lao-Dse* (6th c.b.C.; the oldest known written text of the *Dao-De-Jing* being dated to the 4th c.b.C.). Therefore there are indicated a few remarks regarding the fundamental figures (1 through 4) in their Chinese setting:

The *philosophical One* is the *Enso.* – In *Zen calligraphy* that is the *circle* drawn in one sole swing of the brush. This is the prime fundamental basis of Creation – in the theosophical language of *Jacob Bœhme* the *«Un-grund»* from which everything comes forth, and whereto everything returns. As a second derivative, this circle is *Absolute Existence*; and as a third one it is the *Individual Self* of things; for, everything (formless things included), is – as soon as it is thought – thought and felt as being a *Unity-Selfness*, too. So it comes hardly as a surprise, and has its philosophical ‹beauty› that the *Enso* is phonetically assonant to the Greek *ᶜεν* – *NUMBER ONE*, and also the *Ain-Soph* of western cabalistic tradition, soring *above* the apex of the *Tree of the Sephiroth, and which in the symbolism of Free-masons* as well plays an important (but less absolute) role.

The *NUMBER TWO* in the Chinese tradition is preceded by *Spirit* – i.e. **I**. This comes forth from the *Absolute One* – YI . **I** also is, by it self, as hinted at already in N° 40, ‹divided› into Yin and Yang as a *twofold Unity*. Chinese symbolic language (pictoglyphs) for the *numbers 1 through 3* draws one to three horizontal lines, while in western symbolism, as is well known, One, i.e. **I** (the ‹Father›) is united with ‹TWO› (a recumbent line ▬ or ark ◡ – the *‹Mother›*), to give ‹THREE› as a × (the *‹Son›*), which as a + corresponds to the Four Elements. – In Ancient China, the *NUMBER THREE* corresponds to the soul. *FOUR as* a subdivided *Square* 四 stands for the force embedded (and manifested) in the physical ‹10'000 things›, the former itself thus acting through the latter. – Chinese numbers thus faithfully depict (as ‹pictograms› do) what the text of N° 42 says. That certain translators write about a *‹Great Square›* here, is therefore defendable, although the text says nothing of the kind. However, the version stating that *«the ‹Great Square has no corners» is definitely going too far...* —

The second line of this text N° 42, most acknowledged translators interpret in a way like *«the creatures turn Yin their back»*, or else, *«carry Yin on their back»* – but Yang *«in their arms»*. In fact, precise translation results in a number of more or less opposing logic pairs: ‹creatures› – the ‹10'000 things› – step out of the *moon* and into the *sun*, from *Darkness* into the *Light*, from *conception* into *begetting*, from *concealment* and *secrecy* into general *publicity* and *obviousness*, from a *negative polarity* into a *positive one*, from *negation* into *preservation*, and, to express it in a more poetic form: from the *shadows of the Night* into its *starlit clarity*. – The *Yin-side* they *«endure, undergo, leave behind, or lose*; – the *Yang*-side instead they *revere, receive, embrace, encompass, caress, guard* – and so forth. – All these pairs are textually precise (!), esoterically relevant, and very expressive. — One Chinese of our days comments:

«That Yin and Yang meet and complete each other is the unalterable Law of material processes of transformation throughout the Universe». He compares verse 42. with N° 39. and 41, proposing even that N° 42 should be positioned «directly between the latter two», and then adds: «The 10'000 things leave darkness behind and seek the Light from which they have all come forth, in order to embrace it and to be harmonized by the breath of the *Great Emptiness* {i.e. GOD}». – The latter statement corresponds precisely to the second sequence of glyphs in the second line of this same text.

All this is completely compatible with the teachings of modern Gnosis: In their moon-like feminine way of concealment and darkness (Dao) the 10'000 things on one side carry *«Yin in their belly»* (this corresponds to the *Materia Prima* of operative Alchemy), and on the other side they *«envelop»* or *«embrace»* and *«press against themselves»* the masculine, sun-like, *revealed Light of Yang* that *«is busy with all living things»*. This long-winded interpretation is nothing more than the *combined* translation of the rare but so *polyvalent* glyphs of the original text!

Like today's gnostic teachings thus, the *Dao-De-Jing* sees the 10'000 things generated by the Four (the latter having come forth from the Three) as the omnipresent manifested dynamic of contraries, without which the Universe could not exist – let alone evolve. And it also sees their zeal *«to gravitate toward each other in the hope of attaining harmony»*, as one more *precise variant* says. – *«... in the hope to attain ...»* says the text, thus indicating that this harmony can't ever be *entire*, as long as Creation and her 10'000 things are not completely healed, sanctified and transformed.

These facts lead to the result that – as the following paragraph and also the modern gnostic teachings say – Man experiences this world as a *desert* – as *«a vale of tears»*, where he is *«homeless and poor»* (namely without knowledge, and unaware of the unity of All with God) – and *«widowed»*, as he lacks his *inner* ‹other half›, who alone would be able to make him whole, and would give him *peace, rest and harmony*. These terms as well correspond precisely to the glyphs of the text: All translations at the beginning of each chapter of our present edition are but *a combined choice*.

If now the text repeatedly states – regarding princes and kings – that they deplore their existence, this may be induced by the fact that it is them primarily whom the *Dao-De-Jing* addresses. But we may also understand it the way N° 41 says: Only *humans with sufficient nobleness oft the soul* are capable to experience the difference between the life of an ordinary bourgeois with all its incidents – and the serene life of a person in pursuit of Dao – and make *the* mindful choice. *Insight and mindful choice* however are but the first foot-hold when entering the Path of inner renewal and transformation on the basis of *self-knowledge and self-initiation!*

The next paragraph explains the Law of cause and effects, viz. the agency of the Law of Karma. The *«he»* mentioned there can only be the *«human living in a desert»*, as writes the Chinese commentator we mentioned before.

«Moreover, the truth is that some things, while they are diminished are elevated; and others are elevated for having been diminished» – a remark rather well known in the West (Lk 14:11).

Another faithful translation would read: *«An earlier imprudence might spoil an advantage for him, while, on the other side, a gain might later on become his doom»*. This clearly emphasizes how few a human with his minute overall view is able to judge what is good for him, and what is not. A human on the Path instead *knows* that every event has its good reason, and that every evil and every pain, contemplated in a bigger frame, will sooner or later bring its fruit: The greater the pain, the greater will– sooner or later – be its benefit for the *growth of the soul*. This is the gently equilibrating effect of much dreaded *Karma*. – At the same time , this same wisdom – badly digested – also produced the unhealthy pietistic and puritan moral, following which «suffering is better than joy». – But who lives attentively, easily understands the positive, life- assenting inner truth of this teaching about DAO and KARMA.

The last part of N° 42, as said earlier, has sparked the vastest discussions in West and East. *«The willful human will not attain his death»* (Ular), is the most fantastic of all interpretations – besides *«who lives irksomely, will die irksomely»*. – Or another one: *«A strong ruler won't take a good end»;* and the most dramatic version: *«Who lives violently will die violently!»*. So strong is negative thinking in today's humans! This goes quite well with the Judeo-Christian mentality of punishment, with the Babylonian *«an eye for an eye ... »* of the Ancient Testament, and it also reminds the word of Jesus: *«All they that take the sword shall perish by the sword»* (Mt 26:52). – The last quoted translation was found by several translators into a ‹Western› language ; but no combination of the present glyphs justifies it. It is *only on behalf of this dilemma* that our version here contains the word *«mighty»*: In view of a ruler as the *backbone of the Empire*, the terms *powerful* or *strong* would be enough.

The shortest precise translation oft the second last line of N° 42, according to Chinese commentators, says: *«A strong rafter* (also *ray*, *beam of rays*, or *beacon*) *will not die»* (but transfigure). – And the last line has *«My purpose is to serve as a teacher and a father»* – or *«as a teacher for priests»*: *‹Chinese English›* repeatedly has *‹father›* for *‹Pater›* in the sense of a *priest and teacher*.

In sacred language of old texts, *variants* are no fix alternatives, but rather enriching *parallel layers* when constructing a spiritual building that lectors need to (may, can, and shall) enliven and realize for themselves through their ‹consciousness› – *their living soul*:

Instead of a rafter, or a bridge, there could stand also a strong *light-ray*, i.e. a strong representative, or witness, of the Path of DAO – one *«really powerfully striving for virtue»*, as says N° 38.

A true witness for The Light is himself a ray of this *Light of the World*, a *bridge* leading from earthly humankind to spiritual humanity – from existence as a human to the existence as a god. He or she is then a human living in constant union with Spirit, and proves this by his or her entire way of *actively living an earthly life*. Such humans are released from the wheel of re-births and re-deaths: When they ‹die›, they attain a corresponding level of existence on «a higher octave» – in a «higher dimension» of existence. Their physical death, thus, is no «death according to Nature» any more. For them one can translate: *«[they] may not be unbendable»* – or else: *«will not die»* – or also: *«may not give up»*. For, to humans who have dedicated their entire life to Gnosis, all this is applicable:

Being *servants of Gnosis in the World* they remain firm in spite of idleness and passive, or even active resistance they may encounter. Incessantly – but «bendably» – they stand in this World as witnesses for the Holy Spirit – divinely human helpers and teachers unto the end of their physical life – and even beyond!

Again: such a *«mighty ray»* does not die anymore according to Nature. – He, the *«highly educated one»* or the «high clerk at the court» has *inverted* his life, has stepped on the Path and never left it, with all the implicit consequences. Now that he has become a *«strong beam»* – a *«column in the Temple»* – a *«supporting rafter» for the Gnosis in the World, he «lives on» for only one goal, for just one reasonable task during his eternal presence*: To propagate the Love-Force of Gnosis *as a «teacher and priest»* of the One good tidings about the Path in Light, Truth and Life:

Leaving Darkness and embracing the Sun —
flooded by the Spirit of God, he enjoys
[the One] Peace!

第四十三章

天下之至柔，馳騁天下之至堅。
無有入無間，吾是以知無爲之有益。
不言之教，無爲之益，天下希及之。

43.

The world is most tender and movable —
The course of the World is most steady and inexorable —
Nothing can slip into it or out of it —
There is no gap – no break.
Thence I have recognized: To be unmoved is the best.
Non-speaking is my teaching – Non-doing is my gain
In this World that is scarcely understood.

The pairs of adjectives in the first three lines stand for just one glyph each that contains both – and more: The *«course of the World»* contains also its *running, its frenzy* and its *galloping*, and therefore this is quite authentic.

Instead of *movable* and *tender*, we might as well say *sensitive* and even *volatile* or subtle (thus e.g. *etheric*) – and even *under the veil of the Mysteries*, for, etymologically, the word *subtle* comes from *«sub tela – under the veil»*. It is the subtle weaving of a spider-web (or of *DAO* – see N° 73); also the warp mounted on the loom – and the flitting shuttle itself – and therefore: the busy and precise action, impact and weaving of DAO as the *Law of the* Universe – the loom for existence and agency of all creatures in all five Reigns. Such is the *subtlety* of *DAO as* the *Law of the World* in its subtle, inviolable continuity.

«Steady» – this also means *stable* – thus, *firm, solid, unshakable* – from the *«house built on a rock»* and the *«tower of strength on the seashore»* over a state's good constitution to the rotating stars on the *unmoved* vault of the firmament *«beyond the Waters»*.

Here, known translations, for the sake of a stylish language, oppose *«the most stable item in the World* to the *most subtle item in the World»* – however: WHAT is the most firm, the most steady item in the World? Is it rock? – Steal? – Water? – Is it the flux of time itself – the stream of coming forth, blooming and perishing? – Is it all that together? – Is it none of all those?

As none of these answers are satisfactory, it appears preferable to come back to the *most subtle item* and to ask: Is it Man's most-inner wanting, his thought and hope and wish? – Is it Life itself? – But what is ‹Life›?) – Is it odors? – Sounds? – Thoughts? – Or is it rather that the purpose of the author of the *Dao-De-Jing* was, to confront – like in verse 36 – greatest tenderness in the World to greatest strength?

The most subtle ‹matter› in physical bodies is their ‹blood›; the most subtle body of Man is his thought-body … or is it the ‹soul›? Is it the ‹mind›? – The most subtle element in the Universe is the primary ether – the world-ether, this universal prime matter – *Prima Materia*, also named the ‹fiery humid root substance› – *humidum radicale*. Lao-Dse instead does not mean a physical body or ‹element› in a physical (nor even in a psychic) understanding.

«Spirit, of course!» – The term was already hovering above the present discourse! – But *what* Spirit? – And *what really is* Spirit?

> «In the flow of life, in the storm of actions
> waving up and down —
> weaving to and fro —
> in birth and death —
> eternal sea —
> a veil fluctuating —
> life self ever blazing —
> I create at the blustering loom of Time
> and enmesh the Divinity's lively robe … !»

The spirit evoked in the quoted scene of *Dr. Faustus* is the *Earth Spirit* – thus an *elemental spirit* of the visibly manifested Nature, who is one with the *Universal Spirit*, who is interweaving the «living robe of the Godhead» – the *Universe*. For, Spirit is all that exits; in Spirit everything is pre-shaped before it is pushed to manifest, and *appears* – as a phenomenon – as *Maya* … – Spirit penetrates every minute particle n the Universe, from a grain of sand onto an iron door handle!

The text of the *Tabula Smaragdina* in the translation into Latin by *Hortulanus* (*Garlandinus*) who says: *«Separate what is subtle from what is dense»* – but this *subtle* item is not the *most subtle thing* evoked by *Lao-Dse* yet. In order to come closer to this ‹thing› we'd rather quote from the *Tabula Smaragdina* in the version of *Balduin/Kriegsmann*:

«And like everything is brought forth from One [thing] through the Word of the One God, thus incessantly all things are reborn from this one Order of Nature … ». – Or, in a different translation of the same text in Latin: «… thus incessantly all things are brought forth from this one thing, according to Nature's arrangement». –

The title of said little book even contains – untranslatably – the revelation of this Mystery![13]

Consequently, this *most subtle ‹thing›* is no thing, but *some force*: It is *an energy! Lao-Dse* names it a *formless force*, for, only what has no form itself can bring forth the *10'000 forms*: Same as the smallest primary cell is not yet differentiated relative to the *form* that shall evolve from it, the universal, all-penetrating *primary energy* is yet undifferentiated relative to *any* manifestation *bound to* (or *that could*, or *that cannot*) emerge from IT – spiritually, etherically or physically in the strict sense.

Now let us imagine the Universe as a macrocosmic being of infinite expansion in time-space – a creature itself, though «unlimited» for our faculties to perceive what so ever. Then we remember the line in verse 41: *«A very big form is never clearly distinguished»* – and also remember the old sentence pronounced in the *Fama Fraternitatis* of the classic Rosicrucians: *«There is no empty space!»*.

The space of the virginal Universe – of this boundless, indescribable *«Un-Grund»* or *Prime Foundation* is – as it were ere any created manifestation appeared – ‹filled› with said cosmic primary energy – the most subtle prime ‹substance› of *creation*. Its *subtlety* instead is – compared to Divine Spirit – already a physical denseness (e.g. like water compared to clouds). Biblical Genesis names it *sludge* – lat. *limus*. This term is related to *limes* – *borderline*, or *dividing line* – in the present case *the transition from pure Spirit rotating in itself*, without its direct aim – DE – being discernable, to *creative Spirit* – **I** – and to the latter's primary imprint in DAO, the all-embracing, universal womb (*Matrix*) of the Universe, whose inner rotation instead is already pre-differentiated (pre-determined) as a pair of *YIN-YANG*. – If this were not so, nothing could come forth: Without a ‹male› predisposing dynamic of formation (YANG) the ‹female› imprinted (*impregnated*) dynamic of manifestation (YIN) couldn't possibly give a *definite* form to what so ever, and could produce nothing: No Creation, not even one single creature could appear!

Among the manifested creatures, there are, as we know, some of a very subtle volatility, and others, of a very high density, or fixity. But because every creature, every form of manifestation, whatever the *Matrix* of the Universe brings forth, is impregnated by that primary Spirit who appears as the Father-Mother of the Universe, and who equally coincides with *DAO* – with that *most subtle* but *shapeless force*, even the most dense bodies – even the most coarse forces are permeated by that unique force who as such is formless, boundless, ineffectual and even essence-less. That is how we may understand what *Lao-Dse* wants to tell us, when he says: *«there is no gap, no break»* – or as others translate: *«The formless force infiltrates even where there is not a single gap [or pore]».*

It is this force, formless for itself, DAO, who – with said archaic forces as mediators – keeps shaping everything, thereby determining everything: It molds the external force and inner order of everything, the path of everything, formulates the *One destination* of everything (see N° 39) and thus elaborates the *fate of everything.*

DAO – for itself ineffectual – is the one that *effects everything.* – And so all doing, as long as it is in harmony with the Universal Order, is not the doing of a specific creature or its force, but the agency of DAO *in and through* the respective creature (like as a shadow of DAO) – *by this force* (as *a hue of Dao*).

Now, as DAO is also the highest One Law – the Law of Love which coincidentally is the absolutely highest force in the whole Universe, we may say, in reference to a word by Paul: *«Whatever I do, I don't do myself, but DAO does it through me»*, resp. *«DAO within myself is doing it».*

If now a person – an Ego – is connected to DAO, its doings are embedded in DAO, and in DAO's universal order of Love. Whoever is *not yet* connected to Dao, therefore still lives *outside* of this global harmony, thus *does do himself,* and therefore constantly creates new causes, which again are predestined to constantly produce new effects (Karma). This is the fatality of so-called «fallen Man» – that human who (erroneously) thinks he is separated from God, because he sees his Ego as his human Self. But, what else is really a ‹human self› separated from God – from DAO – if not a twofold illusion?

Therefore, a *mature Initiate* (this is the significance of the name of *Lao-Dse*) *«has recognized the advantage of non-doing»*; – and thus he denies all doings of an Ego-Self: Whatever a personality thinks, or says, or does, plants new causes; – whatever a person thinks, says, or does, thus sows effects! – So simple it is, really, to understand all this!

But – *is it* really as simple as that?

Of course it is easy to «understand all this» *intellectually.* For an individual who has attained a mature, deep insight and a fully awakened consciousness, it is even relatively easy to make a positive decision. But lo! – how hard is it even for a spiritually predestined and well oriented personality to follow the *new*, the *pure Path* amidst the daily magnetic fields of our hustling world full of causes and effects – amidst the swamp of karmic burdens and temptations – wholly enveloped in DAO – wholly in concord with DAO – wholly in harmony with ones Self, with Gnosis and with the Universal Law – the arch-Mother of all thinking, talking and acting!

Thus, if *Lao Dse* says: *«Only a few [persons] under the sky achieve this»*, he does not say so as one who has reached IT and therefore can look down upon all others, as on some spiritually underdeveloped ones. – No, he says so as one who *has experienced*: It is not sufficient to have attained it once and for ever – on the contrary: It is very hard to hold IT fast, as long as our being is stuck in a physical Ego-personality – and be he or she the most pure, the most humble person, the most profoundly penetrated by Gnosis – not just firmly connected to it – but a truly *divinely human* personality!

«Under the Heaven ... », i.e. *«in the World»*. – The Chinese often use this term in the sense of *in Humanity* – here thus for *«only few humans»*. But it is quite similar for very highly evolved *spiritual* beings who dwell in the exalted regions of *Devachan* and still have not yet achieved – or chosen – absolute liberation: A *spiritual* personality in *that* world is akin to a *physical personality* in *ours*. Therefore, the above statement – mixed with a sorrowful undertone as it were – is valid even for those beings who out of free will remain *in this* liberation from The Wheel – out of compassion – and out of the magnanimity of the highest helpers ‹beyond›, in favor of those humans who still err around on the coarse crust of our Planet Earth – seeking – finding – and never the less suffering.

«Teachings without speaking – actions without doing ... »: The World *«has still not understood (seized) it»* (Joh 1:10). – But whoever understands IT, and seizes IT, and achieves IT, will be able to say – still in full conformity of our text:

The peculiarity of this World induced me to IT!

德

第四十四章

名與身孰親？身與貨孰多？得與亡孰病？
甚愛必大費；多藏必厚亡。
故知足不辱，知止不殆，可以長久。

44.

Glory or Life – what do you prefer?
Life or goods –what is more momentous to you?
When you will have to die – what will distress you more?
The dearer you hold something, the dearer you got to pay it.
Who has accumulated very much, would certainly prefer to die.
Therefore:
Frugality will not be decried. —
Moderation will not be put to shame
and can be upheld for an indefinite time.

This text again appears mainly as a tuition for a high clerk, a prince, or a king: Ordinary people often were content to be capable of surviving – particularly during the epoch of the sovereignty of the Mongols, when, during their sometimes short tenure of office, clerks mainly sought to accumulate as much power and possessions as possible. From this point of view the first five lines here are easy to understand – also, many translators are in agreement with each other. For the second part instead – depending of what combination of glyphs is preferred – so many interpretations are possible that once more the rare occurring analogies *needs must* have been plagiarized. –

The first question raised here would be a purely rhetorical one, if not put it into relation with said era: In the caste of the *Samurai* with their extremely strict codex of honor it was a principle and had to be every one's ambition – to not only *«laugh in the face of danger»*, but indeed even to *seek out* danger. When through (un-) lucky circumstances one survived, this shame could be cleared off only by committing ritual suicide.

In the case of a clerk or prince however, we can interpret that same first question with quite different an outlook – and this with so much more certainty as the two lines of the text immediately following the first one are commenting the appreciation of *spiritual Life:* They are oriented toward giving the interrogated person a kind of decisive impulse, so that he or she should cautiously chose their weights and priorities – namely in harmony with the *Path of DAO* – thus, in the sense of *Gnosis.*

Now the interrogated person might answer the *second question* like this: «*What do you want? – My life I have as long as I have it; and my possessions multiply without my making any effort!*» – In that case however, the *third line* would be enough to make this person think – namely with regard to his position during the hours of his death, and in the aftermath to that.

Within the systems of Sufism, and in early Islam, this question plays a preponderant role. Muhammad *Al-Ghazali*, one of the most scholarly literate Sufis of the 11th c.a.D., in his book *Letter to the Disciple*, describes the moment of his own *repentance* – hence the instance of his *conversion toward true Life*, and his orientation towards the spiritual Path in these words:

«*I looked back at my work ... – lo! I had wasted so much effort on a science that relative to the future life (after dying) was without any value or utility. I looked at the intent of my studies; – oh! they had not been honestly directed at the honor and glorification of God, but to gain praise myself and to enhance my own reputation in the world. And I came to the conclusion that I found myself at the brink of a yawning abyss, and would soon taste the fire of Hell, lest I made an effort to completely change my life ...* »[14]

Until here, our remarks about the text under consideration affect just the life of an ordinary, albeit educated and cultivated worldly person. But let us go deeper and ask: «*What is Life? – What is the aim of those questions regarding the spiritual Path of DAO that are supposed to make the main content of the Dao-De-Jing?*» – At that point, the term *Life* at once carries the meaning of *spiritual Life* – the so-called *Life eternal.*

With that is introduced a statement not expressively formulated here: «*The spiritual Life of Gnosis excels all the rest – it is worth more than possessions and honor – and indeed higher than physical life itself!*» This gives even more weight to the subsequent statement: «*The dearer you hold something, the higher is the price you got to pay for it*». This simultaneously corresponds to a fundamental law of both the physical and the spiritual worlds – namely, that throughout the whole Universe *everything has its price*.

In the tale of *The Little Mermaid* worked up poetically by both *Hans Christian Andersen* and *Oscar Wilde*, this same affirmation is made a central statement: «*Everything has its price!*». – Another declaration just there is that love is more precious than everything else in the whole World – and the third one is, that who forsakes his love must pay for it with his or her own life. –

Our present text leaves all those questions without an answer. It only puts the questions – including, but not voicing, the last one: *«What is Life?»*. – This of course brings the Candidate more puzzlement rather than knowledge. But then: This last question – is it not the positively ‹last question› of all?

The following line addresses higher knowledge as well as material well-being. *«Where there is your treasure, there is your heart»*, said The Master. Who on his path has acquired a lot of experience and knowledge – and also a lot of redeeming quality of the soul, and given that he or she remain faithful to this highest love, would like to acquire ever more of it and share it with as many others as possible. – He would rather die than relinquish this treasure. This is the background of every reasonable martyrdom throughout all centuries and millennia of human history.

But for spiritual goods as well as for material ones, one we are to remember: One must not want too much;One must not – as the *Veda* says – *«over-question»* – i.e., transgress the limits of permissible investigation and accumulation of knowledge. The boarder between benign and pernicious magic, or for legitimate and ruinous knowledge, thought, speech and even listening is quite narrow:

«Who is able to limit himself, – who respects natural and divine limits – will not run into danger (comp. N° 32 and 59), viz. *will not be threatened»* – as have other variants of translations to the same passage. The previous line might as well be interpreted as: *«Who knows to content himself* – or: *Who knows contentedness – will experience no shame».* – Who instead accumulates too much, runs the risk to lose much, too. – Exactly: *Everything has its price!»*

The last line of this text is formulated in a most unclear way. But seeing the great number of possible interpretations, and given that he or she remain faithful to their highest love, its significance is easy to guess: *« ... can be upheld for an indefinite time»* is the most precise one: Besides of being related to the prudently acquired (spiritual) treasure it also addresses the person who acquired it.

Moreover, the large fan of existing interpretations in every language offers thousand and one versions, like: *«... and will live long and happily»*; – *«... one can get old and last for a long time»;* – or: *«... This leads to true inner and outer continuity»;* – and also*: «...*

This is the condition to achieve incorruptibility»; – «and will live for long years and in prosperity» … – Thus reads a bouquet of interpretations, some of which, when taking a deeper look, prove to completely disregard what they should not overlook, even though they remain strictly on the materialistic plane, namely: that in China the wish for someone to live a long life – «a hundred years of life!» –was – and still is – the best possible wish of all.

However: *live a long life* – what for? – In order to enjoy for so many more years earthly ‹happiness› and toils?

For a human on the Path of growing consciousness, life in this world – in spite of its countless and unconceivable wonders – soon and progressively becomes a heavy burden: So tiresome is the continuous hindrance of Spirit due to unconsciousness of most of humanity! – So pressing the invincible, the deadly embrace of the soul by matter! – Glory, riches, knowledge, personal ties: the best of all these still must undergo the inevitable dichotomy of every creature the Universe includes!– «Oh! If only all of this were soon overcome!»

The ‹Wise› therefore see a really precious issue in this Nature of growth and decay only when and where they thereby can augment and fasten the treasure of personal Gnosis in the World – when they can prolong their testimony and their endeavour to animate the message of Light in this same World. – For, again: What is *real Life*? – What is growing happiness? Nothing but that growth by *«walking in The Light, the way He is walking in the Light»*!

But here as well, the cosmic law keeps its authority:

The dearer you hold something,
the higher is the price you got to pay for it!

德

Green crown of jade (Zhou-Dynasty, 1200-221 b.C.)

第四十五章

大成若缺，其用不弊。
大盈若沖，其用不窮。
大直若屈，大巧若拙，大辯若訥。
靜勝躁，寒勝熱。清靜爲天下正。

45.

To achieve great things, appears as a blemish, but
to take advantage of success is no shame.
Great plenitude appears to be appalling,
but who exploits it is not indigent.
Great righteousness appears as an insult —
Great skill appears as laziness —
great eloquence appears as stammering —
Impassibility overcomes hot temper —
Coolness overcomes excitement —
Tranquil lucidity puts the world in order.

One should not take this text too ‹literally›, as it runs on various levels at a time.

The interpretation offered here imitates the Chinese preference for a pleasant literary *form* (repetitions, esthetic symmetry, un-outspoken allusions) – rather than the aspect of academic unambiguity – of, let us say: the frontal message. For us Westerners, two dozens of glyphs (letters) suffice in order to *formulate* even the most complex abstract thoughts by capturing them within a *form* of innumerable ‹literal› (picturesque) *formalisms*. Never the less, there occur many misunderstandings: regular speech, the human way of thinking, and other conventions incessantly undergo alterations; the meaning of a phrase therefore is likely to change often and even drastically.

Ancient China – until around 200 b.C. – used about 4000 *ideograms* as ‹vessels› for a suggestively *pictorial* language. The development of *intellective* thought during the last two millennia, and flattening of spiritual notions – not to mention industrialization and worldwide Americanization during he last two centuries – brought with them many modern and abstract concepts demanding for their own adapted language and terminology. These had to be integrated into today's Chinese with its ‹only› 2000 remaining pictograms. Of these, an average Chinese today remembers no more than 200 to 600 glyphs. – Therefore, even today's Chinese have a problem interpreting with certainty most texts taken from the *Dao-De-Jing*. Also, today's new generations in China ignore the surroundings and conditions among which this venerable text was written down for the first time. – All this makes interpretation *for all lectors of today* quite a challenge.

In view of the different linguistic conventions and cultural backgrounds here and there, one will not take too ‹literally› the present attempts of interpretation but rather understand them as a basis for autonomous consideration and meditation. In conformity to their westerly oriented background as it were, the comments offered here seem to *nail down* things that are to be visualized as moving between the tangible and the spiritual worlds rather, and – despite precise verbalization – are to be imagined as *floating* through a space-time continuum: Here everything lives in a frame of spiritual allegories and metaphors: The *Dao-De-Jing* is indeed a Scripture for Initiation!

Both great social, economical, scientific or other *success*, and social, economical scientific or other *riches* are looked upon throughout ordinary society as the most enviable achievements a human could plume himself up on. – With regard to evolution of the soul instead, both appear as a blemish, so to speak. By right one catchphrase in N° 63 says: *«Therefore the wise will reach a point where he does not achieve great things anymore – and thus he will be able to achieve the one great thing».*

This – let us emphasize it once more – has nothing in common with a culture of abnegation or self-castigation, and even less with cultivating a good image of outward poverty and inactivity – in the contrary: Even (and especially) a spiritually oriented person on the Path towards renewal of his soul and spirit is summoned to develop and apply as intelligently and fruitfully as possible the talents that his personality has been furnished with. Whom the destiny has donated a *gift* (whatever kind), is thereby also given the *responsibility* to make the best possible use of it. And this *good use* is not to accumulate worldly glory and wealth, but to foster the spiritual evolution of Humanity – eventually also using some worldly means (techniques, funds a.s.f.). Remember here the allegory of the talents in Mt 25:14-30. – And also: Who does not *give* anything likens someone who *has nothing*!

If for the Disciple of Gnosis said ‹social privileges› are depreciated as ‹blemish› all the same, then it is because on one hand they may be experienced as attachments to the material world of Illusions: The previous text in N° 44 has made this quite clear. – On the other hand, said privileges are also connected to challenges that, with regard to spirituality one could indeed downright call temptations: Who possesses, might crave for more; – Who knows better or can better, might forget the plights linked to ‹successfully› following *The Path*, and aspire to a position from where he might exercise power and influence – maybe even in view of the best of all ‹good› humanistic aims. But in this world nothing is perfectly good and without a disadvantage. – In the contrary: What ever «inspired better thing» a human might undertake to foster, will at the end entail more evil than before. Thus, the spiritual Path excludes every sort of personal ambition – and indeed any subjective wanting at all. At the same time there is no question of an explicit or even strict – ‹prohibition›: A human on the Path towards knowledge, liberation and redemption enjoys the greatest possible freedom and autonomy – and in turn is charged with the greatest possible *auto-responsibility*. – How will he or she meet this great challenge? – Will they ‹fail› and be ‹defeated›, or will they gain blessings from it?

So the well-meant teachings about abstinence with regard to mundane desires is itself a potential starting point to cultivate one's ‹perfect› personality on one side – and for the crystallization of a good doctrine into a dogma about attaining blissfulness through conformity, on the other. Therefore, the third plane of temptation the Candidate might be enticed to adopt consists in denying his talents and worldly duties, and to disregards the responsibility for his specific personal talents: Who means to serve the gnostic teachings of transformation and Transfiguration with too much zealous ardor, might risk really rather to damage them; for, with this ‹Abelian› scrupulousness he really might as well contribute to their crystallization.

The first objective of the present text is thus easy to make out. – But how about the other intents? What is it that the seven opposing duals about the decay of moral want to convey to the lector? – Here we are not talking about social conduct anymore – not about questions of orthodoxy or correct behaviour in life, but rather about the fact that for a transfiguristic occultist – and even more so for a follower of Christ – every thing, every thought, every ‹truth› is vinculated to its counterpart, which often appears as its pure contrary: The deeper insight delves, the wider the horizon stretches, the more are present the relativizing counter-poises to every statement one could possibly make.

As an aftermath of this remark it is easy to comprehend: If we understand *righteousness* as *justice*, it is presently accompanied by the momentum of *injustice*. If we understand *righteousness* as *honesty*, then presently appears at its side – one – the hurtful austerity, with which truth is proclaimed, or – two – the direct *material disadvantage* that very often has to be put off with; and finally – three – the retaliation by the established system punishing others for speaking the truth.

Great skill will not downright appear as clumsiness, but rather as idleness, because the effortless ease of who posses it, can, and often does, scandalize others. –

Great eloquence can indeed appear as stammering – namely to the ‹eloquent speaker› himself wo experiences the impossibility to verbally express his highest thoughts, images and feelings with adequate finesse and precision: ‹Precise› words often are ‹precisely wrong›!

To close this chapter, *Lao-Dse* speaks of *tranquility and stillness* – and this neither in an allegory, nor with a riddle, nor even through a request or warning, but again using for an example two naturally opposing duals: in a double statement of a common significance and equal conciseness, which as a literary trick are crossed, and, cast into one, result in the avowal: *«keep your neutral lucidity, and your world will be in order»*. – Indeed, if *everybody* would do so, *the whole world* would be ‹in order›!

With that, the text of N° 45 has obviously come down from the heights of dialectical, egocentric *self-affirmation*, along the valley of *self-examination*, down to the basin of silent, unobtrusive *self-forgetfulness*: Here there is left no zeal and no desire anymore; here there reign neither judgment nor self-reproach – neither old dogmata nor new, world-changing ideas. Here, our text – Humanity – the World – find themselves in the tranquil center of the Wheel – in the groove of the axle that alone remains immobile – «unmovable» as *Lao-Dse* wants it – in DAO.

All zeal and all desires indeed come forth from the incessant astral agitation of the ordinary personality. – Judgements and self-condemnation sparkle from the persistent mental maelstrom of flashing blood-impulses, feelings and images (imaginations). This creates a constantly wavering steam of heat – a fiery whirl-wind of turbulent *existence,* quivering *essence* , and stumbling *divergence*; – a relentless to-and-fro, up-and-down … – but not embedded in the interweaving harmony of the Universe as quoted for the Earth-Spirit in an earlier chapter, but captured in the shrill coercive detention of a typical ego-personality – madly buzzing about like a wasp captured in a bottle.

What a difference from here to the inner stillness and outer calm of the ‹Wise› reposing in Dao: This is no enforced immobility like of a human who submits himself to some exercise of self-discipline like in a monastery, nor is it one of those Asiatic Yoga rituals as they are transmitted by Tibetans or Zen-Buddhists. No, this is the perfect, neutral harmony of balanced stillness and calm in the Gnosis – without any purpose or goal!

The mental haste, the astral heat, the impetuous movements of hands, lips, and eyes have given way to complete inner relaxation – a relaxation embedded in intensive concentration; – and this amidst daily life – amidst the ordinary world's jostle! This is a *concentration* aiming only at what is immediately linked to the Present – yet in the meantime one with the World and with the harmony and continuity of the Universe.

So, entirely secured in the permanent *Triple Presence* of past, present and future – so, entirely returned into the simplicity of conscious *existence in essentiality* the ego-personality has become silent, listening to the music of the Spheres of the original divine World! – This is a kind of *non-doing*, and yet (*«nothing remains undone»*) a very potent, transforming, *silent agency*!

Silence fills the person, including his blood: The latter's blazing has cooled down; its seesawing has found peace; its disquieted murmur and rush have fallen silent. This silence fills every corner of spirit, soul and body: Such a human rests in his own Self – at first only for moments perhaps, but then more and more – until, *«at the end of days»* of his ego-personality – as the *New Divine Man* – he will not just *see* the World of entirety and stillness, but also will *dwell in it in all-presence*. This is the status where the word will finally have become a factual reality:

«In this World, still — yet not of this World anymore»!

德

第四十六章

天下有道，卻走馬以糞。天下無道，戎馬生于郊。
禍莫大于不知足；咎莫大于欲得。故知足之足，常足矣。

46.

With DAO in the World,
passing horses will drop their dung all the same.
If the World is without DAO,
arms and horses multiply in the suburbs.

By far the worst mischief consists in
that one ignores how much is enough. —
The greatest aberration is greediness.
Therefore: Do know that enough is enough —
and for sure you will have enough forever.

The first part of this chapter contains several possibilities and riddles. Our present interpretation represents the most sober choice of so many possibilities regarding the aim and the purpose of this text. We just simplified some of the ambiguities, others we left out, or we integrated them into a polyvalent expression in English. It is now up to the interested lector to study the plethora of romantic interpretations by other translators who, desiring to be outstanding, reject the obvious – and again, without any detectable philosophical justification, chose what is linguistically out of place. – The *Dao-De-Jing* is indeed a quite extraordinary text – picturesque, and yet quite exclusively precise.

In order to shed some light upon the wealth of Chinese writing often surprising the Western reader, let us examine the present text with the aim to understand the wealth of this language and said versatility. This must not be done intellectually only, but with the help of *deep empathy* on a high spiritual level.

The fact that in most instances we prefer our own interpretations does not mean that all others are entirely *wrong*: The latter often sound nicer and are even rhymed and otherwise adorned – ours instead are sober, factual, and almost crude.

The two principal statements of this text here are quite simple and obvious: *«Dao is in the World ... »* – and: *«Dao is not in the World ... »*. – We Westerners – used as we are to see things *or* white – *or* black; *or* 1 – *or* 0, therefore might expect the classical opposed Duals – and who seeks will also find, so that many translators painted such Duals in the most beautiful colors. But unless they are clearly plagiarized they don't liken each others ...

The elements of the second package of five glyphs, each alone, yield, firstly, *«but, in the contrary, all the more»* – as well as: *«reject, refuse, discard»* and so on; – second: *«run, trot, march, ride* (a vehicle), *pull; let, relinquish, secrete, discharge* … and so on; – third: literally *«buck»*, or *«horse»*; – fourth: *use, utilize,* and so on; – fifth: *«excrement, dung, crap»*, and so on. – The first and second glyph *together* mean *«was gone»*; – the second an third together give: *«gallop»*; – one through five together: *«but on the surface there lie excrements»*.

The known versions therefore let *racing horses, war horses,* or simply *horses*, but also *«withdrawn horses»* (sic!) *gallop*, or *pull manure cars*, – or even *«refused or returned horses pull the plough»*; – and our esteemed lectors now know whence this came.

In the same manner – to just show a few results – emerged the respective opposing statements. Thus *«stand»* – or *«are raised»* – or even *«keep watch»* – *«war-horses at the frontier»*; or they are *«born at the frontier»*. Also they *«pull soldiers over the field»*; they *«leave the suburbs»*, *«are grazing in the field»*, *«trample down the hinterland»* (a possible literal variant could indeed mean: *«Horses devastate the suburbs »*). – The most romantic one we found is: *«foals are born at places far from home»* (Hundhausen).

A curious thing with this text is that who just takes the individual glyphs while following an anticipated or projected meaning, will, adding a pinch of imagination, really arrive at most of said nonsensical interpretations – But the most curious thing is that – what ever variant one takes, the main statement remains the same: Peace as a vision of *order in DAO* – War as a paragon for *«disorder and turmoil of all kind»* (see N° 38). – Indeed, the indirect cause for the *Warring States Period* in China (475-221 b.C.) is found in the Confucian *ban against old customs*, which is well known to be mainly held up by the traditionally conservative peasantry.

If now one sticks precisely to what is written in the text, the latter shows itself as we have rendered it above – without any understandable signification *at its surface*. To a lector with a gnostic orientation instead, the meaning of this text is immediately clear:

Where and when DAO – the universal Law – rules the World, there prevail order, peace and welfare. But the nature of the Universe remains the same: germination, prosperity, and decay follow each other unavoidably; and even the most harmonious comfort generates abuse, injustice and distress in the World. – The only escape is DAO.

And so it must be! For, if all and everything were protected in unmovable peace, welfare and harmony, the World would stand still: No desire for evolution and change, no question like those regarding the basic gist behind the sufferings in this world could arise; – there would be nothing but an aimless, senseless rotation of *the Wheel*, from one birth to the next – from one death to the next – without the least hope for improvement or elevation of any kind …

Instead, let us look at an Initiate of our modern days, who is orienting his senses and thoughts entirely toward DAO – toward Spirit and Eternity, toward transformation and Transfiguration – thus a person who, in his *Small World* – his *microcosmos* – has already brought DAO to life as his daily practice, albeit, maybe, not yet completely and exclusively: – What about DAO, manure, war and frontiers in this case?

«With DAO in the World, passing horses will drop their dung all the same». – As long as Gnosis lives in the microcosm of a person born according to nature – but not as its exclusive ruler – if, thus, this personality – as is the case for most human personalities –is not yet sufficiently pure, not yet in complete and interrupted harmony with divine super-nature, mistakes, failures and lapses are inevitable: Vulgar language speaks of *«producing crap».*

Even a human who in complete insight has entirely surrendered to the Gnosis, will yet, again and again, be invited by so many intrinsic counter-forces, to deviate from *The Path*: illusions, old impressions, fixed ideas, judgments, misjudgments, biases, unconscious fears and habits – and this very often with success. At the beginning of the Path, these so-called *temptations* arise on quite simple fields of existence; but when the Candidate of the Gnosis has learnt to distinguish and avoid the grossest impulses, there come others, more subtle ones: These subtle inducements *«penetrate what is solid»* and *«infiltrate where there seems to be no gap».* Narrower and narrower stretches the Path – more and more subtle are the methods used by «the Adversary»; and so the determination and strength of the Candidate is tested again and again – preferably where and when he believes he is quite safe.

His determination is tested by defying his decisions, by knocking down his achievements, and by questioning insights thought to be secure. – Or, some dramatic unexpected event may throw him out of all painfully acquired securities – out of his precious harmony – flinging him out on the street, so to speak, with one fatal blow. This is the hardest test for the firmness of his faith (this unshakable faith that is the corner-stone of all his endeavors) and of his newly acquired *New Will.* – Will he be victorious?

Fortunately, no Candidate is on his way all alone – not even if he lives all by himself: When he decided to seek the communion with the Gnosis, and as he remained faithful to his decision, he simultaneously became part of it and could feel himself protected in it, experiencing again and again proof that the so-called *Universal Brotherhood* of those who preceded him on The Path, really exists; that he may call them for help and will also receive this help (albeit not always the expected way), and that many challenges and obstacles are dissolved even before their ‹dung› fell upon him. With growing lucidity he becomes aware that the Gnosis, that DAO really has entered his small world – his *microcosmos* – even before he was capable to cast off the dominance of his old Ego entirely.

In the meantime, and even though Gnosis has already begun to *«make its abode within him»*, as the Gospel says, (Jo 14, 23): the *«passing horses»* – i.e. the impulses of his beastly-human nature – *will drop their dung all the same»*. These horses he really feels gallop, pull the plough, devastate the suburbs … —

So he needs must become more and more attentive – if not, soon the same old war will reign inside him, the ‹horses› will devastate his suburbs, and in the worst case, more and more new ‹warriors› will be born in his ‹hinterland› – in his astral body – until he gives up!

At the end of this chapter, *Lao-Dse* mentions two important obstacles on the path toward growing purity, insight and inner knowledge due to the Candidate's *practical experience* with the Gnosis:

The druidic Triads mention ignorance relative to God as the «fundamental ignorance» and the *«greatest sin»*.

Closely examined, ignorance is indeed *the only* real ‹sin›; all other errors and failures are the latter's natural consequences. But *«ignorance does not protect against punishment*, as already the Roman *Codex Juris* proclaimed: What one *can know*, one *must learn* – especially in our present era, where we are flooded with information, practically day and night. – But in the meantime we need to protect our microcosmic atmosphere, our *«respiration field»* against the noisy chit-chat around us, excluding useless talk, purely academic erudition (*«sinful»* in the sense of the *Veda*), and whatever chains us to this world. – *Lao-Dse, he* names ignorance *«the greatest misfortune – the worst catastrophe befalling Man, and worse than war»!*

As another main obstacle when approaching Gnosis – i.e. DAO – *Lao-Dse* mentions *greed.* Here however we should understand this expression in a much larger sense than what is the custom among ordinary humans: Greed does not strive for material goods alone, but also for spiritual, social, and emotional acquirements and accumulations, which mostly are not aspired and clung to because of blunt ignorance, but as a consequence of *egomania.* – In short: The more the Ego wants, intends, and defends, the more difficult – not to say down right *impracticable* – becomes the path toward true initiation. – To call *greed a shame* makes sense only under this point of view – for: Is it not a shame when a Candidate, by *his own energy*, and by his own cravings, thoughts and actions contrary to The Path, continuously blocks the golden trail toward the ultimate goal he pretends to strive for?

But then, *Lao-Dse* promptly also indicates the cardinal remedy apt to suspend and even annihilate all obstacles: It is the firm conviction that *«enough is enough»* – how much or how few of what so ever is enough. The good measure (*«moderation»* of the four cardinal virtues) can always keep the Candidate on the good track. This concerns not only the *«enough!»* in what one can seize, have, achieve, and keep. It stretches unto *letting go* of what the Buddha named the *discommendable attachments*: to let go of knowledge, of renouncement, of obedience – and indeed even *letting go of the will to follow The Path*!

In other words: When *Lao-Dse* speaks of *moderation*, he not only means modesty and humility, but also the consciousness of the fact that every effort in the world needs to retain its healthy proportion – *harmony* – in order to earn its blessing, its grace, and thereby its ‹reward›. – And all this must occur with the Candidate knowing that only *« Gnosis inside myself»* can achieve IT:

«Without me you can do nothing!», said the Master; and the Candidate accordingly: *«Not by myself I can do all this, but the force of The inter-cosmic Christos in me does it through me».* – Or as the Psalm says: *«According to a gift of Grace that everyone has revived ... so that in everything Gnosis should be exalted.»* (1 Pt 4:11). – For, as says Jo 3:28: «Not I am the Christos, but

I am only his messenger!»

第四十七章

不出戶，知天下；不窺牖，見天道。其出彌遠，其知彌少。
是以聖人不行而知，不見而明，不爲而成。

47.

To know the world, without leaving the house —
To see Dao of the Heavens, without looking out of the window —

The farther one travels, the more knowledge one is missing.
The true Saint is aware without traveling about —
he has the knowledge without having seen —
He achieves without doing.

Let us anticipate: A *Saint* has a priori nothing to do with any *Religion*, even less with any *church*. A *Saint* is a human who has become *sane, holy* or *whole* – physically, spiritually and regarding the soul. – He therefore also can heal others, or else impart to them some methods of healing and of hallowing themselves and others, using *gnostic magic* – conveying *healing forces for their salvation* on the three planes mentioned above. – *«Physical, psychic and spiritual well-being»* is the official definition of *health* by the WHO, and this again is *a priori* not just related to mundane medicine.

Regretfully, the English language does not offer itself to form a whole linguistic family in this context, as do other languages – especially German, Latin and Arab, where the root *hel-* is connected with whatever stands for *Light and clarity* – from our cosmic Sun (*helios* in Greek) and the antique *Heliand* (Saviour) to the exclamation of *hallel-u-Jah*, and down to *Hel(l)* with its prince, *Lucifer – the Light-Bearer*. Even the well-known *halo* of the Saints has its origin there, as well as the word *salvation* itself, while the alchemical transmutation of *hel-* and *hal-* has become *sal-* (i.e. *salt*). – So, what is the significance of *health* in our present context?

Apparently it has to do with light. – Light understood as *influx* from the skies «high above» – same as the *morning-dew* falling during the months from March to May, and revered especially by the classical Alchemists, along with the *Missale Romanum.* Therefore it also is some celestial force, and a *healing* state of mind apt to release humans from their bindings to the material world – from their forfeits, flaws and illusions. The sacral iconography overflows with images stressing this timeless tradition. The *halo* itself is an iconographic indicator of *«illumination»*, i.e. of a state of evolution where one's higher thinking body, called *Buddhi* is definitely born, and the head emanates a golden glow (see pictures on pp. 10 and 11.

So, when *Lao-Dse* speaks of a *Saint*, he means to say the same as the term *«the Wise»*, namely someone who has attained access to his higher ‹thinking members› and to communication with higher spiritual powers. Therefore, a *«true Saint» is no thinker of the ordinary kind*, but one noticing things in a *higher sense*: One who does *know* things not just subjectively, but in a higher manner; – one who beyond subjective ‹realities› sees *the whole* – namely *the Truth* (comp. Paul's words relative to the mirror in 1 Cor. 13:12 – viz. the word of Jesus in Jo 14:10: *«The words that I speak unto you I don't speak of myself, but the Father that dwells in me ... »*).

As for the present text of this N° 47, our preliminary comments regarding *the* Saint – i.e. concerning the very advanced Candidate on the Path of DAO – the *Master*, the *Wise* as we may name him – they have already anticipated the essence of its message: From the point of view of *achievement or perfection*, simultaneously all other remarks can be easily understood. The *Neophyte*, the beginning ‹pilgrim› or ‹pupil› on *The Path* instead, primarily needs to *learn* this ‹new› way of cognizance. He, or she, or rather their *‹soul-eye›*, needs to firstly open up for this ‹new› *manner of viewing, of perceiving, and of realizing*. A modern Chinese commentator formulates it like this (we translate his ‹Babylonian English› into a more comprehensible one):

«This chapter is about the philosophical theory of cognizance. The crucial point here is this: Pure intellect and sensual experience are unreliable. It being impossible to advance by them, we are required to penetrate things by inner cognizance, without «understanding» them. Here in particular it is human reasoning that interferes, really. The point thereof is, thus, to understand that all these things can be penetrated only by silent inner perception. – One should confide onto self-reflection really, and endeavour to understand ‹Heaven› through independent inner research, remembering that in the course of evolution all things are indeed subject to changes. The academic way of discussion with its ambitious philosophical theories of cognizance, often reinforces the idealistic opinion that it transcends human subjectivity, while holding in disdain all other views as {or by, rather} ignorance, deriding the practice of knowledge through apperception, and overestimating rational comprehension. – In this chapter rational analysis with its onerous [academical] debates is thus opposed to silent apperception in serene autonomy.»

Our attentive lectors will – even in this succinct formulation – appreciate the Chinese tendency to favor polyvalent phraseology and non-verbal communication. Our modern way of discussion thus has partially evinced the ancient Chinese way of thinking, but on the other hand, it also has enriched it by what we may name a Western (analytical) component.

As a matter of fact, above mentioned *«verbal understanding»* finally hardly differs of what Western spiritual science also names the *«inner loquacity»*, thus critically addressing the thought-storms in the mind with its arguments battling against themselves, and drowning every clear conception and cognizance, while depriving the Candidate of his fertile calmness, in order to keep him prisoner of thousand infertile speculations and emotions.

«Why roam in the far distance – see: all good things are so close!» as an old proverb used to say ... – This proverb has been silenced completely in our hectic times of weekend flights, all-included vacations, and world tours: it was too unprofitable for the turn-over of tourist offices.

– But traveling «broadens the mind» – does it not?

– Well, of course it does, and that was true also in earlier centuries. But the *‹Wise›* of our chapter has learnt that, if travelling lets us *see* many things from different angles, *judge* them under different aspects, *distinguish* them following different criteria, he also has recognized that the essential conclusions and deepest insights come up in the quiet solitude of our personal cubicle – not in some ‹easy jet› – nor flitting comfortably through today's world.

Moreover, the point is not to *see*, to *interpret*, to *‹measure›* and to *‹prove›* as many things in the Universe as possible (i.e. to *compare* them to some official norm or gauge). The point is to recognize and understand the *causes and dynamics* that make happen everything – that Humanity evolves, and that Worlds emerge and melt away. –

Faust in his anxious *urge to know,* expresses it like this: *«... that I might cognize what holds together the whole World, viewing all fundamental forces and seeds, no more needing to grope for words!»* – *Lao-Dse* says the same: *«A true Saint is no thinker, but a realizer; – no know-all, but an all-perceiver!»* —

Indeed, the Path opens itself to inner contemplation, but is obstructed by that penetrant intellectual craving doomed to rummage always in its own assessments, labyrinths and limits, because no human can by *‹his own›* efforts – i.e. using his own *centripetal* thought-power – *«by his own hairs»* – pull himself out of the mud of human ignorance.

By the way: How slow and tiresome indeed is physical voyaging as compared to the speed of thought by which inner view instantaneously propels itself to the most distant country or galaxy – and even into any suitable *zeitgeist*! The new Age, i.e. the astronomical era, which our humanity has entered a few decennia ago – partly in superstitious fear, partly in pioneer-like enthusiasm, partly in dumb ignorance; – this Age, in which the *hypnosis by Matter* will dissolve, and gravity will finally be overcome, will, besides of famous ‹teleportation› also open the *omnipresent and perfect view* on whatever the *new human Mind* can grasp.

Probably (but we cannot know it for sure) what *Lao-Dse* had in mind was not this new cosmic phenomenon; – he rather thought about microcosmic experiences and about the Hermetic law he surely knew : *«As above, so below – as is the big, so is the small – as outside, so inside … »*. The modern Chinese commentator with his expression of *«self-reflection»* appears to have thought of those antique words of wisdom, too: *«Who knows himself, knows the world; – who knows the world, will cognize God!»*. – But the starting-point and first achievement is *self-knowledge*!

Fulcanelli in his book *Dwellings oft the Adepts* evokes the same wisdom by quoting the inscription on the mantelpiece of a French fireplace: • SE • COGNESTRE • ESTRE • NON • PARESTRE • – *«To know oneself, to be, not to pretend»* – commenting it like this:

«Our Adept is quite right: self-knowledge is the key to, the aim and meaning of Life, the fundament for every true value. This force that elevates the industrious who can acquire it, prompts him to persist in the modest but noble simplicity that is the eminent virtue of sublime spirits. This is an axiom the Masters repeated to their Disciples, and by which they indicated to them the sole means to attain higher wisdom: „If you want to get acquainted with true Wisdom – so they said – get to know yourself thoroughly – and you will get familiar with it“». [15]

Who gets to know himself in-depth (and this depth is indeed an abyss!), will get acquainted *ad nauseam* with the omnipresence of his egocentric forces: From pure instinct of self-preservation to the fight for power and to cruelty; from self-pity to the wrath of vengeance – the scale is most varied even for apparently (and normally) charming sweet people! In those depths, a menagerie of impulses and instincts creeps around, *«beastlier than any beast»*, as says Mephistophélès. Who gets to know himself like this, will also see that his Ego joins him on *The Path* – not to acquire, knowledge, however, but to gain a new sublime ego-value: *«Oh glory, to be an Initiate! – Oh glory, to be One Who Knows!»*

The wake, sober pilgrim unmasks this temptation: As a true seeker he also has learnt that *«all our knowledge is but half-knowledge»* (C.G. Jung); – *«that we cannot [definitely] know anything»* (Faust); and he experiences the truth of Socratic *«I know that I don't know!»*. – Not that he'd know *nothing* (or else he could not have coined that phrase); – but in the course of his mind growing, penetrating deeper, and getting a broader view, he simultaneously understands how much more he ignores. The academic arrogance of *Wagner* in Gœthe's *Dr. Faustus* – *«I know very much, but I'd wish to know it all!»* cedes to the surprising, and in the meantime frustrating, insight: *«The more one can recognize, the more knowledge one is missing!»* –

Many a translator overstates this experience interpreting said sentence as *«the more one sees, the fewer one knows»*. – This can indeed occur, but only when the seeker gets stuck in his own academically biased positivistic thinking habits … –

Now, instead of falling into desperation like Faust, Nietzsche, and many others, the ‹Wise› always can know that he *is on the Path*, *«knowing and feeling and tasting»* (*Valentin Weigel*), that this Path is a reality, and that, notwithstanding all his personal limitations, his reward will be his *absolute liberation*:

«Not being himself the Light, but bearing witness for the Light», as says Jo 1: 9. — Or as *Lao-Dse* might say: *Not one who himself is IT – but one who is conquering IT:*

knowing without learning — achieving without doing.

見

第四十八章

爲學日益，爲道日損。損之又損，以至于無爲。
無爲而無不爲。取天下常以無事，及其有事，不足以取天下。

48.

He who learns, increases day after day —
He who walks The Path shrinks day after day.
Increasing more and more, one attains non-doing:
Nothing is done – but nothing remains un-done.
Often conquers the World he who does not attempt to do so —
and likewise:
Who attempts to do so, is unworthy to receive the World.

This chapter can be seen as connected to other chapters, like e.g. 20, 29 and 47: All these (and more) endeavour to comment aspects of *non-doing*. All of them say that DAO cannot be found in worldly knowledge, nor in worldly activity, nor in worldly power, nor in worldly ingenuity, and that IT is indeed incompatible with all those. At the same time, they also say that this fact must neither serve as a pretext to avoid doing anything of the sort, nor as a motivation to avoid *The Path* all together. But rather, the *Art of DAO* consists in attributing their due place to both of them – and specially, to *let things happen* through the sole agency of DAO. – *DAO as a path* means: to *consciously let things happen by concentrated non-doing*.

Modern worldly humans with their hectic and with their greed for false knowledge and power, live on no reasonable basis any more, following no equitable aim any more, because they think their activities to be the basis, measure and aim of the World. Spiritual activity instead – a spiritual Path – appear in this gloomy light as something incidental – hardly tolerable, but surely not worth-while.

At the turn of the 14th century instead, there had begun the foundation of universities in Europe. As platforms with the aim to foster *universal knowledge in unanimity* – thus all knowledge of all humanity, and to convey it to everybody, this was meant to produce universal savants who, among other, were meant to direct public institutions in wisdom, potency and beauty. That's why there also existed the seven *«Faculties of Arts»*, following the myth of the seven Muses of classic Antiquity who served *Apollon*, the *God of Light*. This was the third great faculty besides *Theology* and *Philosophy*, i.e. *Natural Sciences*. – Oswald Croll, a medical doctor, Alchemist and Theosophist, writes in his book *Basilica Chymica*, published , in Paris and Hamburg (1608, in German, French and Latin):

«The works of God are bipartite: The works and ways of Nature are dealt with by Philosophy (i.e. Alchemy as the compendium of all natural sciences); but the works and ways of Christ by Theology: On these two ways we should employ our fleeting time, so that we may die in peace and joy. Of this follows that every true Theologist needs to be a philosopher (thus, a natural scientist), and every true philosopher, a Theologist.

After Paracelsus ... very educated men have endeavored to follow this straight and shortened path, instructed and illuminated as they were – not in the sensual school of beginners, nor in the rational one like the increasing ones, but in the third one, the Pentecostal School of the Perfect ones, in which have been studying without toil nor weariness: prophets Apostles and almost all those well instructed men who followed the life and the footsteps of Christ».

The main agents to unite theology and natural sciences (‹philosophy›) in the classic sense however were not the universities, but the monasteries.: The top of all universities in the world however was the University of Takshashilah (Kashmir/India) with its monastery of Nananda (founded 700 b.C., destroyed by the Muslim during the 7th, and again in the 13th and 20th centuries a.D.), together with its monumental library named *«Mountain of Wisdom».* During its active time, this at the time most famous international University, where studied even Greeks and Chinese) is stated to have covered a territory a mile long and half a mile wide; with 300 auditoria and a large astronomical observatory. One Chinese wandering monk, *Hien-Tsang,* wrote (mid-7th century), that there he met 10'000 Students and 200 Professors, teaching over 30 disciplines *including fine arts and martial arts*.

In Europe, the best scientists were the *Benedictines* (like *Basilius Valentinus*[16]) and the *Jesuits* (like *Athanasius Kircher*[17]). Later – i.e. at the beginning of the Century of ‹Enlightenment› – classic erudition and universal genius waned: More and more pseudo-scientific specialties developed. From originally three faculties, many more emerged; each discipline splitting off all others. – During the 20th century, still more institutes came up, multiplying their premises, personnel, and expenses – but, alas! not their knowledge and wisdom. Their *real knowledge* even diminished over time, attaining a level lower than that of an average person in the Middle Ages, creating illiteracy and today even real analphabetism in good old Europe!

This degeneration began already more than 2000 years ago: Even the Bible declares: *«The wisdom of this world is foolishness before God»*

(1. Cor 1:21), leading to the sentence coined during the Renaissance: «*Vanitas vanitatum et omnia vanitas*», a book entitled the *Fool's Boat (Narrenschiff)* by Sebastian Brandt (1494), the *Praise of Folly (Lob der Torheit)* by Erasmus of Rotterdam (1515), the *Vanitas Mundi* by Jacoponus (1650), and corresponding critical art works: an etching by de *Pieter Steenwijck*, 1633–1656, a painting by Philippe de Champagne, 1646 or 1671, a book by J.ohann Valentin Andreæ), – and so forth.

Lao-Dse very distinctly comments the terms *to learn, to understand, to know*: A person learning by heart the content of an encyclopedia (as in fact would not exceed the human cerebral capacity), must certainly be a great fool. If instead he would *really understand* this content, together with causes and outlooks of it, he were a Sage. –

To learn in a positively philosophical sense is the *meaningful* inner gathering of knowledge serving firstly to understand oneself, the Universe, and God, and secondly to foster the spiritual evolution of Humanity on its way towards its Creator. – In fact, *to learn* is no blind compilation of data, like bees who moreover cover their honey, but conscious *composition*, grain after grain, of small complementary elements of knowledge in view of their *usefulness regarding the growth of Gnosis throughout the World.*

Now, as has shown the previous N° 47, growth in true knowledge is inevitably linked to growth in humility. To coin an aphorism, one might even express it like this: «*The more one learns, the more one becomes humble; – the more one wants to become humble, the more one ought to learn!*» – In this light, the first two sequences of text in N° 48 explain themselves by themselves.

A secondary consequence of self-knowledge is the acknowledgment of how very few a human can do out of his personal knowledge, from his personal effort, and with his personal strength, even when he thinks otherwise: The overwhelming part of his doings issues from some third party knowledge, from unconscious impulses, and from unknown imprints out of unknown sources. (images, judgments, norms, habits) – hence, from some ‹dynamic› *not inherent to himself*. That's why human activities mostly don't follow the actual purpose of the human himself – not even if he aspires to a spiritual goal (Initiation, Illumination, Liberation): So much follows the manipulation by his Ego, by his Super-Ego – his so-called ‹Auric Being›: «*Flesh ... and spirit are contrary one to each other, so that you cannot do the things that you would*» *(Gal 5:17)*. – Hence the sentence of the Christ: «*Without me, you cannot achieve anything*».

As soon as a human reaches this insight, it becomes easier for him to retain his impulses – to withhold himself, and to let many things *be done by themselves*, without his active interference. Hence the teaching following which the Godhead principally interferes with no individual destiny – and indeed hardly with the destiny of this World, since the time when Humanity entered its ‹puberty›, so to speak – thus since just a few centuries ago, really. Correspondingly, the pupil of wisdom lore will learn *not to interfere* with the destiny of individuals, nor in some occurring detailed destiny: He will train himself in *non-doing*, in spite of how active he may be otherwise, in worldly or spiritual things to which he is summoned. And he will learn, first with astonishment, then with joy and gratitude, that *nothing remains un-done*, as already N° 38 said; – that many things simply *happen in perfection* – entirely without his *doing* anything.

Gratitude, not because he is ‹spared of doing anything›, but because he becomes a witness of the sublime laws in the Universe following which no needed action remains un-done, and nothing will happen that is not allowed to happen. – Together with this joy and gratitude grows his *faith by lived experience – Gnosis*. Great tings can happen that way without a major effort (that even might have spoiled the whole thing). – Thus, great things can be attained and achieved, because the ‹Sage› has «become a tool»: a conscious servant of the One Great Œuvre, that is entirely dedicated to the evolution of the Universe until arriving at the level where who is human today, will become a Creator of new worlds himself, even of a new Universe perhaps; – at least this is what gnostic lore teaches us.

Regarding the text of N° 48 this means: Wo from amidst the old ambitious, jostling, greedy world of earthly humanity desires to grasp the most high things, is not ripe yet to achieve such great and important goals. Outwardly rich as he or she might appear: they will remain inwardly poor.

Who accumulates a big heap of knowledge, but does not pass it on to others and to the profit of the One Great spiritual Work, likens one who *knows nothing at all.* Who hoards material treasures but does not spend them with others for the profit of all, is like one who possesses nothing at all. – Who has ben *«entrusted with a talent»,* but buries it, in order to guard it as his entrusted possession, or in order to ‹be modest›, will be found to be a faithless and unworthy servant, and chased away. Who through adequate learning grows in insight and comprehension, needs also to grow in generous, impersonal love (but will always feel that it is still not enough). Those who as (for every day they see how very much they still ignore), they will also grow in inner distance and in wake awareness regarding the ‹10'000 things›. Who, finally, through growing knowledge enters *kind-hearted non-doing*, to him all things destined for him will be devolved like ripe fruits – and were it «the whole World»!

A modern Chinese commentator writes about this situation: «Who charges himself with politics is indeed unworthy to rule the country ».

This declaration goes very far. – In the frame of an interpretation regarding ‹successfully› following The transfiguristic Path of Humanity, it signifies: Who *remains attached* to outwardly institutions and to instruments that are linked to walking the routinely path of Humanity (the so-called *hamster-wheel*); or who, while following *The Path* seeks, or even just hopes for, any kind of personal advantage for himself, including Transfiguration, is unworthy to be admitted to the Great process of all this. Who still fosters his own person while striving for fundamental renewal, isn't fit yet to enter the Kingdom of God. The ‹Golden Wedding Robe› of Liberation is not some goal to be aimed at. It is uniquely the *lawful result* and the certain attest that a human, in the service for the microcosmos entrusted to him, has attained the *Good End*. – Or, as Rev. 22:14 says, combining and translating precisely two Greek versions:

«Blissful are those who fulfill His mandates, and purify their robes, so that they are entrusted with the power over the Tree of Life, and may enter the portals that allow entering The Town!»

Often conquers the whole World who makes no effort to do so!

德

第四十九章

聖人常無心，以百姓心爲心。
善者，吾善之；不善者，吾亦善之；德善。
信者，吾信之；不信者，吾亦信之；德信。
聖人在天下，歙歙焉，爲天下渾其心，
百姓皆注其耳目，聖人皆孩之。

49.

A sage is ordinarily without any intention —
He makes the motives of ordinary people his intention:

To who is good, I am good —
To who is not good, I am good as well: DE is goodness.
To who is honest, I am honest —
To who is dishonest, I am honest as well:
DE is honesty.

When the sage tarries in public, his reservation is so great that
to the populace, his heart is impenetrable.
Simple people notice his most trifling gestures and words —
therefore, to the sage, they all are like children.

To begin with: The pictoglyph for HEART – 心 – *c*an mean *courage, intention, motivation, opinion, thoughts,* and *heart*, thus it is very polyvalent. Moreover, the glyph itself shows a little heart with its main parting vessels *and their opposed flow*. The glyph 德 for *DE*, with all six meanings simultaneously present, could be broken down, pictographically, as: *«growing, learning»*, or *«live heart dominated by a noble motivation* (the *imperial crown*)*»*. The *ordinary populace* stands in contrast to the nobler people or *subjects*, including the clerks and dignitaries who are thought to be capable of *individual judgment*. And throughout the *Dao-De-Jing*, the *«Wise»*, or *«Sage»* silently includes the *wise ruler*, who is supposed to have, at his nomination or earlier, *«entered DAO»* (see. N° 62). – Interesting minor fact: The Chinese glyph for *heart* – 心, *«sin»* – is found also in the Hebrew sign ש – *«sin»* – for *«fire»* and *«light»*.

The elements of *purpose – will* and *ego-will* – have been given a few thoughts in earlier chapters. There, they were opposed to *non-doing*. Here instead, a more profound aspect of *«will»* is considered, but which is equally connected to non-involvement. Therefore, a few more remarks are in order here:

It is inadmissible – it would even be paradoxical, really – to sustain (as most earlier translations do) – that the ‹Wise› has *no will of himself»*, *«no opinion of his own »*, *«no resolute mind»*, *«no in-*

dividual consciousness» and so forth – and even *«no heart of his own»*. An independent opinion (the capacity to discriminate, and a sane judgment), courage, resoluteness and resolve are quite indispensable in order to follow *The Path* in autonomy and mature independence, in auto-responsibility and with wake awareness!

All those *«no ... at all ...»* also smell that *esoteric pietism* – that forcibly cultured behaviour hardly different from that of ordinary humanistic do-goodders: This is a cultivated kind of consciousness hat hides rather well the human beast – but unleashes the latter as soon as there is an opportunity to do so.

No, the expression *«his heart is intransparent»* is brought here in a more differentiated sense, and goes deeper than any pietistic renunciation or well-trained humility. Also, the second line promptly explains the real meaning oft the term as a reasonable *clearsightedness*: The *‹Saint›*, or *‹Sage›* has, as for himself, quite certainly his own views and opinions; for he has the complete view of whatever occurs in the World. He has the experience of one wo has reached self-knowledge, knowledge of the world, and knowledge of God – thus, one who is able to assess in no time any situation, and the adequate behavior for the occasion. But when he dwells among humans, whose knowledge is more superficial, whose consciousness is more clouded than his own, and who with their ordinary endeavours want to follow a goal adequate to them, the *‹Wise›* will stay back and conceal his opinion (unless he is actually asked for it). He will follow the rule of *non-doing* – and let things happen the way the law of cause and effects wants to steer them. – A Chinese commentator in this respect talks of *tolerance and freedom of thought and expression.*

From his high level of consciousness, the *‹Sage›* thus grants the *freedom of error* to all his ‹subjects› – without anger nor malicious joy, but in loving compassion. He knows: if his judgment were like theirs, he would act like they do. Therefore, one could as well translate: *«A Saint often keeps his determination for himself»*. – And this is certainly true for a sovereign ruler.

Based on the same loving compassion, the following lines are to be understood as well: Here, too, goodness and confidence are no expressions of a well behaved personality, but those of that unconditional Love that *«hopes all, believes all, endures all ... »* (1 Cor 13:7). – The ‹Saint› also knows who will *«betray him»*. Only, he may not lightly permit any fellow man to saddle himself with such guilt – and both of them with some new Karma. Therefore he will always follow the commandment, that a ‹sage› shall be *«as smart as a snake, and as good-natured as a dove».*

Also it is quite logical that especially there where every look of his eyes, and each of his casual *(«sideward»)* words are observed, interpreted and commented, he will keep the most possible reservation. The Chinese commentator explains the glyphs *«reservation so great»* (that cannot as such be translated into English), as *«shrinks nose-respiration».* So we understand that his ‹heart› is really intransparent for all (text-wise precisely as *muddy, dull* – see the *wells catfish* in N° 36). And this again corresponds to the teachings by *Sun-Dse*, where the wise general and his army *«are undiscernible»* – impenetrable – and *«cannot be known».*

Similarly, the ‹Master› of Gnosis and his teachings appear to «the World» as strange and even inconceivable: To them, all this is objectionable foolishness, for, contrarily to the Disciple or devout Apostle, they lack positive empathy and tolerance. For this reason as well *«his heart is impenetrable for the World».*

However: if surrounding people laude him or criticize him – if they are scandalized by him, or if they admire him: they painstakingly observe *whatever* he does, and *how* he does it. Every person occupying a representative position is conscious of this fact, and holds himself back correspondingly. While he simply and heartily meets the *«simple populace»*, he continuously observes his own behavior, his speech, and indeed all his thoughts, too, including the accompanying mimics. His subjects observe him, like children mimicking their parents. Therefore, to him they are like children for whom he is the good example, and who are confided to his awareness and his farsightedness.

By right the Chinese commentator says: *«The World is like a large family under the guidance of a loving mother».* – This mother is DAO; – her representative on Earth is the *wise ruler.*

DE is goodness – DE is honesty – DE is empathy and awareness!

德

第五十章

出生入死。生之徒，十有三；死之徒，十有三；
人之生，動之于死地，亦十有三。
夫何故？以其生之厚。蓋聞善攝生者，路行不遇兕虎，
入軍不被甲兵；兕無所投其角，虎無所用其爪，兵無所容其刃。
夫何故？以其無死地。

50.

To come forth into life means to enter death.
Bound up with Life are three among ten —
Bound up with Death are another three among ten —
Humans born to rush into the claws of Death are
another three among ten. —
Oh humans – why?
Because their ignorance is so complete.

[Hear] a teaching disciples should listen to and carefully follow:
To undertake a voyage
without being attacked by a rhinoceros or a tiger —
To walk as a warrior among warriors without wearing a helmet:
The rhinoceros finds no spot to sink in his horn—
the tiger finds no spot to thrust ***in his claws—***
No soldier finds a spot that would take in his sword —
Oh humans – why?
Because he lacks the basis for dying.

The translation here is again as concise as possible. In addition, the commentary offers a few alternatives.

The text begins on a purely creatural plane – but the «teaching» is a metaphor. The final point and culmination is to be understood completely in a transfiguristic sense, and even makes a most unusual statement. For, the *One of ten*, who needs to fear neither rhinoceros, nor tiger, nor warfare, is indeed the *‹perfect one›* – he who has attained the *‹New Soul-Vestment›* and the *‹New Serpent Fire›*.

Three questions sum up this text:

1° What is Life – viz: what is Death?

2° What is ignorance – viz: what is knowledge?

3° What is the *One of ten* doing differently, so that he becomes immortal? [18]

In the creatural world – as says the short, tough statement of the first four glyphs – whatever «steps out into life» is bound to «enter death»; and this is indeed the fundamental fact throughout the whole created Universe. To be born, to grow, flourish, bring fruits, wither, decompose and be purified – such is the prescribed biography of every creature – every stone, every plant, every beast or human, and also the gods (see the *twilight of the gods* in Germanic lore); – even every idea, every invention, and all physical and non-physical facts and occurrences in this world are subject to the same principal law. The ‹*Universal Doctrine*› emphasizes these conditions, again and again.

Even the most convinced materialists acknowledge this reality, and secretly ask themselves the same anxious question as emerges in the present text: *«Oh man – what about all this? – What is the pivot, around which constantly rotates this wheel of births and ‹deaths›, – since millions of years, and probably for as many millions of years to come?»* – So-called ‹practical reasoning› as well agrees that who could reach said pivot, would be exempted of the apparently pointless revolution of that Wheel: *«To live only to die – oh man! – why all this – and what for? – Is there really no exit from this tragedy?»*.

The present text gives the definite answer to this cry for help – and much more.

Primarily, let us remember that on the creatural plane ‹*Life*› represents a form of *Yang*, but ‹*death*› is a form of *Yin*. Indeed, to a human *microcosmos*, an earthly life is a phase of its *active experiences and agencies* – its *exhaling.* Its existence in the transitory regions between death and birth instead is a phase of its *passive learning* – its *inhaling*. Now, as a human has the *possibility*, and thus also the *responsibility* to freely shape his physical existence in the frame of chances and talents given to him, there necessarily arise different motives in life for each and every human:

One main motive has *Life itself* as an epicenter – be it solely in pleasures and benefits, be it in aims and activities for a constructive outlet, or be it just for some humanistic ideals. The text emphasizes, however, that even the most noble activities cannot annihilate the circuit of births and deceases. The question remains: *«Oh you humans: – why and what for ... ?»*

A second possible motive is death, says the text. This may be constant *fear of death*, or *active killing* – as a soldier or as an executioner, or it might be, so to speak, *instrumental killing* of plants and animals, as in the food-industry. This example can be understood much more generally, as demonstrates the famous quotation from *Rudolf Steiner* who coined the phrase: *«When I breathe, the air dies!»*

Regarding Ancient China we also need to remember the *caste of warriors*, and the knightly Order of the Samuraï: Men who had passed an extremely strict education and training, abiding severest ritual obligations, besides an even more exacting codex of honor. For, in oldest times, warriors were Initiates: *sacred fighters,* the noblest ‹duty› of whom it was *to love their adversaries.* The round *petasoi* worn by the soldiers of the famous terracotta army at Xian, very much reminds the hardly more recent Mithrean *libetra.* – But even this impressing level of initiation does not stifle the anxious question: *«Oh you humans – why all this, and what for?»*

The third life motivation is none, really – at least none consciously chosen: It is the idle, vain existence *«from birth to death»* – an existence lived insensibly and thoughtlessly: *«Things are as they are ... »* – and the great mass of society lives like that. This is the way of life that emerged in the ‹enlightened› Hemisphere of our Planet during industrialization with its automatic production lines, with its unemployment and the subsequent ‹schnapps misery›. It is the same mentality of *«no future»* as in today's dumping society, where good people – young or old – are trashed for being less rentable than a machine or an AI-bot. Even some of the most powerful men of today wake up to become aware of the senselessness of the constant chase for goods and power, but are incapable to let go of it. They are, as our text says, marching *«to meet the claws of Death»*, without any aim befitting a human being ... – *«oh you humans – why??»*

The answer according to interprets of East and West is: «Because they live a life too pompous, or too dissolute – completely stuck in *Maya*, the *World of illusions!*[19]

It is *through ignorance* that so many ‹good people› sacrifice themselves – often for some real ideal, more often for a false one. For in the end, even the most noble ideals *«serve death»* instead of life, though so many are fostering with so much toil and renouncement what is supposed to be ‹The Good›! – *Through ignorance* so many give away their life – as hero's, or as martyrs, or just in a cardiac infarction! – *Through ignorance* so many believe in some great leader or magical redeemer, some enterprise or institution or cosmic event to bring durable happiness to the World! – *Ignorance* is the core cause of *all* sufferings in the World. – *Ignorance* is the true *‹original sin of humanity›*, bequeathed as it is *since The Beginning* by parents and grand-parents to their children and grand-children –

and this – *«oh you humans, why?»* – Because the *One Path* towards *true Life* is ignored! – *Therefore indeed* nine of ten humans are – one way or another– since their birth doomed to die; and no end to this lively nightmare is in sight – unless there happens something dramatic, something so special, in them and with them, that they become unassailable for all kind of evil.

Existential dread and conformism keep all ignorance going; Powerful people exploit this unconsciousness and lack of bravery and fuel it even more: so their power increases, still. — Greed for power, too, is a result of *ignorance!* – So, what makes the difference between *the one* and the other *nine*?

It is the acquaintance with the *Path of GNOSIS – the Path of DAO.* It is the insight that nothing *issuing from this world* can mitigate, let alone heal, the pain of this same world. – It is only from this insight that can surge the decision to *«leave father and mother»,* to dedicate oneself to a *fundamentally different* way of life, and to surrender to it. – The *one of ten* has made exactly this decision, and begun to realize it in practice. He has *stepped on the Path*, says the text; – he has become a ‹voyager› – a ‹pilgrim› or ‹pupil› on the Path toward true knowledge. Only *this path*, followed steadily, can save a human from that death sentence everybody receives right at birth. In other words: The One *condemned to die since birth* can only be ‹pardoned› provided he quits his ‹zone of comfort› – that is the way of life he so dearly mourns – *stepping onto the Path, following it*, and *through his own efforts* fulfills the required conditions. Only like that the Grace of redemption becomes possible. – All cultures know this path, although under different names. – All speak of conditions to be fulfilled, or tests that have to be passed in order to *liberate oneself* off the Wheel of re-birth and re-death.

The *Dao-De-Jing* tells us *how* this Grace can be obtained. Chapter 50 mentions he result that undeniably follows the serious efforts on the path of *self-initiation*: When the Disciple of Gnosis reaches the *hub oft the wheel*; when as a ‹pure› or a ‹righteous› he has entered the sphere of renewal and transformation, then he becomes invulnerable fort the attacks from the base world – from the old ‹serpent fire› of his own low Self.: He just needs lift up his eyes to look at the Golden Serpent of his *New State of the Soul* – and every danger is banned at once. Neither blind force nor its unpredictability; – neither smart persecution nor rapacious greed will from now on keep clouding his purified personality – and so he does no more attract them from the outside. *This is* why he needs no ‹protecting helmet› anymore when he goes to meet the World. – The end of the gospel following *Markos* says it in these words;

«Who as one faithful [to The Path] is baptized (βαπτισθεις = overwhelmed, drunk of the Holy Spirit), ... – in my name they will expel demons; in new tongues they will speak; snakes they will conjure, and when they have drunken a poisonous drink they have nothing to fear. To the sick and discouraged they will impose their hands; and the latter will be upright and strong again». [20]

One exception however needs to be mentioned: The fact that ‹the World› is afraid when suddenly confronted to the positive fluid emanated by Gnosis – by the pure Light coming from the One Light. The strong radiation of Strength, Light and Love of a ‹Saint› – of a perfect one – can be perceived by ordinary people of the ordinary world – but they cannot reasonably be assessed by them, and therefore people may get *embarrassed, and afraid.* This insecurity though very often leads to aggressive behavior and actions – reactions like those of dogs and snakes (see N° 55), and as we also know them from the Christian myth of the Passion, and from corresponding fairytales and other myths (Baldur). Thus, many humans react with fear and aggressiveness – also because they feel as if their way of looking at life, their conduct of life, their view of life were questioned and challenged by these *new views* ... –

The ‹Wise› therefore will thoroughly hold back his irresistible emanation of a spirit-soul-human, and only hesitantly let it permeate to outsiders.[21] – The *Hagakuré* therefore teaches us: *«On the top level, you will look as if you had not the slightest idea of anything!»* [22] – If now said *«one of ten»* should be attacked all the same, he knows that this attack is not aimed at him personally, and on the other hand, that these humans *cannot react otherwise*, but by attacking the Forces of Purity and Love, wishing to destroy them – same as the *liver,* at the begin of the contact with the Light, eliminates the gnostic tint, or coloration of the blood. – *That is why* Jesus, already crucified, prayed for those who killed him: *«Father forgive them, for they don't know what they are doing »* —

Their ignorance is too great!

第五十一章

道生之，德畜之，物形之，勢成之。
是以萬物莫不尊道而貴德。
道之尊，德之貴，夫莫之命而常自然。
故道生之，德畜之；長之育之；成之熟之；養之覆之。
生而不有，爲而不恃，長而不宰。是謂玄德。

51.

DAO brings them forth —
DE lets them thrive —
Substance gives them shape —
Strength completes them:
Of the 10'000 things there is none
that would not adore DAO and revere DE.
DAO they adore, and DE they revere —
nothing and nobody commands it, but the eternal order of Nature—
for:
DAO brings them forth —
DE lets them thrive —
These [two] bring forth their thriving —
They protect them against their fiends —
They shield them against their annihilation.

To bring forth life, without taking anything —
To build, without relying on it —
To direct without dominating:
That is what is called the secret of DE.

Same as Brahmanism has its ‹*Prakriti*›, so in Daoism DAO is, in a macrocosmic way, the *cause of all phenomena*, the nameless one, the inconceivable one (Bœhme's ‹*Ungrund*›). – *Cosmically,* DAO is – like ‹*Prakriti*› – the *Arch-Mother* or ‹*humid radical*› – *substance*, from which everything comes forth as a manifestation of divine Spirit – *Brahma*, Daoist **I** – He who *calls out* all that is coming forth. The ‹10'000 things› materialize from DAO who contains them all, *generates* them all, shelters them all, and pushes them all forward. – Spirit – *the Logos* – *«the Force»* – perfections them.

Incarnation of the Spirit is hardly mentioned in Daoism: *«The birth of the Child is a divine secret».*[23] – This corresponds to the Divine Purusha of the Veda – the *Logos* or *Christ-Force* that is born within the human heart, as the *microcosmic Purusha.*[24]

DAO in the sense of *order* within the *universal harmony* of all things, on a *cosmic plane* appears mainly as the ideal society with its human forms of existence and activities. However, what is it that encourages humans to strive for this order and to maintain it within the personal microcosm – respectively, to carry it out of the microcosmical sphere and into society and its world? – It is DE – ‹*Virtue*› as the totality of human virtues, in its *supra-human* form, named *Gnosis* (see also N° 38).

Now, same as *DAO* on said planes brings forth everything, so *Virtue*, too – *DE* – conveys to everything its positive *dynamic*– inwardly and outwardly – and therefore its thriving and its *shape*.

But in order that this shape can manifest itself as a sensible and eventually also visible figure, *substance* is needed – be it gross matter, be it a subtly physical (etheric or spiritual) substance, or be it an individual *being,* independent as such. This is a form of *Life* – of *self-reliant Life* even, in spite of dwelling on a very low level, with no self-consciousness at all, as is the case with minerals. –

The *perfection of a creature as a manifest* ‹thing› however, consists in its consciousness: in its self-awareness (*«I am»*) and in its self-reflection (*«I am I»*), in its conscious *doing* (*«I want»*) and in its *non-doing* (*«No!»*). In other words: the apex of evolution of any form of manifestation as such is its *self-conscious Ego!*[25]

These steps of perfection of a manifestation are, so to speak, like cast into the prepared mold (creative thought), like in the case of injection molding in today's plastic industry: The shape, or mold, is given, and for a specific species remains always the same. – Its quality as well as its *applicability* instead depend on the character of the *substance* that fills the yet invisible, etheric shape, when out of the *forces* driving the process ‹*Prakriti*› fashions the final manifestation.[26]

That's why in nations or human races with a low degree of individualization, the similitude of individuals can be so compelling that a stranger is hardly capable of distinguishing them: The stranger may perceive the analogy of *«the mold»* (the race), but not the *individual ‹substance›* (‹Self›).

Now, as soon as said creature has developed its consciousness up to a certain degree, it becomes conscious of its own existence as well as of its dependency from outer and inner factors and mechanisms. This is the moment where it develops its *religiosity*: its consciousness of being bound up in a more and more conscious connection with outer and inner forces: *forces of Nature, spirits and gods*. – Out of these concepts it soon formulates the hierarchy that in the pantheon of every nation gets its specific structure.

Thus, a human becomes conscious of his own forces, talents and virtues along with – finally – self-consciousness and a clear idea of his highest God who is the origin of all and everything. It is a spiritual performance especially reserved to Man, to consciously become aware of this sublime power, and address It – even while rationally denying It, as we often can observe with *‹atheists›*; for, of what does not exist, *no complete denial* is possible, either!

Instead, an *unconscious, unwilling acknowledgment* of DAO begins much earlier: Even an embryo already orients itself in a certain sense toward DAO – and even more strongly toward DE – the virtues of its surroundings, like virtues and vices of its mother or other people, and like climatic or health-affecting habits of the latter.

Minerals, plants and animals follow the inherent laws of DAO; and analogous virtues take their place in the Cosmos relative to their surroundings. A human sensitive to vibrations of cosmic and microcosmic harmony – i.e. to such subtle vibrations and radiations as those of well-being and order, will equally sense the expression of joy, happiness, fear or harm of other creatures, along with creatural communities: a forest, a school of wales, the artful formations in a stalactite cavern, or a group of unanimous humans.

Such is he *worshiping devotion of the 10'000 things»* Lao-Dse talks about; this awe combined with happiness and gratitude that a living human can *consciously experience*, too, although being unable to describe it in words: «*The DAO one can understand is not he One Universal DAO!*»

Such is the universal spiritual dimension of DAO: DAO as the ‹Mother› – as the directing, pressing and perfecting universal force, as the carrier wave of *spiritual renewal, transformation and transfiguration.* – Such is the *universal Gnosis.* – *Individual Gnosis* is ‹inner virtue› – the DE of the individual, who «underlies himself to the Savior», as the cantata of J.S. Bach, BWV 48 says (see our N° 58) – growing and thriving in this sacred devotion, until reaching perfection: Such is the harmonious cooperation of a human awakened to full consciousness of the universal Divine Plan and Process – from strength to strength, and from Glory to Glory:

DAO brings them forth — DE lets them thrive —
Strength accomplishes them!

德

第五十二章

天下有始，以爲天下母。既得其母，以知其子，復守其母，沒身不殆。
塞其兌，閉其門，終身不勤。開其兌，濟其事，終身不救。
見小曰明，守柔曰強。用其光，復歸其明，無遺身殃;
是爲襲常。

52.

The World has a beginning
that thought out the World's Mother —As soon as someone accepts his mother,
he knows thereby to be her child —
for him who re-gains the cozy security inside of his mother,
the body's dying off is without danger.
To ignore one's inner to-and-fro, and to bolt the door, means to be carefree at the end of one's life.
To continue one's to-and-fro, and to keep up one's entanglements means to be without salvage at the end of one's life.
Respect for the lowly is an honor —
Safeguard for the weak is strength.[27]
To apply one's clarity and to win back one's splendor
and then to relinquish one's body, is no misfortune:
Righteous demeanor inherits Eternity.

This text again shows various ambiguities, and if nobody can insist to have found the *one correct translation* for these words *of Lao-Dse*, the version offered here is surely in harmony with the ensemble of the *Dao-De-Jing* and is coherent in itself. The signification becomes recognizable if one is familiar with the Universal Gnostic Doctrine. Some possible variants are mentioned just by the way.

First of all, it would be good to know several myths around the emergence oft the Universe – especially the ones that begin earlier than biblical Genesis, which starts only in the second phase of materializations. The first phase is the *«State of Emptiness»*, where the Creator creates himself, like *Brahma* who inside an egg (the *Egg of the World* as in later myths) generates himself by *thinking out* himself – exactly as says our present N° 52.

This first and unique All-God is the *Spirit*. This *universal Spirit* – YI – in turn brings forth the *Mother* – DAO – which already is ‹bipolar›, as is ‹He› Himself, and as the *Yin-Yang* indicates it. The *inner Law* of the Mother already contains DAO as *the Path*, and the human who follows the spiritual path, vivifies himself as the inner-own presence of God: This, now, is his own *microcosmic* DAO – his personal state as a *child of God*.

The First DAO, however – the ‹Mother› – is named *The Beginning*, as says the *Corpus Hermeticum*:

«All things depend of One Beginning; and this beginning depends of Him who is One and unique ». – Or – likewise in the *Corpus Hermeticum*, in the chapter about *the cratèr and the Monas*: *«One thing is the beginning of all things, for it gives all things; and if I name it the Good, then I mean the one who is entirely and truly good, always.* – And again in chapter XII/36: *For the Good cannot be surpassed; – it is unlimited and infinite, without a beginning for itself; – but to us it seems to have a beginning ... ».*[28]

What follows now in the *Dao-De-Jing* is a *compendium* of the whole spiritual path of evolution of Humankind: It begins, as mentioned earlier, when Man becomes aware of his *dependence* of DAO as of the Mother of all things, and therefore also as *the mother of himself.* Acknowledging this as an inner experience – not just believing it – the human *recognizes* himself as a *child of the Mother* – as such also named: *Son of the Widow*. He likens a newly born baby who *«recognizes his mother».* So he becomes a *child of God* again, as the Gospel of John mentions very shortly, and as say also the classical Rosicrucians of the 17th century: *«Ex Deo Nascimur – from God we are born».*

Now, as a father and a mother *never abandon* their child, it is self-understood that for a human who has without any doubt recognized himself as a child of God, physical death – the *«deposition of his physical body»* looses its fright.

If now he should succeed making some progress on the path of renewal and transformation, the Candidate needs to make a decisive, conscious effort. Earlier chapters have therefore indicated the *«Wu-Wei»* – the *non-doing* on an already higher level. The present chapter begins on the first level: *purification of the heart.* – This is to say: From your entire system, from the so-called body of thoughts (*mental body*) wipe out the earthly human restlessness – the inner *to-and-fro*. From your body of desires, (*astral* body) the confusion; from the physical body: the whirling impulses; the constant turmoil. – The translation intentionally says *wipe out*, not *thrust aside*: the latter would be a forcible reaction, and this is precisely what must be avoided. The Candidate is to thoroughly eliminate all those pressing impulses, by applying his *consciousness and orientation* – not by any compulsory effort: This is what the picturesque expression *«shut the doors»* is meant to suggest..

Other interpretations propose things like: *«Close the senses»,* or *«close the mouth»*; – but this is a purely materialistic reflection, and inaccurate. The capacity to differentiate with objective clarity of expressions must increasingly be *sharpened*, even if (or because) sparse talk is very important. Neither may the correct interpretation say: *undisturbed for his entire life*, for that is impossible in this world – even in the wake of greatest inner tranquility: The text here alludes to dying as the ‹end-product› of every physical existence – and to the mentality of envisaging this termination with imperturbable calm: Who has reached this inner calm and purity, knowing that he is accepted by the Gnosis (adopted, as by a mother), may truly be said to be braced for the great moment of decease – But who instead continues to feed his worldly human confusion is lost without any rescue – that's what the text means to say. The term *rescue* is brought here with an ideogram containing both the *‹Chrisma›* and the *‹Chiasma›* of the Christian symbolism (see Note 29 with its two vignettes), and thus underlines the parenthood of Christian symbols with the old oriental tradition.[29]

To finish, our text emphasizes the importance of awareness, brotherly togetherness and Love, the way the Candidate is obliged to feel and act toward every other creature; for, while that purity of the heart, of all thoughts and of all doings is indispensable, *«the greatest of them all is Love»* (1 Cor 13:13).

Love in the gnostic sense – this is simultaneously the *new radiance of the Candidate's new soul*[30] – a radiance issuing from him toward all those who suffer, those who still feed the confusion of the World – seeking and erring … – due to *general ignorance*.

The pilgrim who in empathy, comprehension and Love embraces all and everything, while imperturbably following his own spiritual evolution, thereby also partakes in actively enhancing the realization of the Divine Plan, in priestly devotion for the evolution of the Universe towards unification of All with the One Light:

This is the realization of doing without doing –
the true Gnostic Magic!

道

第五十三章

使我介然有知，行于大道，唯施是畏。
大道甚夷，而人好徑。朝甚除，田甚蕪，倉甚虛；
服文采，帶利劍，厭飲食，財貨有餘；是爲盜夸。非道也哉！

Our basic text has 采 = *to tear, to pluck* (here in the meaning of *stealing*); – Wang-Bi has 綵 = *colorfully embroidered*.

53.

When rightly applying my knowledge I travel on the large road,
concerned to do nothing but what is right.
The large road is exceedingly smooth and secure,
but humans like the tortuous trails.
The palace so far away —
The fields overgrown with weeds —
The granges completely voided —
The useful documents all torn —
The belt equipped with a pointy dagger —
Surfeited with drinking and eating —
The remains of money and goods all robbed —
Justice dispensed by who brags with his felonies ... —
Oh the ever too excessive heartlessness!

This text has induced many to fall for a fundamental misunderstanding: Most Western translators have found here social criticism based on exploitation by the nobility. In reality, here the *elevated Path* of Virtue (DAO) is opposed to the devious ways of criminality. The term DAO – 道 – appears *explicitly as such,* at the beginning: instead of *Large Road* one may also read *Great* DAO. And at the end, DAO appears *implicitly*, in connection with its *complete absence*. The 失 of 失道 as in N° 38 (*neglect* DAO), resp. 无道 as in N° 46 (*no* DAO) becomes here 非 (*to lack*, with the marginal signification of *error, sin*) in 非道 – the latter, when *read as separate glyphs,* signifying *absence of* DAO, but when read as a twin expression, meaning *wickedness, infamy, heartlessness*.

It is impossible to correctly integrate this text into the series of the *Dao-De-Jing*, unless we understand it – one – as a warning example for a prince, and – two – if we remember well the historically documented Hunnish and Mongolian nomads and marauding gangs of brigands pillaging villages and individuals alike during many centuries, throughout the Asian continent between Danube and Indus:

Far off in the country-side there are manors and small ranches; the Capital (the *palace*, as a glyph synonym with both the *rightful justices* and the *rising sun*) is *«so far away»*. Marauding robbers –

probably also deserted soldiers as they existed in every century – haunted the solitary regions – raiding and ravaging without restraint. The famous movie *The Seven Samuraï* gives a very lively impression of how these things happened.

Besides *«palace (Commanders and Supreme Court) far away»*, also the less literal *«farm destroyed»* would be adequate. Yet the text nowhere speaks of *nobility* suppressing the people, but quite clearly of a rural population abandoned to all kind of pillaging villains, because they are *not protected* by their over-lords. A version in the sense of social criticism cannot even be found in today's commentaries in communist China.

But, how about assuming this to be meant as a didactic metaphor?

The text is built *from mirroring pairs of opposites*: Torn documents and robber's law oppose the far-off palace; – void granges oppose surfeited brigands; – the speaker of this verse who affirms that he is anxious to do only what is in tune with DAO, opposes the villains boasting of their evil deeds. – The misery where one fears the pointed dagger or sharpened sword of ruthless robbers opposes the secure *main road* of the *Great DAO*; – and the torn *poetry or manuscripts* oppose *the knowledge* the author wants to *apply* in order to exclusively follow the right path. –

Chinese commentators also speak of *writings on silk*. For the alternative by some Westerners reading *«tender, colorfully embroidered robes»* there lacks a corresponding Chinese verb. At any rate, *heartlessness and ruthless violence* are shown to have ousted noble education and *refined cultivation*, because the regent neglects his province.

In spite of the many possible variants, we may assume with certainty that precisely this symmetry of contraries was meant to be the asset of this chapter. It is also possible that like in N° 41 there was contained a *prophecy*, if the *Dao-De-Jing* was authored during the 6th century – or else a historical account of the 4th century.

The question about which of the historical or textual variants is more to the point, remains unanswered. This is no big loss, though, for there exactly lies the wealth of Chinese written language and the art of a cultivated author, along with the level of education and understanding of the reader.

Now, in order to look at the *microcosmic Path* – the *Path of* DAO – this text is quite as unambiguous as N° 46 (*«With DAO in the World, passing horses will drop their dung all the same»*): As a contrary to Western (biblical) tradition, here the *broad street* is the Path of Dao, and therefore is looked at as being the *norm.* This corresponds to the notion already mentioned above: DAO as a universal law all and everything abide to. The whole account can be understood as the *enhancement of the microcosmic to-and-fro* the reader has been warned against earlier: If once one allows to the ‹thieves› to unleash their instincts and desires, one might easily have to submit to them completely.

If this happened, the *palace of the King* – the *«House of the Father»* the pilgrim meant to enter on his path of complete renewal and transformation – would truly be removed to a *distance far, faraway.* Finished the tender *Robe of Light* he was summoned to weave; and all the *good Scriptures* – even if they were written on silk – would be *«torn to pieces»*, or *«snatched from his hands»,* as the text can be interpreted as well. Thus the disinherited Candidate would be left behind, naked and poorer than a beggar, while his opposing forces could *«boast of their looting».*
It appears however that such an interpretation would go too far after all. – For, whence could then come the desperate exclamation: *Oh the ever too excessive heartlessness!»* ? – Maybe the idea of a didactical metaphor is closer to the truth after all: that it is an encouragement for one who shall learn to be well taking care as a ruler, supervising and protecting the lands, farmsteads, cattle and humans confided to him. Instead of becoming a ‹chief-robber›, he is to become a just clerk or ruler, who honors and sustains loyalty, confidence, classic traditions and cultural values – same as the Candidate of the *Mysteries* cares for, and protects, the *Gnosis* entrusted ton him. Both was, is and will be a very recommendable encouragement and warning – independently of any epoch one might think of.

Thus, this chapter N° 53 as a whole links up seamlessly with the preceding one. The present commentary may therefore be closed quite fittingly with these words taken from the latter, and indeed is quite *opposed to it*:

Respect for the lowly is an honor –
Safeguard for the weak is strength —
Righteous demeanor inherits Eternity.

第五十四章

善建者不拔，善抱者不脫，子孫以祭祀不輟。
修之于身，其德乃眞；修之于家，其德乃餘；
修之于鄉，其德乃長；修之于邦，其德乃丰；
修之于天下，其德乃普。
故以身觀身，以家觀家，以鄉觀鄉，以邦觀邦，以天下觀天下。
吾何以知天下然哉？以此。

54.

A well informed person will not be seduced —
Who holds on fast will not be unsaddled —
Children and grandchildren will sacrifice to him, forever.
The virtue of him who ennobles himself will be genuine.
The virtue of who ennobles his house, will be the neighbor's.
The virtue of him who ennobles his village, will expand.
The virtue of him who ennobles his county, will be over-rich.
The virtue of who ennobles the Empire, will be all-embracing.

Therefore:
Regarding a human, look at his way of life —
Regarding a family, look at its home —
Regarding a village, look at its community —
Regarding a county, look at its townships —,
Regarding a land, look at its condition —
Regarding an Empire, look at its subjects —

And whence do I know that the World is so, alas?
Exactly thence.

This chapter is again addressed to a sovereign clerk, or to some prince. We spontaneously remember the phrase of the Swiss pastor, politician and socio-critical author, Jeremias Gotthelf (Albert Bitzius, 1797-1854): *«In the house must begin, what shall flourish throughout the nation!»*. – The time-frame for this quotation shows us how fast a social obviousness can become an almost obsolete, utopian epigram; and this not by abuse or misuse, but because social customs have been changing so radically, world-wide.

The family-clans, customary as they were at the time of the origin of the *Dao-De-Jing*, melted down, due to human individualization and political inflation: first to become small families, then couples intentionally remaining without issue, and finally individual flats, and this specifically in all ‹civilized› nations. Education toward civilized cohabitation became a socialization problem – viz. a program for resocialization by psychologists. Good education within the family has become a rarity; Housing estates and even whole skyscrapers have become mere dormitory-silos; neighbors don't even great each other. Regional or national celebrations, once meaningful, have become noisy festivals in some closed circles, and while xenophobe nationalism – and today anti-human globalism – are actually growing into totalitarian dimensions, there is no real feeling for a true homeland left. Nor is there hardly a remembrance of the cosmic citizenship of every human on Earth ... —

Now, there can be no question about *«strengthening things in order to prevent their superannuation»*, as the next chapter will say: Individualization by itself would be a commendable process in the development of new self-consciousness, self-assessment, self-determination, self-responsibility, and finally both self-conquest and self-realization of an individual, if only the basis for all that was still given: The *«self-refinement»* with which the present text begins, firstly needs one or more examples, then good self-knowledge and self-discipline, and, third, the public esteem for civility, respect for people and things, and a broad education.

That the latter as well has progressively crumbled, has become the fundamental problem of all so-called civilized societies. – And why is that? – Because the first two lines of this text are not applicable to the vast majority of humans any more – and this is true for ‹developing countries› and for ‹developed› countries alike:

Lacking education, formation and cultivation combined with irreligiosity, cannot but lead to the *loss of orientation, to instability and weakness* – and the latter in turn allows for *seduction* on all levels of existence.

«Never were things as precarious as today ! – The care for any kind of fundamental values and education or ‹cultivation› never was as poor, firmness of the character never was so overpowered by faintness and manipulability – and therefore, seductibility and readiness for violence never were as pronounced as today!»

That is what even *Lao-Dse* complained about during his time: The text of his N° 54 culminates in the same sad exclamation: *«Alas!»*, as in N° 53. – And that precisely is what gives it the inexorable feeling of tragic urgency.

As a last remark to the social aspect of the present text, let us emphasize its third line: The prospect to receive sacrifices until long after death – maybe for years and even for centuries, as far as an Emperor might have been concerned, was *per se* enough encouragement to lead a life as ‹good› as possible. In today's ‹developed› societies, the cult for the death is abolished officially, but continues happily with a political or religious pretext, as is the case with Memorial Day and Halloween. Other examples are the tomb of some relative, its flowers being periodically replaced, or the monument for some forgotten hero, or the yearly jubilee honoring the fallen soldiers of some lost war, and so forth …

The reputation after one's death nobody takes very much in account anymore today …

But things look quite different indeed as soon as our text is applied to the pilgrim on *The Path* toward transfiguration: He or she neither expects, nor wishes, any cult after having passed away – quite the contrary! – But they know that during their condition almost immediately following their decease, they will be confronted with their past actions and events during the lifetime they just terminated: The less self-restraint they put on themselves during their physical life-time, the longer they might have to dwell in those rather unpleasant astral regions of the great Beyond.

Instead, if they are serious about their efforts regarding renewal and transformation – thus, if they strive for the *birth of a new soul* and the latter's subsequent union with the divine Spirit – they will make every effort to achieve that *«their DE – their ‹virtue› – be genuine»*. So they will endeavour to *«refine and ennoble»* themselves – not in a mundane humanistic way how ever, but in the sense of Gnosis – in the sense of that *«diminishing»* and of that *«non-doing»*, which the *Dao-De-Jing* mentions ever so often.

Every Candidate on The Path attaining this higher spiritual level will become conscious that it is not sufficient to *follow and imitate* some ideal, but that he is to *become an ideal example himself* – be it for some specific close persons, be it for the general community surrounding him: e.g. the persons of his family – his ‹house›. One level up, there begins the endeavour to stand amidst the World as a shining example – as a luminous witness for the Light; for the advanced pilgrim knows that every effort in this direction contributes to the ascent of the Universe along the giant spiral of its evolution – and be it just a tiny wee-bit. The result of it will show immediately – around him- and her-self – in his direct surroundings, and in the World!

And whence does he know that this is so?
Precisely thence!

德

第五十五章

含「德」之厚，比于赤子。毒虫不螫，猛獸不據，攫鳥不搏。
骨弱筋柔而握固。未知牝牡之合而朘作，精之至也。
終日號而不嗄，和之至也。
知和曰「常」，知常曰「明」。益生曰祥。心使氣曰強。
物壯則老，謂之不道，不道早已。

55.

Who fearlessly accepts Gnosis,
resembles a new-born Child:
Poisonous insects don't annoy it,
Wild beasts don't assail it,
Predatory birds don't claw it.

Its bones are weak, its muscles are delicate,
and yet its grip is firm.
Unaware of the union of man and wife,
its member yet stands up:
Vital force it feels in abundancy.
The whole day long it cries without pain:
Harmony it feels in abundancy.

To know harmony, one names [eternity] —
To know eternity, one names [wisdom] —
Unexpected kindness one names luck —
To build up one's soul courageously, one names strength —

To strengthen things in order to oppose aging, means:
one is not on the right path —
far off the right path since long.

Only very few texts have been translated and interpreted in as many different ways as the present one – even in today's China, and while elaborating our own interpretation. The first and fourth line of our Chinese original each contain one term in a sort of brackets. These are interpolations, and therefore uncertain. –

While all earlier translations of this text conveyed the inserted term 德 – i.e. *DE (‹virtue›)* as *The Path*, we here have directly put the term *Gnosis*. – The second part of the text appears to be addressed to an already advanced Candidate; but for the first part instead we see the assumption that the Neophyte who steps on *The Path* can be compared to a new-born baby who, as N° 52 says, *«accepts its mother and thereby acknowledges being her child»*. This child is described, on one hand, as pure and innocent – and on the other, as energetically grasping this new life, manifesting it in any form of vitality flowing through this new being:

With firm little fists it grips Gnosis, while tender still are its bones (knowledge of the esoteric teachings) as well as its muscles (consciousness). – Its comprehension (intellect) is yet small, but its joy is great, and its sexual vitality (*magical spirituality)* emerges spontaneously; – it ignores yet what this signifies, nor that it is so. *«Unconsciousness of the union of man and wife»* in this present instance – signifies the Candidate's unconsciousness relative to *Yin and Yang* – hence regarding the *dichotomy of the Universe* as well as the concern of the ‹pupil› to *unite* with Gnosis, and simultaneously to *consciously contribute to the re-union of contraries* – within himself as well as throughout the Cosmos.

The author here manifests a sane knowledge of the characteristics of infant children and their ways of expressing themselves, as he does not interpret the baby's immoderate crying as an expression of pain and discontentment, but as one of overwhelming self-awareness without any notion of ‹good› and ‹evil› – as an abundance of sane overall vitality; i.e. as an expression of the tendency of its *‹Ch'I›*, to *establish* and to *manifest* harmony. For, if the little baby crying shows all signals of greatest effort, it (normally) expresses none of real pain. – This reality has often alarmed and made feel insecure many young parents. —

Said *innocent purity* of every infant has its good reason: He does not yet know the *astral storms*, for it lacks the ‹organ› for that: the *astral body*. – He does not know fears nor aggressions yet; and therefore he does not yet trigger aggression in otherwise usually aggressive ‹beasts›. The situation of the gnostic Neophyte is a similar one: The *opposing forces* – the *adversaries of Gnosis* – hardly touch him. But the Candidate of Gnosis may easily lose this innocence, when he loses his infant-like spontaneity by all to painstakingly following the rules of conduct and *moral teachings*: *«I had not known sin but by the law. For, I had not known lust, except the Law had said: „Thou shalt not desire ...!"» (Ro. 7:7).*

Now our text makes a jump of several years and continues where the Candidate has already developed a new way of being, namely, the calm and serenity that are the prerequisites in order to attain the wanted *Wu-Wei* – the *self-effective non-doing.*

Having acquired a new view of things, the Candidate has begun to differentiate what is helpful for his path and what is hindering it, respectively, what definitely might *leas him astray.* – Not that he had already achieved the attitude necessary in order to *«hold fast and not be unsaddled»*, as chapter 54 puts it: With Paul (Phil 3:12) he says: *«Not that I had already seized it, or that I'd be perfect already; but I chase after it, so that I might seize it after all; being myself seized by it»*. – This *«pursuit»* some Gnostics of our days name it their *Endurá* – i.e. their devotion to *accept and endure* whatever lot and tribulation they might be charged with as they follow the Path of gnostic pilgrimage – overcoming all obstacles in *forbearance* and *imperturbability*.[31]

There are big differences in the versions and interpretations of this text both in East and West. It is important, though, not to take all the *redundant polyvalent glyphs* as meaning the same, but to recognize them as an expression of *textual esthetics*.

The essence the four parts of the text have in common, ma be called: *«Natural harmony as the basis to experience eternity»*. This *natural harmony* shows itself, first, by the spontaneous demeanor of the ‹baby›; second, in the calmness and forbearance while accepting the Endurá; third, by avoiding purely academical disputes – in favor of *sane natural reasoning* out of the cognizance of the esoteric teachings and traditions; – and fourth, by adaptation and *syntony* with surrounding conditions, the latter including aging and trespassing of all *forms, and the random conditions* encountered while following the Path. – This tenure cannot avoid *death*, but it really enables *growth and redemption*. The contrary would be to *stick to* things and conditions as they are today, in order to *oppose* aging and ‹death› while believing in *«strengthening things, with the idea to compensate their aging process»* to be a good thing to do.

At the same time, it is not recommendable to rely on so-called ‹lucky chances›: *The Path* can be followed with positive effects only on the basis of clear determination and strength, notwithstanding all opposing forces. As understanding, joy and gratitude grow with growing absorption of Gnosis – i.e. growing union with divine Spirit – this union will be more and more *clearly felt, even physically*: This is the purest possible experience of eternity, and it grows within the ‹void› live *being*, through letting go of all existence, *steadfast in serenity*. – Hence, inverting the formula of our text, we may say:

***To strengthen things which foster the Great Renewal,
indicates that one is on the right path — now!***

VERSION ON INTERNET (ORIGINAL SOURCE UNKNOWN):

[知者不言。
言者不知。]

塞其兌，閉其門；
挫其銳,解其紛；和其光y, 同其塵；是謂玄同。
故
不可得而親;不可得而疏；不可得而利;不可得而害;
不可得而貴,不可得而賤。故為天下貴。
者實際去 智者實際去...

VERSION OF WANG-BI:

知者不言。
言者不知。
挫其銳,解其紛,和其光,同其塵,是謂玄同。
故
不可得而親。不可得而疏。不可得而利。
不可得而害。不可得而貴。不可得而賤。
故為天下貴。

OUR BASIC VERSION (ORIGINAL SOURCE UNKNOWN):

第五十六章

知者不言，言者不知。
挫其銳，解其紛，和其光，同其塵，是謂「玄同」。
故不可得而親，不可得而疏；不可得而利，不可得而害；
不可得而貴，不可得而賤。故爲天下貴。

56.

Who knows IT, does not talk about IT —
Who talks about IT, does not know IT.
To turn off one's to-and-fro —
To bolt one's doors —
To overcome one's fierceness —
To clear one's muddle —
To bring some harmony into one's lights —
To become akin to one's dust:
That is what is named by right: the secret oft The Path —
and this regardless
if one has a family and is cherished —
if one lives alone and disregarded —
if one earns kindness and profits —
if one meets with hate and losses —
if one lives nobly and grandly —
if one is of a lowly condition and poor:
That is why IT is highly esteemed throughout the world.

When a person has truly attained IT, he goes on —
A Wise is one who has truly attained IT, and goes on ...

For this ‹well known› text there exist – besides some Western interpretations – thousands of Chinese pages on Internet. The differences between all these are quite impressing. There also appear additional passages (here printed in blue), that are missing in other Chinese text versions we have encountered. This permits us to link the present chapter with several others in an appropriate way. To this end, a few additional remarks are indicated. The third line, namely 塞其兌 閉其門, is exactly the same as the beginning of the second part of N° 52. Let us also emphasize that in the second part of the present text we render *two meanings for one and the same Chinese expression*: one rather material, the other rather ‹moral› and spiritual. All these are a selection of *a great many equally valid expressions*, in order to convey an adequate overall-impression of this text – for:

The deeper we penetrate into this polyvalent speech, the more the inner signification of the textual tissue (texture) reveals itself. The author especially points out that DAO can neither be named nor described the way it really is (see. N° 01). – Next, he explains *how* one can get access to DAO; and then, *who* is predestined for DAO – namely *all humans of good will*, notwithstanding their social conditions! – Moreover again – what a great rarity throughout the entire sacral literature! – there is a discreet indication that *when Transfiguration is achieved, The Path has not met its* end, but just *begins again* on a higher level of *anothercoil of the Great Helix*!

The message of the present ‹renown› text with its discrimination between *erudition* and *knowledge* is:

Who possesses *inner knowledge*, needs not talk a big lot: Whom should he talk to? – To those who know what he knows? Shared knowledge needs only few words, and so few can be said about IT! – To those who have *no knowledge*? Not even a thousand words could explain IT to them! Instead, there is no need for secret signs nor grips in order to share the inexplicable among those who participate in the unspeakable. – Here, to share means to understand each other, to combine individual knowledge, thus strengthening it together – and in so doing *to let IT grow among all*.

The vanity of the Ego how ever makes that a person speaks when he has nothing to say (or because he fears the potency of silence); – that he gets heated where he does not see any issue; – and least of all he is silent in his thoughts.

Fulcanelli explains the renown phrase by Zoroaster: *«to know · to be able · to will · to dare · to do · to mum»* – ending with these words, while addressing the *Adeptate of the Philosopher's Stone*:

«Finally, when the success of many, many years has crowned all this toiling and sweating; when all his wishes have been fulfilled, the sage, full of disdain for the vanities of this world, will approach the humble and disinherited – all who down here are suffering, fighting, groaning and despairing. As an anonymous and mute Disciple of eternal Nature – as an Apostle of infinite mercifulness – he will remain faithful to his vow to keep silence. In knowledge and in charity, the Adept is obliged to his everlasting SILENCE.».[32]

«Knowledge – ability – courage – action – silence» could as well be a valuable slogan and guide-line for the adept of mystical Gnosis. But how to *«climb the steps leading to true understanding and knowledge»*? – *Lao-Dse* gives us a succinct but positive answer:

The main issue – for the Neophyte as a theoretical rule, for the advanced Candidate as a practice on a daily basis, but for the ‹perfect wise› at any moment, is the *silence* of the physical, astral and mental unrest: *Let go* of nervous activism of this World, until reaching perfect *neutrality and calm serenity* that leads to complete *«knowledge of Eternity»*, as explained in N° 55 of the *Dao-De-Jing*.

Human nature manifests Life through *tension and relaxation*: excitement and agitation until reaching feverishness; inconsistency until reaching madness; inner dispersal until reaching Chaos. What is most typical for humans is their *astral and mental unrest*. Incessant turmoil of thoughts and sorrows, of fears and desires, and the rarely ceasing ‹dialog› of the dialectical Ego with itself: Narcisse speaking to himself in the mirror of his own agitation – emotions, thoughts, activities. This constant turmoil must be interrupted; the doors of senses and sensual organs must be closed and bolted – and all this, while yet working actively *in tune with this World* – in *neutral syntony and sympathy* with it – *but without going astray with it* !

All the *«in-and-out»*, the *«to-and-fro»*, the constant agitation of the human soul, of hopes and fears, of sympathies and antipathies; this glowing and fleeing, this getting hot and getting scorched, this cooling down and freezing stiff … – this storm of excitements keeps the soul completely breathless. Sensations, distractions disturbances continuously inundate it, sowing a thousand germs for new illusions, delusions and pains! With that come influences – be it by humans, be it by ‹demons› and ‹spirits›, or be it by seemingly unanimated beings, emanating all the same heat and movement … – What a relief to be able to bolt all the doors!

The astral and mental storm we all know so well, to which we are ever so strongly bound and submitted, is thus to be unmasked, to be observed in neutrality, and to be called by its name: What can be called by its name can also become controllable, normally. – To control *the storm of the Ego* means, to let go completely of the latter, thus, not to fight against it: *«Do not oppose Evil!»*, says Scripture. But to *distinguish and choose* is what the Candidate is summoned to do – between agitation and coolness, between heat and stillness, the way N° 45 describes it. This is to say: Choose stillness and silence, and in fact and reality *be still before the Lord!*

Three corner-stones of stillness are mentioned by our text: First, to ‹lose› all kinds of *fierceness* – growing from placidity unto leaving behind the old *Ego-will* – that egocentric force *par excellence* that is visible even in the *physical shadow* a person projects on the pavement before him: Fierceness can be much subtler than what ordinary people think! Who in this point learns to control himself, is really *«stronger than who overthrows a city»*! –

Second: *«to become akin to one's dust»* – or *«to follow the Path in the soot»*, as can be read this phrase as well: The glyphs 其尘 include the meaning of *«one's shadow»* as well as of *«one's corpse»*, and also of *«one's ash»*. –

The third and extremely important corner-stone of this *guideline to achieve neutrality*, as one could as well name this passage, is the recommendation: *«To bring harmony into one's lights»*.

The Universal Doctrine regarding human ‹bodies› and Chakra's could explain these things like this:

The *subtle bodies* of Man, and his *Chakras* radiate in different colors, which to the Initiate are known, but which psychic people can see even. And through the relative *purity, luminescence and harmony* of these colors, there radiates the actual condition of the soul and sprit of a person, for *the whole World to see*! – This expression wants to strongly emphasize the *personal responsibility of every human – conscious or not* – for the energies that he or she emanates, thus blessing or hurting the Universe. It also shows how the Pilgrim on the Path must clearly understand said energetic relations, which will in a near future become visible for everybody in the World!

The *I-Ging* once mentions *the lights of the eyes* and the *«lateral lights of the ears»*. This mention could be compared to the *«ears that hear, and eyes that see»* mentioned by the Gospels. – *That is why* the relative glyphs in N° 49 were interpreted as *«randomly remarks»*, and not glyph-by-glyph, as *eyes and ears*.

«Examine the spirits, if they are from God», says the Scripture (1. John 4:1). Yet, *distinction of the spirits* is one of the gifts by the Spirit to the *true Disciples*. But of this, there can be no question in the present state of a Neophyte – and even less of him dominating spirits who are in the service of the Adversary: The drive of the latter is to deviate, at any possible moment, Candidates, Disciples or Apostles from the straight, the proper path, whenever this is possible. –

Now it would be vane to fight against all these counter-forces who act inside and outside of the Candidate. It is much preferable *«to close the doors »*, *«to put guardians before one's thoughts, feelings and actions»*, and to concentrate all forces on keeping up the positive orientation towards *the One sacred task* – i.e. to build up both the cosmic and one's microcosmic ‹New Jerusalem›:

«Do not relish, however, that the spirits are submitted to you, but rather rejoice that your names are written down in the Book of Life!», proclaims the Master in Luke 10:20.

Who is there still talking about ‹fallen humans›? *To experience the secret of The Path*; – to unite with the Light of Gnosis – this annihilates all separation! To understand, deep inside, that separation is *a fundamental illusion* of the centripetal, ignorant human with his agitations and fiery flames of his Will! – *To feel*, deep inside, that *the reign is within oneself* – that God and His Disciples – His children – are *eternally inseparable*! – *Separation from God* can appear ‹real› only to those who don't know DAO – those who don't know GNOSIS: *This is* THE fundamental ignorance!

The Disciple *knows* that there is *much – oh so much! – he ignores*. But one thing he *knows with certainty*: He is one with God, one with the Universe and with every creature, small or big; and therefore he is one also with this World of which actually he is not really part any more. –

And yet: Is there a human living as an incarnate personality who may talk about such *true knowledge* without fearing to be himself a victim of the most abominable deception? – *«Follow your Path ... with fear and trembling!»*

When the Candidate knows that he is one with all creatures, he returns towards them in true *compassion*. – *‹Knowing› in this way*, he can accept everybody's opinion (see N° 49!): He can see, and feel with the conscience of every-one. To those who yet don't know DAO – Gnosis –, he imparts as much as they are capable to adopt. – He doesn't stand higher than they. He is one with them – dust amidst dust – thanks to his new way of thinking, thanks to his deep empathy and his undivided love. – He shares with them his *knowledge – Gnosis* – with the same joy as when sharing it with those who know what he knows. In this way the whole grows bigger and bigger, radiating more and more, and becoming more and more whole. – *United*, the living witnesses for The Light march towards the perfect transformation and Transfiguration!

And when their *Newly Divine Human* arises? – As servants of universal Gnosis, and as helpers for the community of all seeking and suffering creatures, they go on and on:

Who has really obtained IT
goes on and on ...!

第五十七章

以正治國，以奇用兵，以無事取天下。吾何以知其然哉？以此：天下多忌諱，而民彌貧；人多利器，國家滋昏；人多伎巧，奇物滋起；法令滋彰，盜賊多有。

故聖人云：「我無爲，而民自化；我好靜，而民自正；我無事，而民自富；我無欲，而民自樸。」

57.

Ruling the state with sincerity, one rarely does need soldiers:
By non-doing one conquers the World. —
And whence do I know that this is so?
By these reasons:

If throughout the empire there are many prohibitions,
subjects will become completely impoverished.
If people have many weapons,
disorder will reign in the villages.
If people set up many smart schemes,
bloody intrigues will spark riots.
If decrees and court sentences regulate things,
Bandits will rove about.

Therefore, the wise [ruler] says:
«I won't interfere at all, so people will keep order themselves.
I'll relax and have a good time —
so people will become honest by themselves.
I won't generate any difficulties —
so people will get rich from themselves —
I won't covet anything —
so people will become modest by themselves».

The two chapters, 57 and 58 are a pair: N° 57 says what a wise ruler *is to do* in order to reign as comfortably and beneficially as possible; N° 58 tells us *how he should be.* Nearly all earlier translations of this chapter assume that said ruler *is indeed at war*. But Daoism really teaches how armed warfare can be avoided: *«Strong is really who needs not fight with arms»*, is what *Sun-Dse* tells us ever again .[33]

That is why here we have preferred the version *«many weapons»*. The *«smart schemes»* could also be interpreted as *«spies»* or as *«secret police»*. – The more precise version: *«strange things»* does not mean *«ruses»*, but (normally bloody) *«incidents»* and *crimes*. –

According to N° 57, the main task of the ruler is, to live as a good example for his people. If his people thrive, then he thrives with them. – *«Benevolent ruling combined with non-doing has a good pay-back»* – that's what the text insists teaching us; for:

By non-doing one conquers the World!

第五十八章

其政悶悶，其民淳淳；其政察察，其民缺缺。
是以聖人方而不割，廉而不劌，直而不肆，光而不耀。
禍兮福之所倚，福兮禍之所伏。孰知其極？其無正也。
正復爲奇，善復爲妖。人之迷，其日固久。

58.

If the government is very sloppy, subjects are very good-natured. —
If the government is very strict, subjects are very blameworthy. —

Therefore:
The truly wise rules powerfully, but not cruelly —
aloof – but not briskly —
sternly – but not tyrannically —
gloriously – but not dazzling.

Misfortune comes – luck cedes it its place —
Luck comes – misfortune is pushed from its place. —
Who does know his lot?

What is straight, appears to be twisted at the same time —
Good effects Evil at the same time.

+

Humans are all fear and confusion:
Their stars are fixed since long.

This is one of the most beautiful texts of the *Dao-De-Jing* – one of the few where the human soul is given a voice to speak straightforwardly the way it really is – and yet without *declaring* what its most inner feelings are: Its true thought remains unspoken.

The first part, as mentioned above, is a pendant to N° 57, explaining *how a wise ruler ought to be*. He is described as the father of his subjects, resembling the German emperor, Kaiser Wilhelm with his «iron chancellor» Bismarck during their best days, at the end of the 19th century. It would be rewarding to study the parallels between the German and the Chinese human mind; and it is interesting that no other European ruler ever came close to this Daoistic ideal …

The second part of this text is a melancholic assessment, as a very experienced person might make it when reviewing his life. We thus may assume that Lao-Dse (or whoever the aged master-author was) has conveyed to his disciples (in his book) his own experience and thoughts, as if they were pronounced by a sage ruler, who has many a year of ruling behind himself – and is expecting to have only a small number of years before him. This is, in the same time, the situation so well known to Man, when at some point of his life he *comes to his senses*. – Gautama Buddha for example had 29 years, when (following his myth) he left his palace and went out for his *askesis*. Hiob instead is reported to have reached this same point only at the age of 70.

This moment of *coming to one's senses* has also been named the *«psychological moment [par excellence]»*. It is a situation that may emerge two or three times during a human lifetime, when the soul startles from its deep psychic slumber, seeing itself confronted with the possibility *to chose a new consciousness*. This *opportunity of a choice* only rarely emerges by an inner impulse – and even more rarely during the youth of a person – unless a youngster who is still in the process of building up the tools of his personality (subtle bodies and chakra's) discover kind of a remembrance, that now vaguely, but then more and more clearly, leads him back to the One Path again. – *Again*, we may say; for, unless there is a core memory of some kind of a quest already at birth, no such dynamic can emerge spontaneously. In some very rare cases there also might occur the possibility that an entity who in a previous lifetime has already begun or even fulfilled the process of Transfiguration through self-initiation, has returned out of free will, in order to once more lead an old microcosmos to its perfection.

It is an impressing fact that such a person is in no way given any privilege, but rather encounters more obstacles than an ordinary Candidate – even physical death among others …

But mostly said ‹re-awakening› brings the painful insight: *«There is no permanent Good in this world; – the only persistent thing is change itself!»* – This is a puzzlement that life with its incidents and contradictions will typically produce: a situation that is lived as a specially bitter delusion, or as a particularly sharp pain, or even as the collapse of the whole, up to then relatively satisfying, existence and its conditions. At this point it can happen that this human – on the basis of great self-pity – exclaims: «*How* can this happen? – *Why* can it happen *to me* – and *why right now*?» So this human will begin to ponder about the inconsistency of all earthly things: about contradictions of forces and counterforces, about pain and injustice – about ‹Good› and ‹Evil ›. – He or she might then burst into the lamentation (like in the cantata of J.S. Bach, BWV 48): *«Oh miserable me – who will redeem me?»*.

All this is made allusion to in this 58th chapter of the *Dao-De-Jing,* where the ruler-to-be or already enthroned is admonished quite early to think in a philosophical way about the essence of Life and the World, but especially about the plight of a ruler: – thoughts meant to guide him toward moderation, leniency, justice and inner humility – and certainly toward earnest religiosity, too – a religiosity in DAO, exceeding by far the piety of the usual imperial sacrificial rituals.

With outstanding subtlety, though, a *vital question* is introduced here – a question that fills the mind of every single person in the World, who is not completely numb, spiritually. It is the anxious question about death and about what might come after it; – and it is introduced here by means of a *tacit statement* where in the present scriptural rendering there stands the cross. It is the statement: *«The only sure thing in life is death!»*. – A statement that certainly was not allowed to be made in a Chinese text of the given era.

That's why the instructions for the wise ruler – this list of *«reflections a wise ruler ought to pursue»* – end with said anxious final conclusion. In a somewhat more comprehensive version, this conclusion would be (the expression 迷 for *«fear»* having a great many different meanings):

«Considering that everything in this World is subject to constant and incalculable change, and that even the greatest ruler cannot defend, nor even usefully prepare himself against it, not even with highest consciousness; – and considering, secondly, that every day luck can turn its back, giving way to an uncertain and quite unknown fate; – and given, third, that the hour of my trespassing has since long been determined by the stars; – I really am left alone with insecurity, fear, trembling and confusion! – Woe!»

Chapter 76 will give an answer to this deep sigh of desperation.

The Samurai-Master Itei said:
What one asks for, one will receive!

德

第五十九章

治人事天，莫若嗇。
夫爲嗇，是謂早服；早服謂之重積德；重積德則無不克；無不克則莫知其極；莫知其極，可以有國；有國之母，可以長久；是謂深根固柢，長生久視之道。

59.

A successful servant of His Majesty must not be measly.
A citizen must serve minutely if he really wants to receive a robe early.
To receive a robe early, results in him accumulating much favor.
To accumulate much favor, effects
that to him nothing is unattainable.
Being able to attain everything, effects: to know no limits;
To know no limits enables him to be given a province
(as a caretaker).
To be given a province [and to be] its Mother, enables him to
participate in success for a long time.
In fact, a strong personality represents a firm basis.
Growing continuously and living long, he dedicates himself to DAO.

This chapter is interesting from a socio-political point of view rather than from a philosophical one: It can be understood and interpreted with some certainty (but not definitely) only if we delve into the live environment of the relative time period and circumstances. A precise translation must not be put before a background of Western thought, nor of that of some benevolent prejudgments, as if this text were to contain a maximum of Daoistic doctrinal essence: Otherwise discrete allusions are overlooked, and only loud words are understood, such as relate to *doing* and *having* {the European way} – but not to *feeling* and *being* {the Chinese way}. Even today's Chinese interpretations are more or less influenced by the latter, the ‹modern› way.

The worst snag comes up right at the beginning, with the ideogram 嗇, which in the same time means *stingy*, *miserable*, *petty*, and even *narrow*, appearing first in the frame of a ‹warning› and then in the course of an encouragement – thus in a *paradoxon* apt to confuse the lector and seducing him to engage in various high-strung speculations.

Translated glyph after glyph, this beginning may be translated as: *«Humans you shall rule – the heavens (the gods) you shall serve; – don't appear petty»* (and even : *«don't act so pettily!»*). – Many translators want – in opposition to the text – *«When ruling humans and serving the Heavens, nothing is as important as parsimony».* – Others, in the contrary, have: *«A successful servant of Heaven* {meaning the Emperor} *must not appear to be petty».* – One Chinese comment, finally, brings the term *pedantic.* All this induced the forthcoming version: *Heavens*, the *Empire*, *His Majesty* very often mean the Emperor himself, and so one may adhere to the basic interpretation that the whole is some sort of *«career planning».* The difference as compared to a modern career plan – and the kernel of the text – is that this career plan – when the highest branches of the tree of success are attained – aims exclusively at dedicating oneself to the study and practice of DAO. From this results that the translation of the second-last line where the term 柢 (*root, fundament, foot, basis, character, personality* ...) occurs twice in a glyphic tautology, might as well be read in a slight differentiation as: *«strong roots are a strong fundament»*; – and this again could be interpreted as: «*Who stems from a good family* (the French *«souche»* precisely corresponds to this), *has good prerequisites».*

The expression 服 at the beginning, by the way, has significations like *to serve, to be useful, to achieve*, but also of *«robe»* and *«attire».* This reminds the oriental custom to donate a *robe of honor* to please some noble guest, or as a sign of promotion or elevation. This custom lives on today in Tibet, with the offering of *sashes of distinct colors*. And these again are in analogy to the various stolæ of many colors priests wrap around themselves – including the latter's specific significance.

The ‹moral of this story› thus is the importance of being given *a new robe* as soon as possible, this promising to attain an early elevation to some higher rank.

The gnostic teaching as well speaks of an *«early vocation»* and of some (metaphoric, viz. ethereal) *«robes of honor»*: the robe of honor here being related to the *New born Soul* and the *Golden Wedding Gown* of the *New Divine Human.* But right at the beginning, the text admonishes the lector: Who is successful is called to be generous forwarding the received gift to others! – This is the same as what was said earlier in the quotation from *Fulcanelli.* – *The aim is: Live a long time, growing in the service of the Gnosis:*

Continually growing and living long,
he dedicates himself to DAO.

Arranging a little ‹ghost house› in today's Taiwan (see text).
Image source: Internet

第六十章

治大國，若烹小鮮。
以道蒞天下，其鬼不神；非其鬼不神，其神不傷人；
非其神不傷人，聖人亦不傷人。夫兩不相傷，故德交歸焉。

60.

To rule a big country
is like frying small fish:
If DAO presides over an empire,
its phantoms are no gods.
When its non-gods are no gods,
God does not trouble humans either.
When no non-gods bother humans,
the wise [ruler] does not bother humans either.
When all (of them) don't bother each other,
virtue and unanimity will move in again.

This chapter leaves the Westerner with a number of riddles: What does *«frying fish»* allude to? – And what is the meaning of phantoms, gods and non-gods in China during the 5th century b.C.?[34]

Regarding the fried fish, this apparently relates to some old Chinese proverb that means to say that a good ruler should rule as unobtrusively as possible. Chapter 60 in essence therefore says the same as N° 57; only that the religious connotation is more emphasized.

A modern Chinese commentator writes:

«There is a sentence ascribed to Mao: *„Tired of being fried, the fish decays; – tired of government the nation* (人) *decays".*»

The message conveyed by the present chapter is understood by the same commentator to be this:

«As long as DAO rules the world, all sorts of incidents (phantoms) are no longer incalculable {gods}. *Not only can the latter effect nothing: In a well ruled nation, incidents can provoke healing crises on a psychological plane. If, however, rulers are corrupt and squeeze out their people, DAO does not preside, and they will lose the support of people ».* {Brackets inserted by the author of the quote}. — And further on:

«When asked if phantoms can harm us, *Kung-Fu-Dse* said:
„How should one who during lifetime could not harm you, harm you as a ghost?" And, when asked if the Ego can die: *„If we don't even know Life – how can we know Death?"*» — This shows the materialistic tendency of *Kung-Fu-Dse* who also persecuted, and almost annihilated, the Daoist movement.

To believe in ghosts and in phantoms (spirits) was common also in China, as in any agricultural nation, remaining so also during the ‹cultural revolution›, and even more today where even Western esotericism is heavily engaged in Spiritism and Shamanism[35]. – One journalist gives this comment:

«The Chines believe every peace of land to be inhabited by at least one spirit. If someone comes to build a house there, he divests that spirit of his home. Now, in order not to offend the dispossessed spirit, one resettles him: To avoid that he is compelled to live together with humans, they build him his own little villa, and furnish it so that it should be a cozy home. In return, the house-spirit is obliged to honor the family living in ‹his dominion›, and to further their well-being. The more the spirit is content, the better he will help them. To assure he is well, he is regularly given small sacrifices: often a small portion of fresh fruit, rice, or cake. Scented flower garlands and jewels adorn the little home, and fumigating sticks are burnt. Sometimes he also receives some liquor, or a Coca-Cola – not because of its taste, but for the red color of the can! – Indeed there is a belief that red is the spirits' preferred color.»

The Chinese author mentioned earlier, comments this chapter as follows:

«According to traditional Chinese opinion, the World is divided into a double circuit of YIN and YANG. Invisible inhabitants of the Netherworld {*Kuei's*} are the counterpoise to the authority of celestial spirits {*Shen's*} … The Sun sees the sacred dominion of the Emperor. Intrusion into the harmonious play of YIN and YANG obfuscates the fact that we all are on the quest for God's will. Man maneuvers between questions around life and death on one side, and uncertainties around daily material welfare on the other. Therefore, the essence of this chapter N° 60 is: *"For a wise ruler of the World in harmony with the Path of DAO, phantoms have nothing in common with god-sent misfortune*" … – Furthermore, in the reality of human mind, ‹phantoms› are mainly related to the souls of ancestors, and those of their ancestors and pre-ancestors … »

It is self-understood that the «wise ruler» will not only take to heart the sentence about fried fish, but also will avoid offending the spirits. Therefore he will – like it was described in N° 39 – punctually continue to perform his ritual offerings for his ancestors, for the *Kuei*'s and for the *Shen*'s – and be it only in order not to start or rattle the people.

In the meantime, *Lao-Dse* also makes clear that a wise man in the sense of Daoism does not revere spirits as gods, but regards DAO as the *sublime Divine Mother* – the way above commentator has subscribed it. Even the Western researcher of the spiritual world knows that spirits must be nourished, should they not literally *starve*. But this exactly is the goal of a gnostic pupil on the Path of purification, renewal and transmutation: Should the God who is hidden in himself awaken and take over the guidance of his life, all other ‹spirits› are to ‹leave› him (or vice-versa). That's why the Disciple needs to keep DAO – Gnosis – in his foremost thought at every moment – or at least in his constant back-ground consciousness, while ever and again relegating the hungry phantoms, until they starve, or else resign and seek for another ‹milking cow› as their source of nutrition.

It will certainly prove useful to shortly mention and underline that many humans who, following the notions of modern medicine, are suffering from ‹cachexia›, in reality are exploited by one or several of these parasites. However those must not be imagined as gruesome Djinn's or Goblins: Even persons of the closest family can – especially when asleep – indulge in this kind of vampirism – and *all* involved persons (who «love each other so much!») remain in the fullest ignorance about it!

For the Candidate on the Path however, it is absolutely indispensable to separate himself from all old ‹spirits› and ‹gods› of his old consciousness, to completely focus his mind on the *One Truth*, the *One high target – on DAO – on GNOSIS* – and to nourish only the germinating *New Soul*: *«You shall have no other gods besides me ... »!* – Only then his ‹phantoms› will be ‹gods› any longer; – only then will they not bother him any more; – only then will he be able to sustain, as a *«wise ruler»*, the new being prone to grow and thrive inside himself, the way he should like to sustain it. – If this is strived for with a new kind of intelligence, peaceful parting will be possible on both sides – and another variant to translate and interpret our N° 60 will become a reality:

And the harmony of DAO will enter him again.

第六十一章

大邦者下流，天下之交，天下之牝。牝常以靜勝牡，以靜爲下。
故大邦以下小邦，則取小邦；小邦以下大邦，則取大邦。
故或下以取，或下而取。大邦不過欲兼畜人，
小邦不過欲入事人。夫兩者各得所欲，大者宜爲下。

61.

A big empire is like some lowland:
The empire is his wife —
To the empire he devotes himself like to a woman.
The woman normally vanquishes the man without moving —
She remains motionless, because she is below.
Therefore:
When the big empire devotes itself to the small one,
the small empire reaches its goals. —
When the small empire devotes itself to the big one,
the big empire reaches its goals. —
Therefore: Or by yielding one wins,
or by devoting oneself one participates in some winnings. —
In fact, the big empire wants more cattle and subjects,
while the small empire in turn wants its people to be furthered. —
Together both achieve what each of them wants,
It fits the big ones to devote themselves, serving.

Immobility – *stillness* – is one of the most important prerequisites to experience DAO, i.e. *equilibrium and harmony* – for the empire as well as for an individual human. It therefore goes without saying that in a nation where harmony is the prevailing good, calm and stillness as well are sought-after and regarded as precious goods – for the Emperor, for his subjects, and for the whole empire as an organic structure. Yet this is no dead silence, but the calm continuity of harmonic dynamics. In Ancient China this is the double dynamic of *Yin and Yang*, the dynamic equilibrium of ‹male› and ‹female› energies – thus, of activity and passivity, of movement and rest, of giving and receiving, of generation and manifestation. Not one harmonious process can be without them – every process in Nature owes its complex perfection to this harmony. The *conscious, unconstrained* conservation of this harmoniously equilibrated dynamic is the characteristic of societies during the periodical so-called *Golden Age*.

When a society lives in harmony with the processes and cycles of Nature, it is free to express itself through images and relations in Nature, without experiencing any *emotion* nor *agitation*. And, given that the two poles – male and female – are in the most obvious ways manifested in Nature, their natural physical mating is the preferred image to represent their harmoniously combined or complementarily opposed activities.

In the case of the *cosmic harmony* of the great Chinese empire it was the task and the duty of the Emperor – the *Celestial Ruler* – to make possible and maintain this natural order «*in the World*», i.e. throughout his empire. Therefore, the ideogram for ‹World›, ‹People› and ‹Empire (China)› is one and the same; and we are allowed to suppose that it was the Chinese Empire that inspired the great *Imperium Romanum* to name itself *The World – orbis terrarum.* –

With regard to the actual chapter of the Dao-De-Jing, there is rather question of a formula for the politics of expansion of the Empire: It is about subordinating oneself, gain confidence and influence in this position, and thereby finally ‹be on top of the other›: This is a most successful pattern. The same way the *Khazars* of the 7th through 10th century took over the Vezirate, then the Khalifate in Baghdad. Quite literally, the empire of the *Habsburg dynasty* defined its politics of expansion with the well-known sentence: «Tu felix Austria nube! – *You, fortunate Austria, marry!*».

On the other hand, there is a manner of apparent or real subordination to spark (seduce) one's adversary to act, and thereby win:

This is a way of *acting following the laws of DAO*. The point here is the *harmony of Yin and Yang* – Today's *fake news* and *‹false-flag events›* are malign ways to shun the rules of DAO. —

Now, to return to our text, the idea is indeed to apply the rules of DAO also in the daily practice of ruling an empire – and this even in a policy of expansion – so that the over-all *harmony* is still preserved, and so that the desires of the annexed nation are taken in account as well as those of the expanding one.

This should give way to no false appearances, though: The smaller nation lets the big one make the firs step (*Sun-Dse*!), so as to be in a position to stipulate good conditions: usually a defense alliance, and such advantages as measures of furtherance (education, raw materials, and care for subsistence). The annexing part (in our case the Emperor) thereby gets a higher tax-income along with reinforcements of the army. If he keeps quiet and agreeable, he has more advantages; else he risks turmoil, revolutions and wars; – and *«after a war the land is always left bleeding»*, says *Sun-Dse*. – Chapters 57, 58 and 60 take extensively care of these aspects.

A peculiarity of Daoism in its begin is hat these teachings were really followed, and – unlike the colonial politics of European world powers since the 16th century – did not abuse the new ‹provinces›. The latter's internal independence, and their reasonable servitudes towards ‹above›, made of the Chinese Empire the vastest formation of the sort ever seen in our history until around 400 b.C. Ancient China's ethnic pluralism and spiritual liberalism (Daoism, Buddhism, Lamaism, Polytheism, Uighures, cult for ancestors, including witchcraft and sorcery, Shamanism, Sun- and Moon-cults etc.; – later also Maniism and Nestorianism) is indeed unmatched. This state of things was for the first time spoiled by official Confucianism, and definitively abolished by Mao's ‹Culture Revolution› (1949-1982) – both of them absolutely totalitarian. – Today, there exists a similar, but much less harmonious multiplicity, as our world lives in a phase of *inflated Yang*, and suppressed *Yin,* where some religions are keenly persecuted (Christians, Uighurs …)

The new era that our world has entered a few decennia ago, and also the presently emerging cosmic and macrocosmic changes are observed by many with superstitious angst – but by the Disciples of Gnosis with great hope and joyful adaptation. It represents a new chance (and a big challenge) for All, to *«re-install virtue and harmony»* (see N° 60). The most important point is that humans should – among each other and each one for their own microcosm – learn again to apply the old Daoist wisdom in the sense of DE – individual inner Gnosis – in today's new reality, as a renewed harmonious power-play of Yin-forces ‹lying below› and Yang-forces ‹lying on top›, in a well-measured equilibrium of give and take – *Each one according to its way and character* :

Together both will obtain what they want! †

† While we are realizing this translation, the whole of humanity is in a state of global insecurity never seen before: An usurped administration in the USA as executive of a handful insane would-be rulers of our Planet and their sycophants usurped power, willing to annihilate what ever humanity has created on this earth. The masses ignore God's and Nature's laws, now threatening to massacre what ever was worth loving during the last several hundred years. – Miserere nobis!

第六十二章

道者萬物之奧。善人之寶，不善人之所保。
美言可以市尊，美行可以加人。人之不善，何棄之有？
故立天子，置三公，雖有拱璧以先駟馬，不如坐進此道。
古之所以貴此道者何？不曰：求以得，有罪以免邪？
故爲天下貴。

62.

DAO is the Mystery of the 10'000 things.
To the worthy, it is a treasure,
to the unworthy it is a refuge.
Nice talk makes you a dignitary of the city.
Nice deeds makes you a dignified human.
An unworthy person – what made him unworthy?
Therefore:
When the Emperor and the three Honorable are inaugurated —
and notwithstanding that he is conferred
the honoring, the crown of jade and the quadriga:
Nothing is as precious as to sit down and enter this DAO.
Why do humans appreciate this DAO so much?
Is there not the saying:
«Ask for it, and you will obtain
forgiveness for your blemishes, and redemption from Evil»?
This is the reason why the World honors IT.

To begin with, here some variants of translation: The term most of them have used, namely *«sins»* – has been omitted here.: it is too heavy with moralistic ecclesiastic connotation. The version we chose, literal as it is, shows how far reach back the roots of the principal Christian prayer – the *«Our Father .... »*

Instead of *«the Mystery»*, the first line could also say *«the Deep»*. This reminds the old gnostic *Valentinian Æonology* (around 100 a.D): The *«Deep»*, or the *«Silence»*, used to be the appellation fort the «I» of Chinese tradition – and at the same time *«DAO»*; hence the *«Mother-Father»* of Essenian texts. So we find the same analogies in Ancient China as in today's Western traditions, in India, in Arabia, in the cultures of the Maya and of the Celts – and no wonder; for *«Out of One All comes – and into One All returns»*, as says the *Corpus Hermeticum* – the most notorious carrier for the tradition of Alexandrian Gnosis.

As for the inauguration and coronation of the Emperor, there are several polyvalent expressions. The term *honouring* replaces the more precise *salute*; – and instead of *«receives»*, the terms *«conferred»* or *«being overwhelmed with»* are more precise. The present interpretation instead makes clear the polyvalence of translations reaching from lapidary *«splendor»*, over *«jade tablets»* and *«medallions»* (in place of a more precise *«pierced Jade of the predecessor»*) until *«scepter» and «jewels»*: The latter show the typically Western, purely materialistic ideas about honors – completely neglecting the symbolic and magic bearing and practical result – of the ritual as well as of the gifts. For, in Ancient China, besides the fact that together with the *tiara* of the predecessor the new ruler was also transferred the latter's obligations *and the whole Karma* of the empire, there *jade was* (and partially still is today) the *magic stone par excellence.* – Finally, this N° 62 seems to show that, far from official historiography, even before the legendary *«yellow Emperor»*, there lived and ruled a real Chinese Emperor, with insignia similar to those in India!

Another most interesting item is the imperial jade crown of the *Ming-Dynasty* (1368-1644) – a *nephrite crown* as depicted on p. 271. It shows the *snout of a fish* from Rishi-times (*Joannan*) plus a symbolic pair of *Phœnixes soaring up from the flames* – a metaphor already used in Ancient Egypt, at the *Benu Feast of the Persian* Manicheans, and again in the Russian tale of the *Fire-Bird*, representing the *‹reborn Son of the Sun*: the *New Soul-Spirit Man*, who has *lived through* the ‹Rebirth from Water, Spirit, and Fire›.

Besides that, one discovers on this jade crown the rests of an ancient gilding: This corresponds, among other, to the awakened mental body with its golden glow, dominated by an ornamental knob equivalent to the *pinealis* – the spiritual center of a conscious human.[36]

So we see that an adequate interpretation of the *Dao-De-Jing* is possible only for who takes the images and symbolic language of it quite seriously, not with a mocking smirk, but carefully penetrating myths, usages and symbolism of Ancient China. The *quadriga* e.g. symbolized the *four cardinal virtues*, the *«four corners of the World»* and much more – already in Ancient India!

A possible parallel to the last line of N° 62 would be: *«Therefore the noble become humble!»*. This can be understood as both an *imperative* or as a simple statement.

The sixth line of this text is an especially important one. It has been translated in the past in ever so many ways – depending on the interpreter – even perverting the question into a statement, or leaving it out entirely. It might be *«A non-good person – what made him evil?»* – or as well: *«what did he give up?»*, respectively: *who has forsaken him?»,* where this *«who»*, or *«what»* may also be associated to ‹luck›, or to good or bad ‹spirits›: Depending of if we ‹read› the whole phrase as a string of single glyphs, or as pairs of glyphs, or as groupings of three or four glyphs at a time, the sense of the whole phrase changes. This exactly is what makes the unmatched and quite inconceivable literary genius of the *Dao-De-Jing* – and the complexity and its impossibility of a fully adequate translation into our modern standard languages with their modern poverty. Moreover, a *«non-worthy»* person is not the same as an *«unworthy»* person!

All these reasons made that the all too typical antithesis of *«good person» – «bad person»* have been relativized and differentiated here: Following its *polyvalence*, the term 不善人 – *«non-worthy person»* from line three – could also be translated – in line six – as a *«poor man»*. For, more adequately than the purely moral statement *«one may not simply reject him»*, is to take this question quite seriously as an important one, namely directed immediately towards the *cause* of this 不善人. This changes the *«non-worthy person»*, or – read as a group of three glyphs – the *«poor person»*, from a social «stumbling block» into an object for *loving charity*.

Why is this new interpretation so important? *Four reasons* prove it:

1° In the frame of the *Path of Initiation of DAO, loving comprehension* is always adequate, but *moral condemnation* rarely is. –

2° Condemnation of the moralistic kind would mean that the opening of our N° 62 has not been understood at all, when it says (in other terms): *«From DAO All comes forward* (‹good ones› and ‹evil ones›); *– and in DAO all is preserved»* (dignitaries and crooks). –

3° One would be neglecting the silent statement: *«If it is appropriate for Emperors and dignitaries to „enter DAO“ as soon as possible, then it certainly is so for ordinary people, too!».* –

4 As the ‹moral conclusion› of this N° 62 is that all those who accept *DAO* are given – *if they ask for it* – to be *forgiven* all their blemishes up to now, as well as to be *redeemed* of all future evil, it should be quite *un-Daoistic* (same as it is quite *un-Christian*) to condemn whom so ever: DAO – GNOSIS – loves them All!

This is why the whole World reveres IT!

德

VERSION FOLLOWING WANG-BI:

為無為，事無事，味無味。
大小多少，
報怨以德。
圖難於其易，為大於其細。
天下難事必作於易。
天下大事必作於細。
是以聖人 終不為大，
故能成其大。
夫輕諾必寡信。
多易必多難。
是以聖人
猶難之，
故終無難矣。

OUR BASIC VERSION :

第六十三章

爲無爲，事無事，味無味。
圖難于其易，爲大于其細；天下難事，必作于易，天下大事，必作于細。是以聖人終不爲大，故能成其大。
夫輕諾必寡信，多易必多難。是以聖人猶難之，故終無難矣。

63.

Do without doing —
Act without acting —
enjoy without enjoying.
Great becomes trivial; much becomes few —
Reproaches here become favors there.
Do plan difficulties in view of their positive solution —
Do big things in view of their trivialities.
The problems of the World will surely serve its best —
The biggest in the World will surely serve the smallest.
A true Wise reaches a point where he does nothing big anymore —
therefore he is able to achieve the greatest.
A person who lightly makes promises,
surely deserves little confidence:
Great carelessness brings great problems.
A true Wise plans problems in advance —
Thus he has no problems at the end.

This chapter seems to recommend things that are relevant only in the world of ‹practical people›, having in common close to nothing with the *«Path towards Virtue»* – with GNOSIS. But this appearance is deceptive: it suffices to replace the word *«problems»* or *«difficulties»* by the word *«adverse forces»*, and one recognizes the plane of *The Path* entirely unknown to *‹practical people›* – thus, to those people who deal with so-called ‹realities› only.

The basis of the pairs of phrases given here is indeed the first line: *«Do without doing!»* – Now, what indeed is the significance of this *‹non-doing›* in reality? It has been explained earlier that it has nothing to do with *doing-nothing*, but is all about concentrated *letting happen* things on a different plane; – and that's the plane where belongs the rest of this text.

In the first place, this *non-doing* is another kind of *doing*: The Candidate or Master *does things* in his exoteric life, without losing his heart and soul in any such activity – i.e. without sacrificing himself away in this outward life; – in other words again, without losing sight of the fact *that* he does what he's doing, *how* and *why* he's doing it – and also that he's doing it not just to fulfill his inevitable physical duty, but also for the glory of DE. – Therefore: even if he does what he does *«in full devotion and perfect self-forgetfulness»*, part of him yet remains *outside of* this visible activity, as he remains more or less consciously oriented toward GNOSIS.

This way of standing outside – this *neutrality* – has two aspects. One of them is defined by the almost unlimited expression of *serenity* (cheerful stillness). This does not just mean *inner* calm, but also *reservation* – i.e. to keep his inner emotional *distance* from the ‹10'000 things›, with whatever they imply, and whatever they emanate: their smell, their noises, forces, vibrations ... —

So the ‹Wise› is really an inhuman brute? – Does he ignore all about human feelings, preferences and fears? – No, of course he knows all that; for, it would be impossible to be *‹wise›* without being deeply human, i.e. knowing all human attitudes like empathy, the ability to discriminate, to chose and to act! – The difference lies in his being conscious that all things on Earth are relative:

What the one enjoys, others dislike. What the one names tasteless, others relish. – What is just noise to the one is music to others – and so forth. The pilgrim *learns* to preserve his *neutrality* amidst feelings and emotions, *thanks to* his knowledge about the relativity of all things, and acknowledging that everybody perceives, experiences differently, judging every thing differently, and depending of actual situations. He therefore avoids discussions with persons bound to assign *absolute* properties and values to things: dogmatists, pseudo-scientists, fanatics, and foremost those many who allow themselves a judgment without having halfway seen *hardly one side* of a thing. – But even them he will not condemn: Ignorance is allowed as much as it is omnipresent; – and what the wisest man *can know* is but a spark amidst the obscurity of what he *ignores*!

On the other hand, this World is made in such a way that everything, every property or feature can in the blink of an eye change to become its own contrary; – and that is the main statement encountered in the present *chapter about «problems»*.

A ‹Wise›, thus, is no inhuman brute – quite the contrary: he *feels* and *knows* he is human, and closely linked to all other humans of this World! It's just that he is clearly conscious of the multiplicity of human error – including his own – *but in full neutrality*. And out of the *neutrality of his observations and experiences* arises his *neutrality in doing*:

Nothing that can be experienced, thought, said and done on the plane of so-called reality is important. For, nothing of all that is *real in an absolute sense.* DAO is absolutely real – and so are the effects of Spirit in the World of would-be realities. – *What is real* is the path of all creatures through the Universe – this Path that leads them – each on its proper trail – *towards meeting HIM who loves them all*!

A second aspect of this neutrality is addressed in our present text: The advanced Initiate on the Path of Gnosis has stopped doing things with the *Marsian will* of the Ego determined to succeed at all costs with its plans; – also he observes himself acting, almost like an outside third party. – However, he does not so as a *split personality*, but out of a newly experienced Oneness: an Oneness where his Ego is only part of himself, and not the entire individual as ordinary people feel when they say: *«I am – I want –I have – I do!»* —

Quite the contrary: The *Initiate through self-initiation* can rightfully say of himself: *«Not I am doing it – but the [force of the cosmic] Christ is doing it through myself!»* – And in the best of circumstances, when the person is completely (i.e. with thoughts, words and deeds) oriented toward oneness with DAO, this force is the force of Gnosis itself: this universal luminous force the Western World in particular names *The Christos* – in the highest and most beautiful understanding one can have of Him – *far off all mythology and theology* – just experiencing IT in pure awe as the universal emanation of the One Universal Force that is *Light, Truth and Life* – and *sublime Love!*

All this is happening in loving awareness, in clear understanding, in an unequivocal orientation towards The One, in an attitude of utmost scientific conscientiousness, and out of *a new Ego* – of *a new Self* that does not *impose* itself, but has *understood* (as a *knowledge*!) what is *a real reality*. – Not that there were no obstacles nor difficulties left – but he does not undergo them as *Fate Almighty* anymore. – And not that there were no fiends either: They exist, even when every cause for fights and disputes is carefully avoided. – They as well are objects to the benevolence of the Wise.

Who does not know this over-all attitude might say: *«This I cannot fulfill! – This is too much, to high, to difficult, too severe an engagement!»* – But the experienced pilgrim follows his trail, *unperturbably*. He *knows:* If in the World he does nothing ‹big› anymore, the *One*, the greatest *inside of him will achieve it*: In the force of Gnosis, all obstacles and enemies melt down into nothing:

«So he will without difficulties attain the Good End!»

德

其安易持，其未兆易
其脆易泮，其微易散。
為之於未有，治之於未亂。
合抱之木 生於毫末。
九層之台 起於累土。
千里之行 始於足下。
為者敗之，執者失之。
是以聖人 無為故無敗，無執故無失。
民之從事常於幾成而敗之。
慎終如始 則無敗事。
是以聖人 欲不欲，不貴難得之貨。
學不學，復眾人之所過，
以輔萬物之自然 而不敢為。

第六十四章

其安易持，其未兆易謀。其脆易泮，其微易散。爲之于未有，
治之于未亂。
合抱之木，生于毫末；九層之台，起于累土；千里之行，
始于足下。
民之從事，常于几成而敗之。愼終如始，則無敗事。

64.

Peace is easier to maintain
when there is no sign of a conspiracy yet. —
What is vulnerable is easy to abolish —
What is very small is easy to dislodge.

Look forward to what is not yet there —
Bridle what is not yet confused.
Do quite understand, and meditate this:

An entire tree grows from a prong thin like a hair —
A terrace of nine steps builds up on a toilsome accretion of soil —
A journey through a thousand villages begins under the feet —
Who acts, destroys —
Who holds fast, looses.

Therefore:
The Wise remains inactive, and therefore destroys nothing —
He does not cling to anything, therefore does not lose anything.

Humans undertake something ... —
Every time they have almost finished it, it fails.
If the end is as wary as the beginning, as a rule nothing fails.

A true Saint wants without will —
he doesn't covet great physical things —
he knows without having seen —
He turns back to the masses of humanity
[helping them] to surmount their condition —
He helps the 10'000 things to attain their true nature —
But he is not allowed to intervene.

This chapter has obviously been transmitted in different versions. The passages of text *absent* from the original used for our present interpretation, are taken from the version by *Wang-Bi*, and rendered here *in blue color*. They are probably inserted by a later hand, for, by their moralizing tone they differ from the rest, where just facts without judgments are connected one to another. –

The text says *«1000 villages» – not «miles», nor «Li»* (市里) really *– wishing to convey: «... begins where one stands»,* and *absolutely not as almost all other translations quote: «with one first step»*! —

The whole relates to a triple teaching that in its core is one and the same, though: *«The Wise uses farsighted activity*; – *«All big things grow from something small; –many small particles make one big thing; — who is careful from the beginning to the finish, will achieve a good end».* – All this is equally true for the follower of the microcosmic path of evolution *under* DAO, for the ruler of a state *in* DAO, and for the evolution of the whole World *towards* DAO.

As long as no temptation nor obstacle surges, it is easy for the pilgrim to keep up his faith and to follow the spiritual ideal, toward which he orients his path. – But who is *«not yet firm on his course»* is easily confused and deviated to some abusive path: The power of the ‹Adversary› therefore is unleashed already at the beginning, and this the more forcefully as the enthusiasm is now on its highest. –

«Ward off the first negative signs!» is the slogan for both sides; and this goes for all those Disciples who wish to encourage a new, not yet firm candidate on his path: Be wary, and carefully further the new little plant that begins to unfold here: your responsibility is a big one! How easily may break the *«prong, thin like a hair»*, and so the giant oak tree – the new birth of a new *Spirit-Soul-Man* remains just a dream, to be reactivated during a next incarnation!

At the same time, any new Candidate of Gnosis must know from the start that *The Path* is no easy little walk: At the beginning, one might even get the impression of climbing a rocky cliff, alone and without any help. This happens when faith and clear comprehension wane, and when one forgets that *The Path* is an unshakeable certitude. – For only he who can see before his inner eye the Hermetic *tower of nine steps* shining in full glory, can in reality build it: first as a bricklayer, then as a master builder.[37] – Only clear imagination of the fully grown gigantic oak tree due to germinate from a humble acorn, can direct its sprouting, its growth and its expansion of branches!

Evenly, on the path toward GNOSIS – the path toward DAO – every new day – indeed every moment – calls for clear consciousness, in order to direct the steps of the Candidate, and keep him moving: *«Here I stand (for I can't do otherwise)*; – *here I go (and I am helped to advance»).* – What at the beginning looked like a carefree stroll may change with sweaty creeping; but thanks to the confidence issued from overcoming the first obstacles, all turns into courageous advancement again.

This is what the *«king of the Path»*, Master *Lao-Dse* meant to say with his sentence: *«Who remains mindful from the beginning, and never lets up: he or she will not get lost [on the way]!».* – This appears to be a repetition of the warning from N° 63, where the recommendation of farsighted activity is uttered: *«Great carelessness brings great sorrow!»*

Looked at it this way, the first ‹blue amendment› appears as a useful recommendation outside the main text; – the second one reinforces the idea of *non-doing* regarding *thinking, feeling and wanting*: The ‹Wise›, or ‹Saint›, *has lost* the old Marsian will of his old personality – albeit not yet completely, maybe. He incorporates a will that does not express itself as crude *«I want!»* anymore, but as a sometimes urgent *«I must ...»*, surging from the spark in his heart and pressing him as a *New Will* to accomplish things he never had thought about before.

Same for his thinking: Several modern versions translate: *«He learns to forget»* – resp. *«he learns non-learning».* The version proposed here – equally ‹literal› – wants to convey two significations: The advanced Candidate learns how from *imagination* and *inspiration* grows *intuition*, opening to him a reasonable entrance to every information – including forgotten and future knowledge. Therefore he often *«knows without knowing» as says Sun-Dse.* – On the other hand he humbly acknowledges: The more he *may know* (for human standard), the clearer he sees how much (as an absolute comparison) he *will ‹never› know*. This is the often quoted *«I know that I do not know [anything for sure]!»*

An important addendum hereto is the *wise discipline* not to explore nor *experiment* erudition out of pure curiosity. There are things ‹forbidden› for Man to know and to do – not because of a decree by some jealous god afraid to lose some of his power, but because of *the One Law*: *DAO – the Mother of all things!* – This wise discipline is growingly discarded by humanity these days – and that will inevitably lead to humanity's doom:

Creation of a chaotic Arch-Creature, as described by the gnostically mythic tale of *Pistis Sophia*, is again a substantial reality. The boundless *«wanting to play God»* must and will evoke a reaction from the outer Universe – a reaction that will shock only the esoterically ignorant ‹Wise of this World›!

The ancient polymaths and researchers of Nature – the Alchemists until late Renaissance – they knew very well that Man is allowed *to shape, to form, and even to generate* – but not to actually *create things*. The author of the book (transl.) *The key to The Twelve Keys by Brother Basilius Valentinus*, in its chapter about the *Universal Spirit*, explicitly mentions this taboo:[38]

«I have ... promised to indicate the corner-stone and rock ... as far as I am allowed to and have been given from above ... ».

In other words: The invulnerability of the Mysteries – particularly the Mystery of Life – is no *mystical* matter, but an absolutely *concrete* one. To disregard this Law, must entail the most fatal consequences.[38-A] – A modern author writes:

«It is Alchemists – but just those who really merit this title – who animate some idle matter and lead it to its divine Apotheosis: from Nature to Super-Nature. By following this Path philosophically, as humble but determined seekers and researchers of Nature, they precede matter on its Way of the Cross – its path through the CRUCIBLE. Through their work with the ‹Three Fires› – physical, metaphysical, and essential; – as ‹Philosophi per Ignem› – philosophers through Fire – they follow their deep-inner hunch about the essence of the Divine – amazed visionaries of the interplay of physical, spiritual and original fires, as a reward by divine Grace for their firm faith (i.e. inner knowledge – Gnosis), and for their long, wearisome steadfast endeavours ... ».[39]

The ‹Wise› knows very well the high value of his efforts for the ‹*10'000 things*› in the Universe: Every liberated soul shines as a small new Sun! But when this is accomplished for himself, the ‹Saint› will not just disappear ‹in Heaven›: He *turns around* to meet all worldly humans, as their helper! This is his *sacred servitude* and sacrifice – effective on a plane completely unintelligible to the Masses: To most of them, his wisdom is pure tomfoolery – but to others it appears as an *existential menace*. – There really lies the *sacrifice of the Wise* for World and Mankind ...

And yet – while he would like, and is, able to, help and counsel others: He must accept that his counsel is derided and scorned, and that he is persecuted even personally, as it has been during many centuries. The *‹Law›* allows him, to teach and promulgate the *Message of Light*, and to give the example by his way of life, but *never to intervene actively* with destiny of individuals, nor with specific occurrences in the World! Thus he is bound *to see, to feel, to know, to remain silent* ... - and ...

——— *to non-doing!* ———

The famous terracotta army of Xuan (3rd c. b.C.)
The morison on the bob of many of the soldiers reminds the (almost contemporary) *Libetra* of the Mithras-cult. (Image source : Internet)

第六十五章

古之善爲道者，非以明民，將以愚之。
民之難治，以其智多。故以智治國，國之賊；不以智治國，國之福。
知此兩者亦稽式。常知稽式，是謂「玄德」。「玄德」深矣，遠矣，與物反矣，然后乃至大順。

65.

In olden times,
persons dedicated to DAO used to keep people dumb:
A nation is difficult to rule when it has great knowledge.
Indeed:
When education dominates the nation,
there are traitors in the lands —
When absence of education dominates the nation,
the land lives in prosperity.
Therefore, consider both sides, and yield to this practice:
Always to remember and to follow this conduct,
is what one names the true secret of DE.
An abysmal secret of DE indeed, and entirely incomprehensible!
And at the same time of an absolutely outraging nature!
Later however, there ensues from it
Greatest submission, order, happiness and welfare,
all in one.

First of all, what needs to be emphasized is that here the term *education* stands for *erudition*. – For «*land*» we might as well read *Nation* or *People or Province*. – *And the terms of the last line are a selection of significations for the one glyph* (順) *of the text*.

What is useful to the ruler of a nation is, in some ways, also applicable for the Candidate of the Gnostic Mysteries, on the *Path of DAO*, or for any other path of initiation. A person with a high standard education will quite naturally also be inclined to apply the way of thinking of the academically scientific world to the teachings of transfiguristic wisdom. Attention especially of humans of our time is averted from the *One Great Whole*, and directed toward a mundane horizon of puzzling details: Modern education, training and formation along the mainstream of ‹survival of the fittest› in a materialistic surrounding, encode, solidify, and fixate the flattening of this horizon, and few are those who escape the seductive song of the *sirens of cultivation* and the compelling suction and grip of the materialistic *Skylla and Charybdis*.[40]

Given that all this has caused obstacles to seekers since Antiquity, the Candidate on *The Path* is always instructed to let go of this ‹old› thinking habits and to adopt a ‹completely new› way of thinking, respectively, to apply himself to spiritual simplicity, and even naïvety. The figures meant to support this concept are multitude: The *‹fool›* of the *Tarot de Marseille* carelessly lifts his foot toward the ditch into which he will presently fall; – *Perceval crossing a bridge as he leaves his mother behind,* is depicted as a *naïve fool*. – *Richard Wagner* nails it down in his *Lohengrin,* coining the phrase: *«Wise through compassion – the pure fool».*

With this are addressed three corner stones as conditions for illumination: In order to attain *«wisdom before God»* that in the same time is named *«foolishness before humans»*, a purity of the heart very close to naivety needs to be developed: This child-like *simplicity* addressed by the *Sermon on the Mount* must not be confounded with childish stupidity by ignorance; it only means exoneration of so much ballast of a civilization binding humans to this Earth: unnecessary comfort, superfluous nutrition, useless teachings, idle thoughts, weird arguments and obsolete actions. – In early times, this correctional training produced mystic hermits: in antique Syria, in Hellenistic Egypt, in Christian-Orthodox Greece, during the European Middle-Ages – including Indish ashrams and Islamic ‹Marabou's› a.s.f., some of which survive until today.

Our present text seems to address no spiritual meaning, but only a harmonious way of ruling an empire. Nowadays, it would be quite welcome, alas!, if the rulers of any state would possess at least *some* wisdom, honesty, simplicity and farsightedness. For – and the later chapters will elucidate this further – as is the king, so will be his subjects. – A real king is a *good example* for his nation!

Generally speaking we might say: Who lives simply – spiritually and physically – can live calmly and content. – Who lives amidst material and spiritual *riches*, complicates his own existence and that of others. He easily gets agitated and diverted, and in his anguish loses from sight the *essence of Life*. – From an intellectual point of view as well as from a material one, the general rule is: *«who possesses much, wants still more ... »*. – Thus, unnecessary goods are accumulated along with erudition that brings *no knowledge*, but averts one from the Right Path.

That's why the recommendation in N° 65 is indeed more profound and more far-reaching than what we thought at first glance, so that our civilized way of thinking could rebel against it. The whole argument therefore is just a matter of deeper understanding:

The whole verse is based on the existence of *illuminated* persons, who bore in mind only the best for *subjects, empire and Emperor,* when they taught people in public. Within the frame of an *inner* teaching of wisdom they served the *One Great Oeuvre* – the great Plan of God. This means: their whole existence and impact were *meant to serve Humanity, Universe and God.* The glyph 天 stands for all three: for *heaven*, for *God who «rules» this heaven*, fort the *World*, the empire and the people, 天下 (*«the Upper and the lower»*) and for the *Emperor* (天下王) who as a representative of God – *«Son of Heaven»* and a *god himself*, rules this world.

Thus, our N° 65, too, shows the antiquity of the wisdom of universal correlations and proportions, and the image of the *Son of God on Earth*, as the *Corpus Hermeticum* teaches us – this Hellenistico-Egyptian compendium of all ancient wisdom that says (here usefully summarized):

«As above – so below, as in the big, so in the small, as in the past, so also in the future and now!»

So this chapter as well is directly applicable to the Path of self-initiation: The Candidate needs to live as simply as possible; he is to be «dumb» for whatever keeps the world spinning in ceaseless agitation, fostering vain hostilities. He may be rich in inner experience, in knowledge, in empathy of heart and head; – he may languish for universal wisdom of Gnosis, augment his knowledge and refine his character: His ‹subjects› – energies and habits of his *inner human personality* – he needs to direct them following gnostic principles, but not as a *pious cultivation* – neither culturally, nor scientifically, nor as a social or religious refinement. He needs to keep content his ‹people› on the level of the physiological necessities of life. If his orientation toward DAO is unambiguous and sufficiently mindful, his intellect can be very useful for his efforts for the World. But the tool *must not* inadvertently become the work piece itself, even if sometimes ‹reason› may contradict vehemently what according to the principles of *DAO* and *DE* is the right thing – and indeed *the sole defendable thing.*

At the beginning, it appears difficult to harmonize both earthly and spiritual desires. But once he has attained this composed equilibrium, the new *witness for The Light* will experience the greatest

Devotion, order, happiness and welfare – all in one!

第六十六章

江海之所以能爲百谷王者，以其善下之，故能爲百谷王。
是以聖人欲上民，必以言下之；欲先民，必以身后之。
是以聖人處上而民不重，處前而民不害。是以天下樂推而不厭。
以其不爭，故天下莫能與之爭。

66.

There is a reason why rivers and the sea are capable
to be the kings of many valleys:
They have the custom to be below —
That's why they can act as kings of many valleys.
When the true Saint is among the people, he certainly wishes
to use a simple language, wishing for what his subjects wish,
in order to rule them so much more assuredly.
He who is really grand, acts with sovereignty,
but without suppressing the people. —
He demands respect – but without offending the people.
Therefore his reign lasts, joyfully and content, without casualties.
He is without a fight,
for his subjects give him no motive for fighting.

At a first glance, this chapter seems to be but a continuation of the *admonitions to a ruler* of N° 62 : to adapt oneself at the right moment, to enjoy one's dominion with so much more certainty – calmly and free of cares. It also is a repetition of the teachings from N° 49: To assimilate one's wishes to the wishes of his people, and to remaining conscious of the fact that they always observe him: Children imitate the attitude, gests and habits of their parents to the tee. – The tone, demeanor and clothing of the superior boss coin the demeanor and clothing of managers and their staff, until down to the office-boy.

By the same token the highest responsible of a community can easily estimate the impact of his subordinates – and thus his own – if he regularly mingles with the most insignificant ones of his employees, notwithstanding the nature or objects of this community. This has been transmitted also regarding the most famous Khaliph of Baghdad, *Harun-ar-Rashid*, immortalized by some curious anecdotes in *Thousand Nights and One Night*: He ruled so calmly and with so much popularity in the 8th c.a.D., that he became famous even in the West. – By right, if we attribute to those tales the extent of credibility they appear to merit.[41]

The ‹bath amidst people› is still common in our time – from a football-hero to minister-presidents popes and the like – only that today's ‹kings› making their public appearance to celebrate their Ego rather than to sympathize with people – and not in order to *«look at the mouth of people»*, as Martin Luther expressed it when he was to produce his translation of the Bible from Latin into the *language of the people*, instead of into that of the Elites. – The ruler presented in our text instead, wishes to get the echo to his way of ruling, by looking into their eyes, while signaling to them in gests and words this benevolence for each and every single one of them.

Now, how can this be translated for the case of the ‹pilgrim› or ‹pupil› on the gnostic *Path of DAO*?

Same as the *«wise ruler»* minds not to be too distant of the people, the Candidate as well must not completely deny worldly things, but outwardly remain connected to the way of life of ‹ordinary people›, without scandalizing them unnecessarily by his difference in demeanor, clothing, or by prescriptions of purity.

The *Fama Fraternitatis* – the first of the three Rosicrucian manifestos of the 17th century, – recommends to all *«Brethren of the Fraternity R.C.»* not to wear some special habit, *«but to adapt to the usages of the land»*. Also, they should not exercise any other occupation but healing the sick – and this for free. On the plane of ‹reality›, this means that they were no concurrence for artisans or traders: Wandering healers always existed without numbers. – On the spiritual plane instead, *healing* means: promulgation of the *Universal Doctrine* among the relatively ignorant (and therefore ‹ill›) people throughout the World.

Now, one might be scandalized because Initiates to the transfiguristic path are compared to kings. The *Dao-De Ging* explains in its 39th chapter, why this comparison is so adequate: *«To serve is the fundament of ruling; dignity is he consequence of simplicity … a king names himself solitary, forsaken, indigent ...»* (comp. N° 39 and N° 42). – The same is true for the Pilgrim on The Path: In spite of living amidst the world he is no part of it anymore. – Connected to it as it were, he nevertheless feels himself to be a stranger …

The conception of *serving* is immediately connected to the notion of humility. This has nothing in common with a cringing sneak or a pietist: Humility *does not advertise*. If it were so visibly exposed, it would just be another form of hypocrisy. – No, some outwardly *«uncouth warrior»* or *«stately dignitary»* can inwardly be far more humble than a shabby beggar who asks for *«money to buy bread»*, but refuses a piece of bread!

The pupil of Gnosis – if he is serious about it – has made a choice to which he subordinates everything else: ‹success›, coziness, an intimate homeland – things ordinary humans enjoy so much. His choice is simply a religious one – but it has its price! This price may consist, for example, in that he is obliged to accept without comment institutional learning in school, the state or church; for this are *the usages*. – Or in that he is obliged to silently obey people who are unfit exactly in the domain where they are ‹specialized› and should excel … –

All this shows in many ways that the comparison of an *«inspired pupil»* and an *«ingenious ruler»* is quite adequate: A *‹Pilgrim›* – a *‹Wise›* in the best case – is at the same time a wise *king*: an *ingenious* ruler over his *impulses* (the commoners), over his *cravings* (the clerks), his *will* (the Generals), his *thoughts* (scientists and priests), his *actions* (dealers and peasants). – Once he is well set in his orientation, he *«acts with sovereignty, but without oppressing his subjects»*, avoiding what might oppose *The Path – «but without offending the people»*, i.e., without self-mortification – or else, sooner or later, a ‹revolution› may break out: The oppressed representatives of the Masses might unexpectedly ‹take for the streets›, blocking all, and eventually annihilating the results of many years of spiritual progress!

Therefore, the Initiate lends his ear to all, like a wise ruler, *«wishing what his subjects wish, in order to rule them so much more assuredly»* – conceding to the former king that he still has a right to speak up – only, maybe, *«not just now!»*

Thus, the whole business is to find the right measures in all: Exceptions of the basic rules as a ‹pupil› are inevitable. – But even if some time things are done that contradict The Path, favoring the millenarian *human beast*: The newly *ruling sovereign king will observe his predecessor with a mocking smile.* As long as these exceptions are not directly *thwarting* the Path he will remain a neutral observer, *«without interfering directly»*, as is fitting for a wise prince: He knows when and where such exceptions are admissible, and will by no means let them promulgate themselves. – That is how he can – *autonomously in full harmony* – continue the *One Path* – *«rejoicing and content, with no casualty»:*

He is without a fight,
for his subjects give him no reason to fight.

第六十七章

天下皆謂我道大，似不肖。夫唯大，故似不肖。若肖，
久矣其細也夫！
我有三寶，持而保之。一曰慈，二曰儉，三曰不敢爲天下先。
慈故能勇；儉故能廣；不敢爲天下先，故能成器長。
今舍慈且勇；舍儉且廣；舍后且先；死矣！
夫慈以戰則勝，以守則固。天將救之，以慈衛之。

67.

Common folks all say:
«DAO is above me; – to me it is worthless!» —
«Man alone is great; therefore IT is worthless!» —
«It may not look bad —
[but] Humanity is miserable since long!»

I have three treasures and hold them fast
as the objective of all my wishes:
The first is named mercy —
The second is named moderation —
The third: To abstain from pressing oneself forward.
Mercy, in order to fight bravely —
Moderation, in order to be able to expand —
To abstain from pressing oneself forward,
in order to eventually become a strong tool.

Nowadays,
mercy has stopped – and bravery too —
moderation has stopped – and expansion too —
reservation has stopped – and responsibility too:
All this is completely dead!
Humanity likes to fight for the victory —
their rules of the game are merciless.
May Heaven save them
and mercifully preserve them!

Known translations here differ from each other all the more as they are more ‹beautiful› to listen – especially when rhymed. If their analysis, based on our three basic Chinese texts, can explain some of these versions, yet in the light of a lecture favoring the truly spiritual significance (and this alone is what the present volume is about) some completely new results come up.

Translating the text glyph after glyph, without anticipating their possible signification (single glyphs, combinations of glyphs, modern Chinese interpretations), this same text leads to a new, indubitable, and in itself harmonious interpretation without any romantic inventions, as soon as the syntax of the phrases is painstakingly respected. – And moreover our text gains utmost actuality with that!

This is true for the whole *Dao-De-Jing*, really – but quite especially for this N° 67. Original Chinese ‹translations› and commentaries make sure that the *autonomy* of the present interpretation is not the result of some *arrogance*: Out of the *328'000 Internet pages* that open in the blink of an eye as we enter the last sequence of just ten glyphs, *ten* variants were studied in detail. *Nine of them* support the present version, *seven* leave no chance to any of the Western variants; *one* mentions another English version that agrees with ours – partly word by word, partly introducing some queer ideas.[42] At any rate, only the present interpretation fulfills all three critical conditions as mentioned in our *Introduction*. –

It is typical for the original arrangement of the text of the *Dao-De-Jing* that the beginning and the conclusion often appear to span an ark, into which is inserted the explaining comment – sort of like the paste into its crust. – And so it is here as well.

The *fundamental thought* of ‹verse› 67 is that today's humans (around 500 b.C.!) have forgotten the old Cardinal Virtues; that they don't know anymore what to do with the primitive (primeval) tradition of DAO; and that in place of goodness, moderation and humility there reign egotism, intemperance and aggressiveness. – Are we not lamenting exactly the same things today?

The ‹crust of dough› of this fundamental thought is filled here with the enumeration of three main virtues and their advantages for society as well as for the individual *fighter on The Path*. This goes also for the Candidate of the Mysteries and for real warriors. Now, as every virtue is mentioned with its advantages, it is illogical to translate as did most others: *«The [specific virtue]* has *completely stopped, is dead»* (thrice 舍); – *[and it (!)] «has been* superseded (thrice 且) by *[its advantage!]»*. – No, it would be better to take the glyph 且 accurately , namely as *«also», «additionally», «furthermore»*, – thus as: *«and therefore also ... »*. – As the present translation follows most accurately the original arrangement, everybody can understand the meaning of each glyph here. –

Now, as for *the esoteric signification* of our N° 67, it is unnecessary to go into all details: The whole text as such explains itself by itself as soon as it is put into relation to the *«pilgrim on The Path of DAO›*:

«Love» as the glyph 慈 stands as the sum of many precise significations, like for *«goodness, mildness, forbearance, good-naturedness, charity, mercy, compassion, empathy, tenderness, gentleness, respect»* etc., the consummation of which however is *Universal* Love as it is defined in the *Letter to the Corinthians* (1 Cor 12:13). This single glyph, then, includes a great number of properties that are to be acquired by the ‹Candidate›, or ‹pupil›, thus becoming authentic in him by the bye; for, without them, he would remain just *«a sounding brass, or a tinkling cymbal»*, as says Paul. The commentary to N° 39 gives a historical explanation for a possible origin of this musical comparison.

Moderateness has been mentioned in an earlier chapter already. It is one of the old *Cardinal Virtues*. For the Candidate this means, in a first place, *simplicity* of his daily requirements. The simpler he lives, the lesser the diversions he undergoes, and the rarer the possibilities for him to be attacked by opposing forces. – One remark to this: *Simplicity* – or, as others want, *frugality* – should be (says the text) a prerequisite for *«expansion»*, hence, for *growing welfare*. Originally that must certainly have meant expansion in space (namely agricultural surfaces and people), but later on, political, economical or simply *personal* expansion as a merchant or clerk. Others put *«generous»* for *«not stingy»*. This reminds us that in the Orient especially, and preferably in context with the spiritual path, a most important habit is: giving alms: For the Muslim this is still part of the five principal virtues of the faithful. – In the Christianized West, only the ‹collect› has remained thereof …

The expression *abstinence* in this regard – let us emphasize it once more – must never be understood as forceful *asceticism*: *Reservation* is a natural and self-understood behavior for the serious Candidate: It is rather the contrary of egotism, ambition, and ruthlessness (see N° 81); – it therefore may be understood also as humility, provided one understands this expression correctly – i.e. *not moralizing*. The previous chapter has already commented on this.

Who knows the Path of DAO from his or her own experience, also knows the comments by many outsiders – people at the fringe of the path, who use to mock our Pilgrim and his demeanor – or by others who even feel themselves scandalized by him – or else, by those who make their deprecatory remarks, shrugging their shoulders, etc.: *«All this is surely but foolishness, and quite useless indeed; – intellectually great* (大)*, but practically worthless* (不肖; compare American *«different»*) … ». And, looked at it from their standpoint of vulgar earthlings, they are completely right …

Even when viewed from the angle of human history of cultures, the forthcoming text contains interesting hints: Reservation, or discretion, is recommended with the aim to *«eventually become a strong tool / organ / talent / vessel»* – hence a useful servant of the World-Empire. – Chinese commentators also mention *ship*, reminding the French *vaisseau, which besides «ship» can also mean* a *vessel* (from *«vase»*). The *modern* (communist) Chinese version of this text uses a different glyph here, meaning today a *«boss»* and *«chairman»* – but not that of a *vessel* or *tool* anymore.

Of this ensues an occasion to mention that the Candidate on the Path toward Gnosis strives to become *a strong tool for The Spirit* – a *transmitter of the Grail*, wherein the wondrous transformation of an earthling becoming a *‹Spirit-man of the Beginning›* can occur – one who then is capable to restore and revive others with the *‹salutary water›* of Gnosis. – It is well known that *Pharaoh*, the prime Adept of Egyptian Gnosis, was repeatedly depicted in a barge steered by the gods (resp. the high-priests wearing their masks) – the so-called *Sun-* or *Light-Barge*.

Here a special feature emphasized in an earlier chapter is worth mentioning once more: The *«sacred warriors»* (that was the caste directly under the Priests, like the Indish Kshatriya) were taught to lead their battle not only without wrath, but even in Love and with noble mercy toward their adversaries (see next chapter!). Direct vision lets us see that the usage to really *kill until death ensues*, arose only in the course of *totally physical incorporation* (crystallization) of the World, and of the degeneration of the human soul: Before that, ‹heroic death› was as reversible as a small fainting (‹blackout›); the fight was a play –but not in the sense of entertainment (like knightly duels), but in the sense of a sacred ritual, wherein ‹the sky› (天) decided of the victory of battling humans (夫) as myths still tell us (e.g. Thor, Sigmund and the Valkyrie). – However, the ritual tournaments degenerated into relentless, merciless fighting and maiming, when the gods – and later the Angels – left Earth … —

As it opened with the formula 天下, *«under the heaven(s)»* – i.e. *«in this World»* – the text of N° 67 closes with an *invocation of Heaven,* and with an intercession for World and Humankind:

May Heaven save them, and mercifully preserve them!

Gilded nephrite crown (hetian jade) with a fish snout (Oannes!) and two Phoinixes in flames. Ming Dynasty (1368-1644). – Image source: ‹Alibaba›.

第六十八章

善爲士者，不武；善戰者，不怒；善勝敵者，不與；善用人者，爲之下。是謂不爭之德，是謂用人之力，是謂配天古之極。

68.

An excellent commander is not bellicose —
An excellent warrior is not enraged —
An excellent conqueror does not attack —
An excellent leader of humans subordinates himself.

By right non-fighting is named a virtue —
By right one names one's servant one's support —
By right, since high and ancient times one names
to espouse Heaven the highest goal.

In our introduction to this book we have named *Daoism a system and most comprehensive science and philosophy with high practical relevance on all domains of life*. The field on which the total sum of antique Daoism can best be illustrated and practiced, is *warfare*. And the most famous early classical book of Daoist philosophy besides the *Dao-De-Jing* and the *I-Jing*, is the book by *Sun-Dse* about the art of highest strategy[43]. This book teaches the *art of war*; but it does not understand war as an *«act of violence, to force the adversary to fulfill our will»*, as writes C. v. Clausewitz in his famous work,[44] but as a method of *avoiding* armed conflicts, to *prevent* combat, to *sidestep* it, or else to lead it so as to cause *the minimum of losses on both sides – «short and forcefully!»*. –

Sun-Dse says:

«Those who assist their Overlord using DAO, do not use weapons in order to coerce the World, for these things have the tendency to pervert themselves into their contrary. Bramble bushes will grow where an army has passed, and miserable years follow a great war» (see Dao-De-Jing N° 30).

Another very Daoistic classic says (see N° 31):

«Weapons are calamitous instruments, and not the tool of an illuminated person. When there remains no other choice, it is best to be calm and free of any sort of passion, and not to celebrate the victory. Those who celebrate their victory are blood-thirsty; and for blood-thirsty people there is no place in this World».[45]

How different of this instead are the many yearly celebrations and parades throughout our modern world – in East and West!

This most famous study and teaching by *Sun-Dse* contains all aspects of Daoism, and it is applicable to the cosmos and every microcosmos, to war and peace. Envisaging all fields of action at a time, it repeatedly stresses the importance of *compassion* – at home as well as on the side of the adversary – plus the *absence of any kind of passion*; thus of hate, anger and cruelty even where and when the combat is fought with toughest rigor.

This conception so different from that of today's warfare could also be named an *esthetic of war*: The Greek αισϑησις – aísthesis – besides sensual apprehension also signifies *insight, consciousness* and *inner apprehension.* – This means: For Daoism, the thing is not just to be ‹victorious› by means of weapons. Every fight must be submitted to the control by *compassion.* – This *duplicity* of matters is also named *«the Daoist paradoxon»*.

Sun-Dse teaches the *mastership of plenitude*, and this in four ways: Mastery of *energy*, mastery of *force*, mastery of adaption, and mastery of *the Heart*. In his *ninth chapter* he writes: *«What counts is uniquely to avoid aggressive action. It is enough to concentrate ones force, to correctly assess the adversary, and to win over people; – that is all»*.

This remarkable concept, when adapted, is absolutely applicable to The Path of a simple ‹Pilgrim› or ‹Disciple› on The Path of DAO. Only that here the ‹person to be won over› is one's proper Ego.

Characteristic for this understanding of warfare is the following quotation after *Zhuge-Liang*, this most famous general at the beginning of the 3rd century b.C., whom we have mentioned before:

«In olden times, those who ruled well did not arm their people; – those who were well armed, wouldn't enroll an army; – those who knew how to cleverly line up their armies, did not fight; – those who were excellent fighters, didn't lose; – those who knew how to lose, didn't perish.»[46]

The *Sun-Dsi-Bing-Fa* by *Sun-Dse* coined an even clearer phrase:

«Entice your adversary to come toward you; do not voluntarily go toward him ... invincibility is a matter of defense, vulnerability is a matter of attacking» (see N° 69).

A competent general excels because of his wisdom: *«To overcome the armies oft others without fighting, is the highest art»*. Daoism names war «a grievance like a surgical operation, but to rule in peace, a wise prophylaxis». Our chapter 68 as well (beside many others where we mentioned it) with its quotations from *Sun-Dse* stresses said unaggressive, unpassionate, impersonal and compassionate ‹warfare with a heart›: Following Sun-Dse, even war submits to the harmony of DE!

The *absence of anger* in physical warfare is reflected by the *absence of quarrel* in the case of the Candidate on *The Path*. This is an important principle regarding his inner self as well as for all his social interactions, the latter being just the external mirror of his inner state of being. Now, of course it is quite impossible in our world of today with its *«merciless rules of the game»*, not to be touched by any conflicts. Instead, the important thing is not to fight through this kind of litigations as do vulgar earthlings – in anger, fear and passion – nor to sneak away, cleverly or cowardly: Where a conflict gets unavoidable, there it should be solved in such a way that for all ‹participants› *the least possible pain* ensues – thus in compassion also for the most aggressive parties – and most of all, in the best possible orientation toward the gnostic Path and its sublime ideal.

The term *«servant»* (here and in N° 59), as well as such expressions as *vessel* or *tool* (N° 67) make abundantly clear, how much in those days the individual (if peasant, clerk or king) felt obliged to their overlord and to common welfare, the highest exponent of which was the Emperor – representative of the Godhead on Earth. All this shows how much sense made the position of priest-kings in eldest times, like in antique *Uruk*, where the priest-king was chosen and even inaugurated (= initiated) by the Nephillim or gods, and taught and protected (or abandoned) by them.[47]

So the old Daoism reflects some oft the original cosmic laws and their harmony, the divine «Law and Order» – that harmonious union of soul, spirit and body in the times of the first Beginning – in the Golden Age of humanity, of which – consciously, or unconsciously like a dream – a memory survives in every human, as an urging yearning of the heart, wishing to return as soon as possible into that ‹celestial›, truly divine harmony, as is the custom in today's bona-fide orders and fraternities with such slogans as *«Liberty, Brotherliness and Love»*:

By right, since high and ancient times, one names
to espouse Heaven the highest goal.

第六十九章

用兵有言：「吾不敢爲主，而爲客；不敢進寸，而退尺。」
是謂行無行；攘無臂；扔無敵；執無兵。
禍莫大于輕敵，輕敵几喪吾寶。
故抗兵相若，哀者勝矣。

69.

Regarding strategy, there is a proverb:
«Rather do not play the guest, but the host —
Rather do not advance by a finger's breadth,
but retreat by a foot's breadth»
By right one says: «Advance without marching forward —
Beat [the adversary], without moving an arm —
Throw [him], without putting up resistance —
Conquer [him] without fighting !»

There is no greater loss
than to underestimate the adversary:
To disregard the adversary, is as good as
losing one's most precious jewel.
Therefore:
Wherever warriors fight each other,
the more empathic part will certainly win.

This text again is connected to the *Art of War* by Master *Sun-Dse*. – The *Dao-De-Jing* loves pictorial language; it likes to take its images from the happenings of war. This is most understandable, assuming the *Dao-De-Jing* to address itself to a ruler in the first place, to whom military things are daily business. As is well known, most rulers were elevated in their high position because they were stout fighters, or victorious generals – as shown by *Zhuge-Liang* (se note 36), and *Hong-Wu I* (see picture on p. 35).

A cardinal element of Daoist practice is the principle of *abundance* and *emptiness*– and this on all levels, not just in war-times. Indeed *Sun-Dse* dedicated to this subject the whole *chapter six*, with many variants in the sector of *stillness and movement*. Generally speaking, one comes to the conclusion: Who *is active, empties himself* (of energy and means); who remains inactive (in *non-doing*), remains in plenitude. Who succeeds triggering others to become *active*, himself remaining in psychic, spiritual and physical composure, preserves his plenitude, but admits, or causes, the others to empty themselves.

This exactly remains the fundamental Daoist concept in all known *martial arts*: It is all about accumulating, guarding, and transforming *Ch'I,* while letting the other(s) dissipate their *Ch'I* in the process. – Who remains ‹full›, will win; – who empties himself, will lose. These principles are valid on all fields of activity – spiritual, psychic, and physical; – when fighting, or ruling, or when negotiating – and in each and every form of inter-human exchange. This also is the meaning of such expressions as regard *subordination*, and/or *«lying below»*, as repeatedly expressed along the *Dao-De-Jing*.

The same principles are taught by another book from Antiquity: It is the *Book of the Masters of Huainan – surnamed Huainan-Dse.*[48] There we read, among other (quoted by *Sun-Dse*, loc. cit., p. 20):

«If generals and officers are ill-disposed towards each other, and if discontent has established itself among the soldiers, one names this emptiness. When civil government acts intelligently, when military commanders are reliable, and when superiors and subordinates have the same focus, and when will and energy act in harmony, one can speak of plenitude. ... Smart people know how to fill their people with energy ... , whereas the incompetent ones, seeing the plenitude of others, rob the latter of their fullness».

This play of emptiness and fullness is what our N° 69 is all about. Right from start it hints at the teachings of *Sun-Dse*:

«Provoke your enemy to come towards you; don't march towards him voluntarily... ».

To leave the initiative to the adversary, but to be ready for him; – to guess his intentions without showing your own, this is the essence of inactivity. To seduce the enemy – even with trifling movements – into precarious activities, is the essence of movement. – Add to this the element of deception – not just by a deceptive attitude or by spies, but by systematically developing an unfathomable attitude.

The latter consists of these two elements: *formlessness* and *invisibility*. By *formlessness* we understand, among other, that the enemy should never be able to know, what means or movements will come up next, nor when. – *Invisibility* quite clearly is an example where the *art of warfare* joins the *philosophy of the individual Path of Dao*.

Regarding invisibility, the *Huainan-Dse* sums up:

«Concerning the arts of war it is essential that the strategy be unfathomable, that the form remain hidden, and that movements occur as a surprise, so that it is impossible to prepare for them. What enables a general to surely be victorious is his unfathomable wisdom and his way of acting that leaves no traces behind.» –

This corresponds to the renown Pythagorean text: *‹Symbola› – the «spiritual traveling money»*. – *Pythagoras* lived around 500 b.C., as probably did Lao-Dse. A complement to the former's *‹Golden Verses›*, where he says: *«When you get up from the litter, take some of it and destroy with it your image»,* reads: *«Blur the traces of your cooking pot in the ashes ».*

The *Huainan-Dse* similarly continues:

«Only what is formless remains untouched by everything. The wise hide themselves in their unfathomable self, so that their feelings elude every kind of observation. They act in what is formless, so that nothing can thwart their plans.»

This needs no further comment: The realization of ‹formlessness› will be developed and realized by every person individually – according to their natural personality. However, the fact of being *unfathomable* must not be confounded with some kind of *mysterious secretiveness* without any spiritual substance behind it!

Equally, the warning, not to underestimate one's adversary is quite appropriate for all ‹Disciples› on The Path: The forces of the ‹Great Adversary› are many; and even if they seem to come from the ‹outside›, mostly the cause of their appearance is still grounded inside of oneself – in one's Ego. Therefore here as well the wise words by *Sun-Dse* are quite advisable:

« He who knows himself and the others is never in danger: – He who does not know the others, but knows himself, will once win and once lose. – But who knows neither the others nor himself, will be in danger in each and every battle».

As a conclusion to this chapter, we need to add the following remark: The Daoist virtues are: *intelligence, credibility, courage and severity combined with humanness.* This means: *compassion* and authentic *cordiality, purity of the heart* together with *mildness and warm-heartedness* ... – in short, what popular speech names *‹Love›* – but preserving the Daoist distance. In fact this is the most desirable ‹virtue›: In it lies the sum of all that has been achieved on The Path. Therefore the Daoist adversaries don't fight *against* each other, but as the text clearly and quite literally says: *together*. The ‹rule of the play› says:

Wherever warriors are fighting together —
The more compassionate part will certainly win!

第七十章

吾言甚易知，甚易行。天下莫能知，莫能行。
言有宗，事有君。夫唯無知，是以不我知。
知我者希，則我者貴。是以聖人被褐而懷玉。

70.

[Really], my teachings are most simple to keep in mind,
and can most easily be put into practice —
[But:] Humanity is incapable to keep them in mind —
And incapable to put them into practice.

Words have a Clan —
Works have a Liege
And yet, humans lack illumination:
they simply don't understand me.
Those who have understood me are rare —
Those who follow me possess nobleness:
The truly wise wear brown cloths on their outside,
but inside they carry a jewel.

Here we are put in front of a purely spiritual text again, which is unrelated to any of the renown standard books of Daoist philosophy (*Jings*), but just simply and directly lets speak Gnosis – or rather: lets DAO itself heave a deep sigh:

«My teaching is so simple; – and so simple are the conditions for the admittance to The Path; – there is so few one really can do, and should do. – Since so many centuries and even millennia humanity listens to the Good News about the Path of self-liberation; – and still – alas! – so few put it into practice in their daily life!»

Since the laments by *prophet Hosea* in the 6th century b.C., the same exclamation resounds – and is still ignored (Ho 4:1-9):

«The Lord has to argue with the inhabitants of the land, because there is no loyalty nor love what so ever, and no knowledge of God is in this land ... – But no-one should quarrel, and no-one shall scold! My people imitate you, you priests. ... My people will be annihilated, because it completely lacks knowledge! ...».

Luther translates the same text even sharper and more precise, writing: «My people is doomed, because they are too lazy to learn!». And the prophesies of the Maya Priests around the year of 1541, say: *«The princes of these people will be captured, because they are without any reason».*

In that far-off past, the same complaint was directed at the priests in their temples only: it was they only who (besides a few privileged persons mostly not including the biblical kings) possessed the esoteric knowledge. – In today's world with its ignorant humankind, not just the priests of the temples alienate knowledge from Humanity, but also the ‹priests› of scientific laboratories within Universities. The representatives of the deeply enrooted centers of political and economic power – and even of elementary schools – define and decide what the Masses should be allowed to know: The slogan by *Machiavelli*: «*Good is what* serves the state» (hence: the government) is actual today more than ever before!

Princes and kings of Antiquity and the Middle-Ages, including the *Medici* of Italian Renaissance, made it their merit to have men of letters visiting their courts.They even kept them as permanent counselors. – In our 21st century instead, a semi-political group named PEN-Club mulls over the question: «*Is literature useful to the State?*»!!

But let us come back to said *ignorance* relative to DAO – in the past and today..

«*Words have a Clan*», *says Lao-Dse* with the voice of Gnosis, and with this he means, among other things, «*One word seldom comes alone*! – Words are embedded in other words; meanings are embedded in other meanings – and all of this is embedded in the background of our world. – «*Works have a Liege* »: someone who commands what must be done, or who allows for what is done, controlling, monitoring, dominating and (in the better case) accounting for these doings. The Liege of the Candidate on The Path, is his New Will controlling him so that he shall use his speech conscientiously and sparsely, and premeditate his actions: Words are a form of energy, just as are deeds. – And so is every unspoken word and even every thought. Hence, it is not as a proverb lightly says: «*Thoughts are free*»![49]

Thus, that people – today as in the past – *don't understand* the teachings of DAO, is not due to the latter's complexity, really: Besides the forces opposing the expansion of the «*Good Tidings*» time and again – this lack of comprehension – it comes from the fact that humanity, since childhood, is trained to believe only complicated and difficult things to be of high value. – The wisdom of Daoism and Gnosis instead is simple, teaching the exact contrary, namely:

To become «*still before the Lord*»; – to keep in check one's thoughts; to well poise one's words and to minimize one's doings in the sense of non-interference and without agitation; – to become ‹unfathomable, ‹formless› and so to speak invisible; «to blur one's traces»; – in short: to ‹diminish ever more› in one's entire existence, and to *let happen* one's effectiveness more and more on a higher level. The ego-will, trained since childhood as it were, is to become as small as possible; – materially oriented and incessantly changing worldly ‹knowledge› needs to be «forgotten» as such, and to be subordinated to lively and spiritual norms unchanged since the beginning of times..

All this will of course have consequences for the existence of a person: Various changes will come into his daily life. And so the Candidate sees himself confronted with a *fundamental question*: Will he choose, for the rest of his earthly existence, to dedicate his whole inner attention and all efforts to *The Path*? – Will he really want to quit his accustomed ‹zone of comfort›, and confide his further existence to this new and very different way of life? Is he – is she – ready to *let happen* for themselves the changes connected to them, and to *consciously cooperate* with them?

Not many who say YES here, are ready to remain with this YES across all impediments: *This is the loyalty* Hosea is speaking of in his lament! – And Gnosis, through the speech of *Lao-Dse*, agrees, regretting that so few humans really comprehend her, and follow Him – the One Spirit. – But some of them *«have nobleness»*!

However, this now is no nobleness as the World applauds it, but a nobleness modest, silent and unobtrusive – *formless, invisible, traceless.* In modern Gnosis we therefore speak of *nobleness of the soul* – and of the *splendor of the soul newly born in* GNOSIS – *in* DAO – *out of the «living waters of God's river»* that John mentions in Jo 3:3-7.

These few then are not wearing any magnificently adorned robe of silk, as did the nobleness and clerks at the time of *Lao-Dse*, (see picture on p. 11). They wear indeed a shining robe: the ‹new robe of the soul›; – but this is seen by only a few: For all others' eyes, they wear a meek brown cloak like ordinary peasants, citizens and servants. In their heart however they carry – fully blossomed out – their flower of the soul: The ‹Rose›, the ‹Lotus›, the wondrous ‹blossom of the heart›, and whatever all the many names may be – depending on the denomination of *The Path*, throughout the World:

In their heart they carry a jewel!

A SMALL SELECTION OF TEXT VARIANTS OF N° 71 [50]

VARIANT WANG-BI :

知不知上，不知知病。
夫唯病病，是以不病。
聖人不病，以其病病。
夫唯病病，是以不病。

Variant MAWANG-DUI (Text B, all there is)

知不知尚矣 不知不知病矣
是以聖人之不□也以亓病= 也是以不病

VARIANT OF THE ‹BASIC TEXT›

知不知，上，不知不知，病。
聖人不病，以其病病，是以不病。

etc.

OUR BASIC TEXT (‹ORIGINAL›):

第七十一章

知不知，尚矣；不知知，病也。聖人不病，以其病病。
夫唯病病，是以不病。

71.

BEST KNOWN VERSIONS COMBINED

To know that one knows not, is commendable —
To ignore what one knows is a bad illness.
Only a person who suffers from his illness is not ill.
The Wise is not ill; for he suffers from his illness —
Only such persons suffer from this illness, as think they are not ill.

THE MOST OCCURRING CHINESE VARIANTS COMBINED

To know that one knows not, and moreover
to ignore what one knows, is a bad suffering.
Only humans suffer from [this] suffering, but this is no illness.
The Wise does not suffer – He considers suffering to be an illness.
People only are the illness —
The illness [itself] is not the illness.

VARIANTS OF THE PRESENT EDITOR, COMBINED

«To know without knowing» is the highest superiority —
To be unconscious of what one knows is a bad nuisance.
However, humans suffer from an illness: they don't suffer of.
The Wise does not suffer any pain —
he suffers with those who suffer.
Only humans suffer pain; [but] this is no illness.

The inserted titles dividing some of the different originals of this ‹verse› indicate it already: there are many manuscripts of this verse, and the possible interpretations to this short and apparently so obvious text are innumerous. Besides several hundred versions in western idioms (of which we have integrated here more than a dozen) the Internet offers no less than 2"110'000 results in Chinese: It suffices to enter only the first little sequence of four glyphs; and all of them are related to this same text!

At last, the basic text is quite clear: The ignorance commented in the previous chapter resembles an *evil illness* – a big evil suffering. But the cause and the effects – conscious or unconscious suffering – are different.

The best known quotation is this: *«I know that I know nothing»*, ascribed – *for sure erroneously* – to *Sokrátès*. This reception of the text would cement the notorious *complex of indignity*, originating from false pietism: Not even the dumbest human knows *nothing*; – but all human knowledge is just half-wit hidden under half-knowledge.

Current translators certainly err when they affirm that the text really means: *«to recognize one's lack of knowledge is the highest»*, when in fact that is rather the basis to real *learning*, and therefore, in the sense of the text, for *new knowledge*. The particle 知 that shows a certain kinship with the glyphs 大, 夫 and 天 – *greatness, Man,* and *God*, has numerous significations: *to announce, to inform* and *to be informed; to learn, to experience, to comprehend, to be able to, to know; knowledge, intelligence, intellect, comprehension, etc.* – Its part 失 alone means *to renounce*. One might, thus, almost ‹read› 知 as: *«to dispense with the writing tablet»*.

This little analysis is no academic play with words! Its *secondary aim* is *to familiarize our lector with the polyvalence and flexibility* of Chinese ‹writing›, thus explaining the rich fertility of the Chinese language – and thereby that of the *Dao-De-Jing*. Its *main goal* however is the stimulation to meditate about what a profound complex of conceptions, emotions and impressions beyond sensual experience can be seized with the sole term of *«to know»*.

So many meanings there are, yet not just in the western sense of a *choice* from which to pick one, but as a multilayered *floating whole* that can change its main weight – depending of which aspects out of the present summation of those in any way accessible to the reader, are preferable in an actual moment. – Yes, the *Dao-De-Jing* is really a *classical sacred scripture!*

This makes understandable why certain interpretations occur only in the West (e.g. with an ascetical judgment) – and others only in China (without a judgment). – Just one single variant adds something fundamentally different here; – something that has a specific importance for Daoism; – and this leads again back to *Sun-Dse* and his teachings about strategies, *embracing all domains of human existence*, as has been pointed out before. This *‹Sun-Dse* *variant* has therefore been integrated into the new, third translation of those published here and now.

The *passages printed in blue* are the alterable parts; the ones in *red* hint at an esthetic parallelism – probably by a copyist – where the silent meanings *«very»,* and *«most»,* has been replaced by the repeated glyph 矣 – an emphasizing particle at the end of the phrase.

This again allows a specific remark: *To speak* pure Mandarin Chinese is *difficult* even for a Chinese who has grown up with a different dialect than Mandarin. The slightest little variant in tone or pronunciation changes the signification. Thus already here, only who possesses the *same vocabulary* as the speaking person can understand the latter. This makes reading the rich texts of Antique Chinese difficult even for modern autochthone Chinese! But it changes when *reading* Chinese, as soon as one drops the thought of confronting something quite un-understandable: The glyphs have their *signification*, their *inner, psycho-logical meaning* – and whoever has enough empathy to do so will find access ... – *in their own language*! – This makes that Chinese writing approaches *Egyptian hieroglyphs*; but the latter are already bound more closely to specific *phonetic values*, and therefore are less versatile than Chinese glyphs. In Chinese, *to know* and *to ignore*, *to learn* and *to discern* are therefore most closely linked to this versatility and polyvalence in general – and with the multi-level purposes of the *Dao-De-Jing* in particular.

Now, in order to enter the many possible interpretations of this short text, let us first look at the combination pulled from the *reasonable western versions*. It is a selection, for many of these versions often are not even logical in themselves; despite containing many poetic garlands. Chinese instead is always sober and clear.

The main purpose from a western perspective is well known: Man should become conscious that ignorance is an illness, lest he must be named *completely ill*. Obviously, the first ‹medicine› to cure this illness is *self-consciousness*, and as a consequence, *humility*. In this case it seems logical that the *‹Wise›* is a non-ill person, because he is so *conscious* of the limitations of all human knowledge – and because he therefore consciously suffers from the illness of ignorance, as this variant wants it, – at least for the western way of thinking. For the Daoist way of thinking however, this understanding is only partially correct:

The philosophy of a Daoist is strictly objective. He does not judge, and therefore has *no emotion* when confronted to a lack (*emptiness*) or ‹culmination› (plenitude) – nor does the Wise suffer pain because of his *partial ignorance*. The western comment about the Wise is evaluated in a typical western way, but for the Daoist, *illness* and *egocentric, self-related suffering* is but a *Reality* (and therefore an illusion) – and yet truths and realties are quite different things!

«Heaven and Earth are not benevolent: they regard the 10'000 things as straw-dogs. – The Wise are not benevolent, they regard humans as straw-dogs», says N° 5 of the *Dao-De-Jing.*

This image relates to the fact that following ancient tradition, in China *living dogs* were sacrificed, but in later times there were only sacrificed *straw puppets of dogs*. – Hence: Looking at the whole Universe, humans without knowledge about DAO are not comparable to *stray dogs*, as one western version of N° 5 wants it, but they really are nothing but *straw dogs* – inanimate straw puppets, just worth to be burned!

N° 76 emphasizes this conception again, as there all dried-up things are associated to Death. – It is significant that – in China as in the West – as ‹civilization› advanced, erstwhile *sacred animals* became the feed of *profane humans* – In China even today young dogs are deemed a delicacy, precisely as lambs in Near East and in Europe. The difference is determined only by the subjective assessment about what is ‹normal›, ‹moral›, or ‹human›.

After these western versions of N° 71; let's see the Chinese view:

As mentioned earlier, the Chinese commentaries as well differ greatly from each other. Even the ‹pseudo-Socratic› version can be found there. The ‹combined Chinese version› coalesces some 40 variants. – It intentionally prefers the ‹Daoist paradoxon›: *«To know that one does not-know,* and in the meantime *to ignore what one knows»* is, on one side, the same as the western ascetic variant. But it can be related also to persons who find themselves embarrassed with *insufficient information* about a subject, but on the other hand have doubts about *available information*. This is the case when – following *Sun-Dse* – one knows neither one-self nor the other, so that one is *inevitably doomed* to fail completely and lose the battle.

As for suffering, illness and being ill, it is necessary to be conscious of the fact that *«humans»* or *«people»* in the present context mean the *‹Masses›*, the *‹Sheeple›*: those who increasingly having become dull and with averted eyes, obtusely pass by whatever their daily material life calls *unimportant*. Stately economy, educational institutes and the mass-media have captured and fashioned these people, and fettered them like flies wrapped up in a spider-net: Numb as they are, they not even realize when the spider returns once more to suck its bounty – a really dramatic state of things, indeed!

Especially those humans suffer from an almost incurable illness. But also those who *believe* they are not ill, and who therefore *don't suffer consciously,* have this illness that is no illness in the common understanding: *«The illness it self is no illness; – people alone are the illness!»*, says today's Chinese Daoist. This statement as well should be deeply meditated.

So the ‹Wise› can come to the conclusion that he is summoned to intervene here and to cure those patients, without being affected by this illness: *«He treats the suffering like an illness»*. – How does he do that? – He does it by trying to make humans attentive to the desperate situation in which they find themselves; – by handing over to people the means to attain a deep insight; – by trying to show them a picture of that Other Path that can lead them from their deadly illness toward healing and recovery. It is the situation of the ‹Preacher in the Desert› – from Buddha and ancient Egyptian Saints of the desert and John the Baptist crying in the wilderness, down to our present time: Each of them went out to show people the *Path towards Life – DAO* – the CHRIST: Didn't He as well say: *«I am The Path»*?

But today as in all times the answer resounds from the street: «We don't want this one! – this one can't be Him! – Not this one, no! – We want Bar-abbas!»[50-A]

Yes, the pain suffered by the witnesses for The Light is a great one! – And yet they remain faithful to their message – to their testimony, to their sacrifice: *«I know I (i.e. my Ego) can't do anything; – and yet I continue!»*. – This as well, by the way, is a neo-Chinese interpretation to the first sequence of this text in N° 71. –

And so we come to the third – to the mitigating version as proposed by the present editor.

The basis for the first line corresponds to the formula in N° 64: *To will without willing*: 欲不欲 – and *to know without learning*: 學不學 – as parallels to N° 63: *To do by non-doing:* 為無為.

It is not possible here to conclusively comment the difference between the two glyphs 不 and 無. This is just about gaining, as well as possible, a Daoist comprehension of this text – namely:

To know without knowing is to say, as an alternative, that one does not stick infinitely to some kind of knowledge, but one is to remain open for any new understanding : *«Know as if you didn't know anything»*; – namely, as if this were *not your* knowledge; – This means the same as that you should possess as if you did not posses *anything at all* (Bœhme, Gichtel[51]). – *Will without binding yourself to your will.* – Always will in a state of flowing adaptation to changing conditions and effects: Thus is the postulate of *Sun-Dse* regarding ‹formlessness› with respect to your *microcosmos*!

So far – so good and classical; – but there is still the announced *‹Sun-Dse-Variant›*. It goes like this: *To know without having been informed* – or also: *without having learned or experienced*:

«(He can) see what others can't see, and know what others don't get to know ... – To feel and to understand when one has acted, is not worth to be named insight; – to achieve anything after having strived for it, is not worth to be named an achievement; – to know anything after having learnt about it, is not worth to be named knowledge.

«Really: To be able to act on something before it has happened; – to foresee something before it becomes active; – to see something before it manifests itself – these are three abilities who develop in close relation of each other. Then nothing is anticipated, but it is understood by insight; nothing is carried out without a result; – and one does not go anywhere without a profitable outcome.» – That's what Sun-Dse has to say about what makes an excellent general.

The dimension that gives to this text its force and its liveliness is the fact that it is deeply embedded in the Daoistic basic mentality of *openness, perviousness* and *formlessness*. – *And all this together in one, is really «the Highest»*!

Equally unlucky as *not* to know how much one *doesn't know*, is not to know what one *does know* – i.e. what one can rely on as a firm belief on the basis of an unshakable *faith through experience*, without firsthand *«having slid the hand into the wound»*. That is why the word of Jesus: *«Hallowed are those who have not seen, and yet do believe!»* (Jo 20:29) doesn't have the least dogmatic touch, but is an encouragement to open oneself in perviousness and intuitiveness (from lat. *intuere – to contemplate and see*) meaning *higher wisdom* – i.e. knowledge *higher than all knowledge and all reason* – and thus also really *to know what one knows.*

The ‹illness› of humans as was already emphasized, lies in that *they don't suffer* from their complete ignorance. – But what about the Wise? – He suffers (says the text), but he does not suffer pain because of *his own* partial ignorance (for this is a neutral fact to him). No, full of pain out of *compassion* he contemplates Humanity reeling from one pain to the next because of their ignorance, *without learning* anything from it (Luther); – and he also suffers from this pain of the others – *«knowing through compassion – the innocent fool ... ».*

Understood this way as well, the ‹Wise› – he who has already progressed on *The Path* –is not ill himself: Indeed, he suffers from the pain of others. In such instances, compassion of ordinary people is usually some kind of *personal emotion*. – The Wise instead suffers *differently* – from a pain *not binding him* to specific persons, but by which through a charitable sacrifice he binds himself to the *Karma of the World*: He suffers as its impersonal servant – as servant of the Great Universal Work of spiritual evolution of *all creatures*! Feeling since long to be one with the Universe and its Creator, he binds himself in his union with Humanity. – And by sacrificing himself in this way, he also contributes to connect humanity with the One Universal divine Plan – albeit ‹Humanity› itself is incapable of recognizing him doing so; but if they could, they would *refuse* to acknowledge it as a factual truth.

So, a few aspects of the inner content of this text could be shown – but by far not all; for the true depth of it cannot be declared – and hardly even be fully appreciated. DAO, the *«Mother of the 10'000 things* who can be described, *is not really* DAO, but just a reflection of IT. Blessed is he who can *«see Her who can not be seen»* – like the seer in the biblical *Revelation* (Rev. 21:11):

Her reflection of The Light was like a very precious stone — like a shining jewel of jade ... !

德

第七十二章

民不畏威，則大威至。
無狎其所居，無厭其所生。夫唯不厭，是以不厭。
是以聖人自知不自見；自愛不自貴。故去彼取此。

72.

When people don't fear the head powers,
the greatest violence will ensue from it, for sure.
Don't penetrate into their homestead —
Don't disdain their way of life —
then they will not disdain to do what is right.
The truly Wise knows himself without being ashamed —
He loves himself without overestimating himself —
Therefore he quits his closest friends — and choses This.

This text is – exoterically speaking – again addressed to the ‹wise ruler› who, in order to fully enjoy his protectorate in peace, and free of problems, can be uncompromising to the point of cruelty – but also goodhearted and generous to the point of motherliness (see N° 59). This motherliness however must stop as soon as the people stop respecting the administration they have been given.

But this again can have two reasons: Or the ruler or his clerks have omitted to follow the *DE* of wise government, bleeding the people white, or demanding too many privileges for themselves; – or they lead a life provoking the people; – or the people have been stirred up by some agitators (see N° 57); – and from this kind of unrest there usually ensues *«greatest violence»* for all!

In the sense of farsighted government (see N° 64), the ruler is – in all these cases – admonished not to harass people in their most intimate environment, and also to respect their working and their other ways of life. A variant to the second line would also be: *«... the law is the imperious power»:*

Instead of promptly revenging himself with retaliations against people's eventually righteous rebelliousness, the ruler is well counseled to solely keep following the *imperial law*. Also, he is invited to take counsel with himself and ask himself if not *he himself* is triggering this insurgence by vexing or offending the people. Using this as an exercise in self-knowledge and self-control, it will be quite possible for him to correct his imperfections, or – if he is culpable of none of that – to reinstall the good order with self-assurance, but in good measure and without any kind of haughtiness nor self-aggrandizement. —

What does this mean again in analogy to the individual journey of a person on his or her *Path of DAO*? We have earlier compared ‹the people› to the totality of imaginations and movements of the earthly personality – and the ‹ruler› to the newly acquired consciousness and new will of the new ‹celestial› personality. When the people disregard this higher authority – this means that the old beast-like human has gotten the upper hand of the pupil, or at least tries to do so. Now the new consciousness and the new will are called for: Will they be able to restore the good order, without sparking a civil war – an inner crisis?

The fundamental element at the beginning of the Path is, so we said, *new insight* into every occurrence in the world and inside the Candidate himself, along with his firm determination to «let wane» the old, earthly personality, as says the Universal Doctrine. This waning of the old personality, the new way of thinking and the new will, may not forcibly perpetrate onto the ‹people›: By forceful actions or by repressing natural desires, the people – old habits – would be overpowered, vexed, and harassed in their intimate surroundings: Too stern a self-criticism, or even self-punishment, will hamper the process more than some liberality. The effect would be extremely serious: The ‹people› would dodge ‹into the underground›, would swear vengeance in secret reunions, and organize retaliations. And then, «one red day», when the ruler is the least ready for it, the outwardly wonderful order breaks down; the people *«shake off their fetters»*: The new ruler falls … —

Now, the thing needs not always to play out in such a catastrophic way. – But the truth is that purification of the personality with all its low impulses (thoughts, words, deeds) along with consequent pursuing of the Path following the laws of the Universal Doctrine cannot be achieved through tough discipline, nor through external reinforcement. The only way is to learn reasonable self-domination, and, by *sympathetically « observing what is happening inside»*, and to ‹un-learn› what is undesired (se N° 77).

This is the phase where the personality is not *educated* and *cultivated* anymore like during the phase of *purification*, but where in a self-enhancing process it is *reduced to a physiological minimum* and replaced by a wholly new ‹celestial› personality: It is the phase of renewal, followed by the phase of transformation and topped by the transmutation of worldly Man into an earthly ‹Son of the Heaven› – into a spiritual emperor!

But even the ‹prince regent› – the Candidate who with a *purified heart* and a *«new soul»* is preparing for his *spiritual birth – for his definite union with The Spirit*, and for subsequent *Transmutation and Transfiguration* – he as well will soon begin to rule the way he would want to do it if he were already a *Son of the Heaven*. Therefore he controls himself with great severity – that is the high-strung self-discipline as is demanded for the serious Candidate – and with the greatest possible indulgence in the same time.

Not subjugating the *primitive instincts* by force, but letting them dissolve through *higher insight and awareness,* and thus leaving them behind, he trains his *new demeanor* and thus makes it authentically his own. He lets happen what comes to pass, and his ‹people› are content and *«get rich»*. So he may – as says chapter N° 59 – rejoice at the constant growth and well-being of the new kingdom – the kingdom *«not of this world»*, inside of himself!

Continually deepening his understanding of everything – but without tormenting himself (thus also without any pietistic complex of inferiority); – loving himself – but without becoming careless (hence also without new bad habits nor artificial self-control); – and least of all with the illusion to have already accomplished everything and being already a real ‹Saint›: This is how he rules his inner ‹kingdom›. So many of those who had already ascended high and far, fell back again and into death: There are not just those who have been *called late* , but also those who have *fallen late*!

In wisdom, and – like in N° 59 – *«living many years and with growing success, he follows DAO»*. This is indeed the only thing a Candidate on his Path *can, and should, do*. – But this sole thing embraces the Universe!

Thus following DAO – now as a Disciple and Master, maybe even as an Apostle, but ever remaining a Pupil – learning, striving and teaching – he more and more leaves behind the matters of ‹ordinary people›; for his ‹clerks› have since long fully accepted his way of ruling his kingdom; – and so he goes on and on – towards the Good End, until being allowed to enter the realm of divine rest and peace.

So he leaves behind those — and attains This!

德

第七十三章

勇于敢則殺，勇于不敢則活。此兩者，或利或害。天之所惡，孰知其故？
天之道，不爭而善勝，不言而善應，不召而自來，□然而善謀。
天網恢恢，疏而不失。

73.

Courageously to dare, entails death —
Courageously not to dare, entails survival:
So both have sometimes advantages, and sometimes disadvantages:

Heaven is cruel – Who knows why?
Heaven as a directing principle:
Do not rebel, but do overcome leniently —
Do not eloquently oppose, but do humbly accept —
Do not conjure IT, but follow IT. —
At all events, bow down, and imperturbably find a solution.

The all-embracing net of Heaven is lose and floppy —
but it does not miss nor neglect anything.

In one of the first chapters of this book we mentioned the code of honor of the old Samurai – the so-called *Knights of Antique China*. This code demands that fulfilling one's mission one should at any rate seek to die: *«To die while fulfilling one's mission is an honor; Not to fulfill ones mission and to stay alive is a shame»* – says the *Hagakuré.*[52] – Thus *« to dare courageously» with great probability entailed death*; – but not to dare, mostly as well!

One anecdote mentioned in *Sun-Dse's* teachings about strategies shows how risky it was, to survive: In one battle an entire Brigade fell to the last man. The general, having fought to the end and returning home as the sole survivor, barely escaped the dead-sentence for ‹illoyality› to the troops.

The *Dao-De-Jing* however advances another meaning, and also promptly explains what its point is: Who lives, undergoes all possible blows of fate, pains and losses, as earthly life brings them: This is the disadvantage of *survival.* To die means to lose ones life with all the comforts earthly life entails, but on the other hand, sufferings and pains have an end (for some time at least). – While our author stresses the painful parts of dying as well as for survival, he takes up the desperate cry of so many people lacking spiritual insight: *«Oh cruel heavens! – How can you allow all this distress?»*

The answer comes immediately, and in quite understandable a form: There is a universal law that functions as an unshakable principle of conduct for whatever happens throughout the World: This law – this universal arrangement – determines what can occur to whom and when and under what conditions. All beings except humans are subject to these happenings without much of a chance to *choose* their reactions. *Humans alone* are given – within the limits of their individual possibilities – the free *choice and free will* to confront all occurrences «allotted to them» – their fate, as it were – one way or another: Will they just passively endure all of it, loudly complaining, or meekly resigning as martyrs? – Or will they realize such incidents as new chances to *actively participate* in shaping their lives – be it by positively tuning in, be it by refuting or even fighting them (and thus most certainly succumbing)? – The latter is what we know as being called: *«to brave destiny»*. – Both ways principally result in the same final acknowledgment: The total sum of all pains remains the same, but the lessons change!

The *Dao-De-Jing* now teaches us: *«Do not oppose your destiny – do not resist it – do not squander your energies complaining and loathing – neither try to evoke a different destiny for yourself. – For, even if you would succeed, the actual test or lesson is not yet passed, but only postponed»*. – Therefore, the Candidate is given the recommendation: *«Overcome all tribulations indulgently. – Be a humble vanquisher. – Try to understand the utility of every adversity, and accept it in a positive mood. – Don't make things worse than what they rally are, like by teaming up with magical forces and powers whom sooner or later you will have to pay back ‹to the last cent›, no mercy granted! –*

«Learn to learn by following your destiny in positive adaptation and cooperation – even if this should entail your physical death: Every experience has the same value; every adventure is part of the entire treasure of experiences your microcosmos needs to collect in order to become perfect, and in an appropriate moment to make use of; – be it in this present lifetime, or in a later one!

«Nothing can happen without a corresponding cause; – every cause will as an effect bounce back to its creator: Sooner or later; in this present life or in a later one! What ever the life of a human may bring to him or her – everything is the result of some previous thought, word or deed sowed consciously or not!»

At such a ‹verdict from Heaven›, most people would shake their heads disapprovingly and at loss: All too strange are these teachings to them. – All too deeply imprinted into their understanding of the World are the modern materialistic theses of Anti-science, and of the powers of this World serving them. But in Ancient China as well things may have been in no better shape. At those times as well a person hearing above suggestions might have answered:

«But how about all the injustice and cruelty of Destiny who favors the ones, while tormenting the others? The ones grow up in welfare, healthiness and glory, enjoying every possible ease without an effort. Even those are eased and fostered by Fate, who have seized for themselves – officially or clandestinely – numerous advantages, by using shady tricks and even criminal activities – and moreover by causing bloodshed! – Others live in poverty, oppression and illness, from the cradle unto the coffin. And whenever they try with all their forces to change their Fate, , their load still keeps growing! – What do you say now, you clever teacher?»

The latter's solace is clear and sound, as he shows that said *«fundamental principle of Heaven»*, based on which humans undergo trials and temptations, also sends ‹rewards› and ‹penalties› as each one has ‹earnt› them – according to how he has lived his life. Today, this fundamental principle is known in the West as the *Law of Karma*, and feared by many: Most people attribute every lenient experience to their own *virtues*, but all nuisances to some *«blow of Destiny»*.

But Karma is no human who gives and takes. Karma is Egyptian *Maat*, Persian *Asha*, stabilizing the equilibrium of the whole Universe: Even the weight of just a *little down feather* impacts the balance: Will the latter be equalized at a life's end? The total sum of all causes must *to a hair* have the same weight as the grand total of all effects.; – and Karma equalizes all with Love: If *a little down feather* suffices to do so, this soul is saved! – The slightest thought moves the balance of *Maat* : *«Not one hair falls from your head, without the Universe trembling»*: *ASHA – MAAT – KARMA – DAO – GOD* … ‹knows›!

«The Law of DAO is like a net», says the author of *Dao-De-Jing*. This net knows neither time nor space. Its sole measure is Eternity: *«There is nothing it will miss, and nothing that will escape it»*. At the *«End of Days»*, everything will be equalized. So, the Wise strives at creating no causes anymore, so that his *Karma* may become perfect *during his or her present lifetime* – thanks to the help of Karma itself – the *Law of Love*. Thus, he bows in the typically Chinese way, as Its awed and thankful servant:

Heaven's all-embracing net does not miss nor neglect anything!

民不畏死，奈何以死懼之。

若使民常畏死，而為奇者，
吾得執而殺之，孰敢。

常有司殺者殺。
夫代司殺者殺，是謂代大匠斲。
夫代大匠斲者，希有不傷其手矣。

第七十四章

民不畏死，奈何以死懼之？若使民常畏死，而爲奇者，
吾得執而殺之，孰敢？
常有司殺者殺。夫代司殺者殺，是謂代大匠斲，
夫代大匠斲者，希有不傷其手矣。

74.

When people don't fear death anymore —
how can one teach them to fear death again?
Supposed, people fear death as usually they do,
but, given a criminal case, I am obliged to catch and kill him —
Who dares to do so?

Normally there is a public office
inflicting the capital penalty on a human. —

When a person replaces the public officer for death-sentences,
this is exactly the same as
replacing a master woodcutter.
When a person replaces a master woodcutter,
it hardly occurs that he does not get bloody hands.

Only few can be said about this bloody chapter in connection with, and leading to, the flourishing lands of Gnostics' spiritual efforts:

A science engaged with life in all its forms as it were, but the adherents of which in the course of centuries more than one time have been persecuted with fire and sword until almost being extinct, would rather shirk this sad chapter of human existence. – But that's too difficult; and in Ancient China it was certainly more difficult than in today's Europe.

In fact, the death sentence is still rather widely in use – in Occident as well as in Orient. Even the European States have rather late stopped all kinds of executions as well as ‹member-punishments› – cutting off of ears, noses, hands and other members. – Particularly in China – and even more under today's Chinese occupation of Tibet – both kinds are still in sway – without mentioning secret torturing methods throughout the World. – And it is only just to mention that several social attitudes throughout modern ‹civilized nations› are quite similar to torturing: from *‹harassing›* and *‹lobbying›* in economy and industry, down to the straight jacket in modern psychiatry and other stately establishments. – But let's return to China!

«The Chinese Empress Wu-Hen ordered all women she had banned in 683, to have hacked off their hands before bereaving them of their lives», as narrates an article about this question, where especially

Russia and France, but also Tartary, Turkey and Egypt play a sad role – hence, cultures who partly in time, partly by their racial roots were or are related to ancient China. Said official research had indeed been sparked by the last line of the present text, with the riddle: *«Is this a ‹bloody hand› by the bloody crime itself, or by the blood of the punishment?»* – The text admits more than one understanding:

On one side, the ruler sees himself confronted with all possible small or big crimes – from simple theft over offense against His Majesty (like unsheathing the sword *in the presence of the ruler*) downright to capital delicts and their official punishment by the public office installed to this purpose.

On the other hand, the ‹wise ruler› – hence the one who follows the Path of DAO – sees himself confronted with the new bloodshed and blood-guilt ensuing from the bloody punishment – be it the hand of the executioner himself, be it the king's – by proxy, as he gives the order. But the *«master-woodcutter»* who according to the universal cosmic law is to *cut down humans*, is ‹Death› Himself. That's why everyone who usurps for himself the right to pronounce a death sentence, gets ‹bloody hands› as well.

With this, the text arrives at the second level, namely the question: What is the attitude of the ‹Wise› – of the Disciple of DAO – regarding the blood sentence? – Does he choose a position on the usual humanistic plane – thus lean to the self-evident protest? – Or will he profit from this question to *deepen his self-consciousness*?

The passages in the original of *Wang-Bi*, here printed in blue, do not exist in the *third text*. They seem to be an insertion by some copyist who interrupts the straight line of *Lao-Dse*'s words by replying in the form of a juristic question, like:

«All this is quite nice and good; – but tell me if you please: how do you see this in practice regarding punishment for crimes that have, since time immemorial, been punished by member-punishment?» – And what is your opinion with regard to physical punishment of any kind and in general? – Where would we go if we would abolish all those existing laws?»

With this question, the seemingly simple, concrete consideration and justification of harsh penal sentences that we thought to be limited to our ordinary every-day's life as simple earthlings, is at once raised to the spiritual plane again: On one side, the penal justice who postulates:

«When humans think they are allowed to play the ‹woodcutter out of personal authority›, so to speak, then the official stately powers are summoned who – as a master-woodcutter – represent the interests of the land, and thus reinstate order». – On the other side, we see the Daoist who raises the same question to *a higher level*, saying: *«Fundamentally, no human can claim the right to hurt others – be it ‹only› by hacking off a hand, or be it to the death. – All this is against cosmic laws: "Thou shalt not kill!" – and full-stop».*

Is that all we can profit from this text? – Not if, as a didactic problem, we raise it *to the third level*: that of deep individual self-knowledge:

1° There lives no human – bei it a male or a female – who didn't in an earlier culture or lifetime have «the hand at the hilt»: as a brigand, as a soldier, as a clerk payed for killing, as a sniper, priest or torturer. Considered in the context of the eternal, all-embracing net of Karma, ALL OF US ARE MURDERERS, THIEVES AND BANDITS ! –

2° We still are that today – and be it only in our thoughts, or in an impulsion of a fraction of a second; – indeed, even when we just have a hostile wish or whim in the context of today's economy, politics and society – or finally, as the most ‹cultivated› carnivore ... – yes, even today ! – How extremely disquieting !

Who wants to be honest against himself, cannot claim this self-reproach to be completely devious relative to him or to her. – Oh yes indeed: the street is long that leads to being a Saint who – really and *in every situation – «couldn't hurt a fly»* – except a human were really above every kind of offence, anger, revenge, judgment, instinct for survival a.s.f. *at every moment*, too !
Why are millions of humans gazing on a TV-screen – or even just in their thoughts or dreams look at all those bloody images? – Why does a human who without any moral conditioning *immediately before* a bull-fight enters the arena, feels some creepy *«I-don't-know-what»*? – Indeed – *what is this ?!*

And why would most humans refuse to put themselves such awkward questions, instead of facing them – let alone getting themselves into a situation where the thing becomes palpably concrete? Fright and trembling are the fruit of ‹earlier› experience: Is every human hand wet with blood? – To any Gnostic a simple fact ! — Oh-yes:

«Blood is a very special sap !»

錦繡中華之一頁　　　裴明龍編

第七十五章

民之飢，以其上食稅之多，是以飢。
民之難治，以其上之有爲，是以難治。
民之輕死，以其上求生之厚，是以輕死。
夫唯無以生爲者，是賢于貴生。

75.

People starve
when their regent levies too many taxes; —
then they starve.
People cannot be ruled,
when their regent treats them as merchandise; —
then the people cannot be ruled.
People take dying easy, when the ruler demands
that they live scarcely, while he lives in abundance; —
then they take dying easy.
Only a man who refuses to treat life as a merchandise
is worth being named a nobleman.

The last sentence of his text lets us suppose that it was written down under the impression of Confucianism. The latter was, as is well known, rather materialistically minded, even if some Daoist elements are contained in it: A great number of Daoist people were executed at the command of Gung-Fu-Dse. – But let us begin with the beginning of this verse N° 75!

This is again a teaching addressed to the ruler of the country, but this time clearly with as a background a *humanistic influence* at a time when serfdom and slavery of entire populations were greatly in vogue, as we remember from the slavery during the colonialist era: The Spaniards since 1492, the English during 18th and 19th centuries' India, the Dutch and French in Africa are the extremes. But until today, European and Chinese, French, Swiss and German companies continue their clandestine slavery in mines, factories and farms (shoos, cocoa, textiles, electronics etc.), while in a most cynical and hypocritical way, disdaining human usages and lives.

During the ‹best› times of world-wide slavery, hence from Antiquity to the late Middle-Ages, some slaves lead a better life than the autochthonous population: comfortably, in dignity, and possibly being promoted even to highest offices (like as Viziers and secretaries of the Kaliphate, as generals, or as trustees of big trading companies).

The same goes for Ancient China. When a lord or ruler did not fulfill these obligations, he was stripped of the power he had received from Heaven. Then, the people had the right to rebel against him, and even to overthrow him. – In Ancient Rome, expressions like *familia*, or *famulus* included the slaves who could even be adopted by their patrician master.

So, the great Ming Dynasty was founded by a simple ex-slave. — However, we know how much pressure is needed until a people of basically peaceful peasants rises in a revolt: They are the best to know that it is often preferable to gain small wages for great work, than to lose everything all together. But once this force breaks lose, it is very difficult to contain it again. The myth of the foundation of the Swiss Confederation is a model for this case.

With this background, N° 75 of the *Dao-De-Jing* gets quite alive: As opposed to N° 57 (the Prince of *non-doing*), N° 60 (frying fish›), or N° 66 (the popular ruler) here the element of *moderation* is featured. We need to remember that the regent of a province – in antique Rome as well as in ancient China – saw his office as a sinecure, off which he was busy to suck the greatest possible fortune in the shortest possible time. – And that is where the spiritual dimension comes into play:

The ruler shall again be the Ego-identity of the Candidate on his Path. – The Empire shall be the microcosmos he inhabits and is striving to animate. The people are the same as earlier.

The aim of the Candidate as a ‹provincial trustee› is still the one who has entirely dedicated his personality to live in the service for *The Path* he is pursuing. His ‹subjects›, thus, are to be as modest and calm as possible, while he himself as the ruler endeavors to accumulate for his microcosmos as much soul-quality as will be possible during his short lifetime: That will be his treasure – his profit as a temporal ‹governor›.

The only difference is that when an Initiate tries to accumulate as much spiritual profit as possible, this really *must* be at the costs of the ‹people›: The latter *must* almost *starve to death*, so that the new kingdom can arrive in Force and Glory. But here this treasure cannot come from the possessions of the people. *«Flesh and blood cannot acquire the Kingdom of Heaven»* (1 Cor 15:50). – Even though the ‹people› are to assist the process of transformation, they cannot contribute a great lot to it: The highly developed *New Vehicle* of the Candidate cannot be built from the fruits of the fields!

On the other hand, here as well the ‹ruler› must not tyrannize his people, as, if he does, they will ‹rebel› against him – e.g. by an illness of the physical body, or even by sudden death: That's when the ‹ruler› is deposed like with one great blow, and the empire – the microcosmos – needs to go and wait for a new ‹king›.

True, this people as well is, in the better case, full of contempt against death, if not quite ready for suicide as were the starving rice peasants of that earlier time (or like those in today's India: modern slaves of today's, purely commercial ‹colonial powers›). – The death of the Pupil however is not wanted at all: The physical build-up of a *New Man* – from a new birth to a useful fundament of experiences, in a surrounding completely different from conditions in a former life, needs like 30 years. Only then a new ‹new consciousness› can begin to really build up.

But there is a fundamental requirement this Prince Initiate needs to fulfill from start, or else everything were good for naught He never must look at himself or any other person as *a thing* – namely as at something completely independent from soul and spirit, that would be annihilated entirely after decease. He or she must be completely conscious of the *responsibility every inhabitant of any microcosmos* has since birth – knowingly or unknowingly: *«Ignorance does not protect from punishment!»* —

In fact, there is another important way to ‹read› the second-last line: *«People refuse to serve [their ruler] only when they are treated as a ‹thing›»*. So, if one wants to follow The Path, the good end of which is the union of a microcosmos with the One, All-embracing Love, then he needs to *start with himself, first*. For our picture of a Chinese province, this means: One can (it must be repeated once more!) neither love unconditionally one's neighbor nor God, unless one has learnt to love one's own personality with all its flaws – looking from the perspective of the would-be ‹celestial› *new personality – with impersonal unconditional love!*

True: the Wise considers all humans – and therefore himself, too – as *«straw-dogs»*. – Nevertheless, Man *is and remains the Crown of Creation* – its *Compendium*, so to speak – and at the same time its most incomprehensible wonder. It is here, especially here, that the sentence about the Daoist paradoxon is most appropriate – for: these irrational, incomprehensible, awesome *«straw-dogs»* really are … — *Gods!*

Only who refuses to treat any kind of life as a «thing» is worth to be named a nobleman!

第七十六章

人之生也柔弱，其死也堅強。
草木之生也柔脆，其死也枯槁。
故堅強者死之徒，柔弱者生之徒。
是以兵強則滅，木強則折。
強大處下，柔弱處上。

76.

When a human is born, he is quite tender and supple —
When he has died, he is quite rigid and stiff.
When a young tree sprouts, it is quite tender and supple —
When it has died, it is quite dry and hard.
Therefore:
Whatever is rigid and desiccated, is related to Death —
Whatever is supple and tender, is related to Life.
And this means:
An all to mighty army is normally doomed to perish —
An all too mighty tree will normally fall.
What is too strong and too big is normally reduced —
What is very tender and flexible, normally will rise.

How very strange: This chapter shows that today's *Chinese translators and commentators* tend to let themselves be inspired by their Western colleagues, and this in the sense of active violence and of radical solutions. But the glyph 死 for *‹death›* and for *‹to die›* also covers *‹lively›* contents – from *rigid* and *stiff* unto *uncompromising* and *merciless*; – and the glyph 折, besides *to break* has many meanings in the sense of *to bend, to deflect* – and from *«to mourn»* onto *«change of mind* (but never *«to fell»*!). – This also corresponds much better to the fundamental Daoist rule of *non-violence*. – Some secondary meanings also are: *«The greatest army must be able to wheel;* – the biggest tree must be able to bend» …: in Chinese, *«a rule», «a habit» and «must»*, are expressed with one and the same glyph.

These linguistic exercises are not to be taken as an intellectual play, but understood *«with the heart»*: *sensed* rather than ‹known›. Modern brain-people understand the depth of this text much better when they can *sense and experience them* (*smell and taste*, as say J. Bœhme and V. Weigel) – the way it is with symbols of all kind.

At any rate, we learn here that whatever is nascent, young or growing, intrinsically already contains its torpor and death: This is the eternal cycle of Life – «from birth to the tomb». And our text underlines that whatever loses its mobility and adaptability, is «doomed to die». – In a certain way, thus, this chapter is the answer to the great existential questions like in chapter 58: *«What is Life? – What is Death? – And what really is the cause and reason of a human life within this cycle? – What is the reason and aim of tis timeless tragedy? — Who ... ?? — Why ... ?? When ... — ??»*

On the basis of these questions, the philosophical intention of this very pictorial chapter meets us in the rather melancholic mood of a person asking himself a great many anxious questions regarding life and death. This becomes even more visible in another possible version for the first two lines: *«When he dies, he is quite rigid and useless»*; – but watch out! In both these images, *aging is not mentioned – but included as partaking in death*!

The seeker on the Path of DAO puts himself the same questions – but, with as a background, higher knowledge and comprehension regarding the cycle of whatever can evolve inside the wheel of *Nature*, in the wheel of *time and space*, in the wheel of *Karma*, in the wheel of *Nemesis*. – This last word best describes the condition of human nature. It is derived from the *green lands* where *«in the First Beginning»* all beasts (including Man) bustled about carelessly, but then developed their being thrown back and forth, from fear to anger, from joy to pain, from pleasant allotments by Fate (good opportunities from ‹Karma›) to fatal reprisals for human arrogance.

Even a person who «knows», still does not know how he will behave in the hour of his death and beyond: It looks as if this final exam at the end of a lifetime – this exam for admittance to a new life-cycle – were ‹lived› anew, every time!

The ancient Samurai were trained not to fear death – not just that they should fight and fall so much more fearlessly; but also in order to learn to disdain worldly life. – The Hagakuré, the very ancient Book *For The Samurai* says:

«Who every morning orients well his heart and is capable to live as if his [physical] body were already dead, gains the freedom of The Path. His whole life will be irreproachable, and he will fulfill his mission with success.»[53]

Why such thoughts in the present chapter of *Dao-De-Jing*? – Because this describes the degeneration and crystallization of young and old only for the sake of emphasizing *survival and raise of what is tender and ‹green›,* thanks to Daoist's flexibility. – Ancient mythology used to attribute the green color to whatever was young and lively and promising – and the term *green* itself is, looking at it from the perspective of linguistics, derived from the source of all earthly life: From the green shield of Perceval[53-A] to the Vitriol of Alchemists!

«Who gets too big and too mighty, normally is doomed to perish; – what remains supple and young, will live!» – Many defeats of Humanity whenever they meant to find their glory and greatness, prove that what grows too big is always *doomed to die*: from the world-empires of *Alexander the Great* or *Napoleon* over the giant *Zeppelin ‹Hindenburg›*, the ocean steamer *‹Titanic›* or the colossal canon *‹Dicke Berta›* unto the dream-empire of the *‹European Union›*, the USA, modern China and back to the stone-age, and *dinosaurs* of a new future in another «Very Beginning».

Today, many people of a so-called *Third Age* run to high school courses, fitness-centers and art-events, hoping to remain young that way. – That's very good, and it may somewhat delay crystallization; – but it does not impede it – nor do cures with fresh cells or *‹adreno-chrome› or hormone boosters*: sooner or later the strongest tree *must fall* – withered despite standing over a fresh-water source!

There is only one source that dispenses the *Water Of Eternal Life* and infinite bliss – yet not in an ordinary, material sense, but in an immortal sense: This is the *One Prime* Source, the *One Water of Life*, the *One multiple Path or fundamental renewal*; – the Path of DAO, the Path of GNOSIS and Sufism, the *‹Path of the Rainbow›* of the Indians ... – whatever we like to call it. This is no way of chemical, surgical or magical rejuvenation, no physical immortality through cloning of cells, by nucleinic acids or by cryo-techniques. It is the Path on which the perishable human personality *«dies before he dies»* (as the language of the Mysteries says), so that the imperishable *New Divine Man* may begin to live before he can really live! – *This is* the ‹tender›, the ‹green› sprout, *«due to live»*, as predicts our text!

The great Sufi Initiate, *Muhammad al-Ghazāli* in his booklet *A Letter to the* Disciple – *Ayuha 'l walad*, writes: *«My son! I assure you that, if you walk on the mystical path, you will see wonders at every step. Sacrifice your soul, for the essence lies in sacrifice.*

– «*As Dū-an-Nūn-al-Misrī said to one of his Disciples: ‹If you can dispose of your life, join me; – if not, don't lose your time with the trivialities of Sufism›.»*[54] – And Jesus said:

«Who abandons his life for the sake of following me, will gain IT!»

德

錦繡中華之一頁　　裴明龍編

第七十七章

天之道，其猶張弓歟？高者抑之，下者舉之；有餘者損之，不足者補之。
天之道，損有餘而補不足。人之道，則不然，損不足以奉有餘。
孰能有餘以奉天下，唯有道者。
是以聖人爲而不恃，功成而不處，其不欲見賢。

77.

The DAO of Heaven —
is it not like bending a crossbow?
Its upper part, one pulls down —
its lower part, one pulls up —
shortening what flies too far —
lengthening what is too short.

The DAO of Heaven —
it collects superabundance and completes what is shortcoming.
The DAO of Man [instead] – is it not of this kind:
offending those who are in needs, while attending the super-rich.
Which human enjoying superabundance serves the World?
— Only a person who lives in DAO!

Therefore, the Wise —
He is effective, but does not rely on whatsoever nor whomsoever —
he serves and achieves, but without calculating —
and he heeds neither shame nor honor.

The Westerner reading this text for the first time finds it difficult to interpret the muddle of crossbow and heaven, of worldly attachment and autonomy. Used to quickly chose a pivotal point, he makes a grab without looking at such details as «too short» or «too long»: «*The pivotal point is clear – the rest must adjust itself!*», he thinks.

So this one lets a bow-maker *equip the bow*; –that one sees *bending the bow* to be an allusion to the biblical verse: «*Every valley will be filled, and every hill will be lowered, and the curved way will become straight – and the bossy ways will become even*». – The third, still simpler, has: «Whoever shall exalt himself shall be abased; and he that shall humble himself shall be exalted».[55] – The fourth, finally, sees therein an instruction for aiming better ... —

But a Daoist does neither moralize nor speculate –and neither does the *Dao-De-Jing*: Whatever it contemplates on the worldly human – the material and visible plane, it sees at the same time on the philosophical plane of Cosmic Order – and moreover on a third level – the one of Gnosis. – That is the universal level, the level where one is in union with God, where everything is Spirit (and so it really is,!) – where everything is in harmony with *the Great Plan of the Universe* (and so it really is as well!) – and where everything lives and weaves and suffers in everything. – And indeed, all a human can do or perceive is, in every single moment, at the same time a divine reality, and a cosmic one. The joint center of all these movements that are spreading like the rings on the surface of a silent pond (each one in interaction with each other) is the *Heart of the World*. The latter's center is the *Heart of the Universe* ; – and the prime source of all this is *DAO*, the *«Mother of all things»* – named «Mother» in all cultures, philosophies and religions of the world.

The present text as well has three levels: one of DAO – the universal source amidst the absolute Light; – one of the World with its human to-and-fro; – and, third, the one of ‹the Wise› as a mediator between heaven and the world – a small world himself. By striving on the Path of DAO, he simultaneously realizes the Cosmic Law (*«not a Iota will be taken from it, until the World perishes»*; Mt. 5:18). Despite living and acting in this local World, he simultaneously is bathing in the «living water of the Stream of God» (Joh 7:38). And while he thus is united with everything, he all the same is also his own small world – a microcosmos … – and all this will be perceived and realized by whoever is exercising himself in the *high art of archery* – that very special and quite exclusive art of striving for DAO.[56]

This excellent philosophical *art of becoming one with the Path* through mediation of the crossbow, is very, very ancient. Even the Veda already mention it: *«The mystic syllable OM is the crossbow; – the soul of the individual is the arrow. – Brahma, the divine prime fundament, is their aim. – He who is not inebriated by the visible world can hit it. – May the latter become one with his aim – like the arrow!»*[57]. – Here we don't only hear some mystic teaching, but also some *lived experience*!

A few sentences by some Masters of the art of archery named *Kyu-Do*, show, what this is all about (no special selection or arrangement made):

«The starting point is that the thinking Ego becomes silent». – What's needed is to «detach oneself of all bindings – become Egoless – standing outside of all stimuli – centering oneself – concentrating one-self: The bent bow comprises the Universe in itself!»

Thus, this art is a realization and visualization of the perfect union of spirit, soul and body – of God, Cosmos and Humanity – as well as of thoughts, feelings and actions. Before a Zen archer is allowed to put an arrow to the string, he has been exercising himself during many months to achieve the proper poise of the body and the correct way to breath, *effortlessly* (!) bending the bow, and *unconsciously* letting slip away the string:

S*ilencing the thinking Ego* is, as is well known, the aim of every mystical Path of becoming conscious. But in archery, it is the *first precondition.* – A critically thinking person might find it curious to learn that deep *self-knowledge* is possible when the Ego has become silent. – So, *what is that* Self? – and *what is that Ego?*

«The real art is aimless, will-less, ego-less ... » said a Master of Daoist archery. – That is exactly what writes the first Theosophist, *Valentin Weigel* in his book *About Praying and Non-praying*, penned in the year 1572:

> *«When a person ... finally arrives at non-praying... , so that he ... forgets all about place and time, and about a creature, becoming nothing at all: In this oblivion, and letting go of himself, this person prays for nothing – and that is non-praying, where God Himself prays in a human. Therefore, to pray in Spirit and Truth is nothing else but to be completely free of sentiments, of activities and of personal wishes. Likewise: time-less, place-less, creature-less, where one desires nothing anymore; where one neither fears nor rejoices, and neither loves nor hates; where one effects nothing with senses or thoughts, where one pays no attention to oneself, at all, and where one remembers nothing about time or place, nor of one, of this or that. – In Summa, where one has entirely died in Christo, and lies hidden in God. – From this death and sepulture indeed resurrects Christ – The New Man!»*[58]

To relax and to breath consciously, so that the energy may flow freely; – achieve the great tension of the bow without tightly stressing one's muscles; not to try hard – indeed not even to think about it – *«to observe friendly what happens inside»; – «purposely becoming purpose-less – this is real presence of the mind!»* – so the Masters of archery keep teaching; – and also: that here there are *things coming to pass that reason cannot grasp. –*

Is the Path of gnostic renewal and transformation not precisely the same? The words of the Masters of *Kyudo* hardly differ from those of the great mystics – from the first begin unto what the Cathars of the 13th century named the ‹Good End›:

«The Spirit born from archery loves humanity, loves all things; – he lives happily in this world». (Ingaki Sensei) – «It is important that everyone exercise himself very carefully on the Path he has chosen » (Myamoto Musashi). – And an anonymous Master said:

«With the upper end of the bow, the archer pierces Heaven, on the lower end there hangs Earth.»

This statement shows in the best way what the beginning of chapter 77 of the *Dao-De-Jing* has to say; and it has been already explained earlier. But here *the DAO of Heaven is the archer himself*! –

Entirely united with DAO himself, the Master – the ‹Wise› – fulfills the actual task of being human amidst the universal creation. In his divinely human roll as a mediator between Heaven and Earth, with the upper end of the ‹bow› he «bends» the celestial forces down to the plane of humans who are well prepared for it; – with the lower end of the ‹bow› he *pulls* humanity up – towards the cognizance *of* DAO, towards the Path *in* DAO, ad towards self-redemption *thanks to* DAO.

The‹ Wise› forms a bridge between cosmic regions – the earthly and the celestial ones – by, so to speak, transforming down to a level endurable for well-prepared humans, the very high divine vibrations that an ordinary human can neither perceive nor endure.

This elevated way of being human largely transcends in efficacy and significance what everybody can take home from this text. It *shows*: DAO as the Law of Karma equalizes and steers – not just material valors and things, but immaterial occurrences in this World as well. Therefore, in the whole Universe *nothing* can come to pass that is not *allowed* to happen.

Who should fear a threatening world cataclysm or other catastrophes, prophesied by numerous groupings and individuals? – The World does not depend of a human hand ready to annihilate its own works – but in the ‹hand› of the sublimest Love, of which it is said:

«God never abandons the works of His hands!»

Only completely insane humans are capable of realizing such a catastrophic event – those who with their pseudo-scientific, political, military and other pernicious experiments could be able to hazardously risk the welfare of the entire Planet Earth and its creatures as if this were a child's play, as at the time of this translation indeed seems to be incumbent: all of this out of Luciferian arrogance and completely lacking intelligent consciousness!

The ‹Wise› instead, the *«human living in DAO»* is very conscious of what he does for Humanity and the World: What he dispenses whenever and wherever he can, cannot be expressed in words. He attempts to mitigate and to mediate. He strives for no dominion but that over himself. Only a few recognize what he is doing; even fewer appreciate it. Many deride him and even ban him, but as for today without hindering him: This is the (wavering) privilege of our time. – Never this service receives any thanks. But this cannot frustrate the ‹Wise›: He feels his inner task and remains loyal to it, on all his ways. He does what has to be done, without measuring. He gives his best and goes on. He sees so many things that ought to be done as well; – only few of them he can achieve; to nothing of it he remains attached. – He serves *«with all his heart, with his entire soul, and with all his capabilities»*, for all his service is service for God – service for the Gnosis – service for DAO.

If he is lauded or criticized, loved or scorned: He remains loyal to his Path, doing his work. He even ignores if he can be named ‹a Wise›. But he knows his union with Gnosis and – beyond time and space – his union with very many brethren and sisters, who form one great Universal Brotherhood – most of whom don't even know each other personally …

And one thing he knows with certainty:

The aim toward which he is flying as an arrow, is reality, beauty and splendor; it is strength and glory; – it is eternal light, unwavering truth and inexhaustible life! One ‹day›, the arrow will have become golden, and amidst the splendor of the spiritual Sun he will fly along – be it into the final goal of All, or be it continuing to serve Humanity and the World. Only few humans have reached this sublime condition; – maybe there are even some living here in our time. – But, as says the unknown Japanese Master of archery: *«Who has attained this condition will be well served doing as if he hadn't attained it!»*

He continues his work
but relies on nothing and on nobody … —

第七十八章

天下莫柔弱于水，而攻堅強者莫之能勝，以其無以易之。
弱之勝強，柔之勝剛，天下莫不知，莫能行。
是以聖人云：
「受國之垢，是謂社稷主；受國不祥，是爲天下王。」
正言若反。

78.

In this World, nothing is softer and suppler than water —
but when it attacks,
not even the strongest thing is able to resist it. —
That is why nothing can be compared to it:

What is supple overcomes what is rigid —
The more adaptable one always prevails —
The whole world knows this – and yet they do not do it.

By right the Wise say:
«Who with devotion serves the country during common misery,
will by right be appointed Lord of the millet-people.
Who has carried the land during its distress,
will by right be made the ruler of the kingdom».
[This is] a striking proverb
with the appearance of a contradiction!

The sequence of the glyphs 社稷主 that here we have transmitted as *Lord of the millet people*, really signifies the ‹Lord› – 主 – of a ‹high, or honorable, society› – 社 . – For 稷 there exists no known interpretation (it may have gone lost in time). Chinese commentaries name ‹millet›; Western translations have *Lord of millet*, *priest of the altar for/of earth and millet,* and similar things – and they ignore the notion of ‹*high*, or *honorable*, *society*›.

Indeed, rice and millet were cultivated as the main nutrient in China already 8000 years ago, and it stands to assume that some of the more than 10 kinds of millet have ‹immigrated› to the West with the army of *Attila's Huns*. – The institution named *Millet society* here, might stand for some agricultural commission, fraternity or cooperative, supervising the collective plantations and harvest. The so-called *‹Lord of the millet-people›* would then, maybe, correspond to an agricultural deputy or high clerk of the land in consideration.

The first glyph of both main paragraphs of the direct speech – thus, of the *proverb* – has a great number of significances – from *endure* and *undergo* over *submit, be defeated, be subject to,* unto *take upon* oneself, and *lead out of* (a place or condition). One of them that could provide the ‹proverb› with a significance clearly linked to the text, would be something in the connotation of *«being subservient»*, as an active and voluntary form of *«underlay oneself»*. – Inexistent in today's language, the idea of it is still found in a mid-18th century cantata of J.S. Bach, BWV 182: *«King of heaven thou art welcome»* – with the aria (the known libretto being weakly translated into English): *«Lie before your Saviour prostrate ... »*, originally not aiming at *submissiveness,* but at *faith, confidence and loving devotion.*

The same is true for the man who in the present N° 78 is so meritorious regarding his country: Full of faith and confidence he has sacrificed his whole being, when famine, epidemics or even war and foreign rule pushed many to quit their home, or even their life, as in N° 75. – So it is only just that this one has been selected as chief of the millet guild – or as the ruler of the World, hence as the Emperor (天下王). – The foundation of the *Ming-Dynasty* has a similar story: In the course of the great *peasant's rebellion* of the year of 1368, an orphan born from peasants, *Zhu-Yuan-Zhang* grew up in a monastery before he became a troop leader and even general – and finally, under the name of *Emperor Hong-Wu I* founded the *Ming-Dynasty.*[59] –

Now what has all this to do with the spiritual starting point of this text of N° 78 – or with the unstoppable strength of the smooth power of water?

Today, *gentle people* are mostly regarded as weaklings – oft even as dumb, because of heir tolerance ad kindness: With such an appearance one cannot make a career – and yet that is the main purpose of life – isn't it? – The *Dao-De-Jing* insists through several chapters that this is not so, but that, what is tender, is stronger than what is hard, more powerful than what is violent, and more unassailable than a strong army. – Moreover, the sequences of glyphs in present N° 78 shows many similarities with N° 76 looking at exactly the same subject – just this time from another point of view.

Our chapter 78 is – as observed before, oriented rather toward *active subservience*, and towards *faith and devotion.* The example and the proverb stress even more *adaptability.* – Maybe, the peasant *Zhu-Yuan-Zhang* also owed his great success to some Daoist tactic he could have learnt in the monastery (besides of his great army that grew to a final number of 250'000 soldiers). – At any rate – and this as well issues from above mentioned comprehensive history – *Zhu* was not only completely devoted to the liberation of his native land: With growing clarity and will-power he strived to attain the *one goal* – the most egregious one: the dignity of an *Emperor* – being a *ruler under the Heaven*! – And as we know, he achieved his aim (see. picture on p. 103)!

Lao-Dse of course could not have in mind the peasant *Zhu* who lived only 1700 or 1800 years later. But the story clearly shows the possibility that a seemingly most unworthy person can become most worthy to achieve *«the Highest»* (se N° 22). But he must not make his efforts just for the sake of his own gain; and instead of leaving his community – the humanity of his world – when things turn out badly, he is to serve them in unshakable devotion – continuing zealously and in inalterable loyalty *«to do what has to be done.*

Is it not quite the same with the Path of DAO – the Path of GNOSIS? – Here as well the one thing that counts is, first of all, the clear determination to go on and on, on the path once chosen – day after day, one pace after the other: in ‹bad weather› as well; even when the crop seems to refuse ripening; even when weariness, inner idleness and other adverse forces advise one to abandon. For there is the certitude that IT will continue, always – and that, wherever one may be, one stands *on the Path*; – that each step is *a step forward*, and that one will always be helped when one asks for help, as long as the efforts don't diminish.

From the moment when in the human heart the light of Gnosis rises anew, one must hold fast on these three pillars: a *firm inner faith* hat this Path is *a reality*; – *unshakable confidence* (‹hope›), that whoever accepts DAO as his lode-star can become a *Son of Heaven* again; – and, third: *love, faithfulness and gratitude* for being able and chosen to *really follow this Path of fundamental renewal*, in deed and verity – and with the help of Gnosis itself, notwithstanding all obstacles – *like water*:

«Go, subserve your Savior! – Don the spotless robe of your faith to encounter Him! – Life and limb and all your facilities / shall now be offered to the King»!

Who serves his community, serves himself. – Who in this highest sense serves himself, serves the Highest. – And so his service falls back upon himself again: He is chosen to be given highest dignity: *«Who has endured all the troubles, who has held on up to the end, notwithstanding mischief and hassle —*

By right he will become a ruler under the Heavens!»

第七十九章

和大怨，必有餘怨；報怨以德，安可以爲善？
是以聖人執左契，而不責于人。有德司契，無德司徹。
天道無親，常與善人。

79.

When pacifying a great dispute
there certainly remains some hostility in the air.
To return resentment with gentleness —
To be able to make peace — did you think this is good enough?

The true Wise holds on to the left part of the agreement,
but does not file a statement of claim.
For the virtuous, there is the office for agreements —
For those lacking virtue, there is the enforcement office for claims.

The DAO of Heaven does nothing personally —
but it always procures satisfaction to people.

When west of the Bosporus there virtually thrived nothing but jungle and wild beasts, China already had its highly developed civilization and culture with comprehensively detailed regulations for commerce and money systems, along with the corresponding public institutions and jurisdiction. – Then, like today, dilatory payers, careless dandies and crooks proliferated. – Then like today, there occurred endless lawsuits devouring heaps of money and energy, the settlement of which inevitably left behind bad feelings.

In today's banking business as well we still know the so-called *swap contract* with its ‹left and right legs›. This means that the two partners are bound to different conditions. If or when the contract is canceled before the due term, the claims of one party are set off against those of the other, and the business is settled amicably. – Similar cases are possible when (as it often happens nowadays) said delayed payers, careless dandies and crooks affirm their insolvency, but at the same time lack nothing for themselves.

How could this possibly be solved without leaving bad feelings on both sides? – Therefore, *Lao-Dse* already some 2500 years ago recommended the creditors not to get flushed over such a case, but to be generous; – not to engage the renitent payer in a possibly year-long litigation, but to find a peaceful arrangement with him. – For, as says by right the author of the *Dao-De-Jing:* even if you win your case, or when in a mediation process a solution acceptable for both parties is achieved: there inevitably will remain bad feelings on both sides!

So it is *not enough* to peacefully settle the whole incident? – What more can be done in such a case, really?

Lao Dse makes an appeal neither to the ‹reason› of the cheated party, nor to the proverb, following which «the wiser caves in»: He makes an appeal to the *wisdom* in Man; – he speaks to *‹the Wise›*.

He says: Hold on to your part of the contract – be ready to accept the other party to be less virtuous than you, and thus to neglect his part. There is indeed a possibility to enforce your right before a justice, but this will bring you much vexation, costs and hassle. – Better let go of the matter – without litigation, without dubious expenses, and without hassle nor wrath!

«This sounds very nice indeed», says the ordinary person hearing such counsel; – *«but how will I get my money?? – I am no charity club for sloppy entrepreneurs!»*

It is here that our understanding needs to quit the level of *ordinary* virtue, and go to the level of *DE* – the level of *Gnosis*, i.e. of living as a person having realized *inner renewal* – the harmonious state of ‹the Wise› as it were; – and this in a triple way:

Firstly, there is the serene composure the ‹Wise› needs no effort to keep anymore, for it has become authentic for him – not as a culture, but integrated in his true character. It is the attitude of soul and spirit as shown in the anecdote about a Zen Master who at the event of a strong earthquake, in his room took the ‹Zen posture›, remaining thus seated, and when the tremor stopped, finished the phrase he had begun when the earthquake started.[60]

Secondly, there is the *«foreknowledge»*, Master *Sun-Dse* is mentioning in his book. – In this specific instance, this means *«to know both the other and oneself»*. In this case, greater difficulties can be avoided because one will simply lend no money to an individual whom one knows to be untrustworthy. – Or else: one lends him the money, *despite well knowing* that he cannot be trusted; – but in the ‹Zen attitude› that, what ever may come of it, one will not feel angry, as one took the money for lost from the beginning.

Third: In chapter 73, DAO has been presented as the ‹Law of Karma› : ‹Karma› or DAO as an «all-embracing net of Heaven, lose and sluggish, but never forgetting or losing anything or anybody». This aspect is of course included in the present case, but not explicitly explained. – So, what is the meaning here?

The fundamental law of Karma is so that a person cannot experience anything – neither ‹*misfortune*› nor ‹*luck*› – unless he or she has caused it beforehand, somewhere in time and space – or *will cause it in the future*! The fact that the cause may also be set in the future, may sound quite silly to ‹enlightened ears›, and *paradox*. Who would indeed willingly do anything that *inevitably must* cause them mishap? – However: What can a human know about his or her future decisions and reactions in some happening that is, and must be, completely unknown to them today?

On the other hand, some debtor who never pays his debt may thus balance some old Karma: The creditor may ‹owe› him this amount from an ancient cause, so to speak. – Or he can create new Karma by which the loser of today will become the winner of tomorrow (see N° 42). – The balance is assured in any case. From this point of view as well it may be wise not to go and sue said debtor. Also today's creditor would then become the origin of new Karma on the level of sentiments and emotions!

Still, the summit of the teaching of this text is not the *personal satisfaction* of today's creditor whose claim thanks to the law of Karma *will be* satisfied, inevitably – or, as just shown, *hereby is* equalized. It is the consciousness that Karma is neither after *you*, nor *me*, nor *them*, but, quite impersonally, preserves *the equilibrium of the entire divine Universe*!

Now, let us step up to the highest level of this example: All that has been said is also valid for the ‹Pupil› or ‹Candidate› on the Path of DAO: Not one single honest effort in pure dedication to *The Path* will remain without reward! – Each and everything will bring its positive result in due time. But the Candidate *must not calculate*: *«He serves and achieves without calculating»*, is what was said already in chapter N° 77. Everything else would be buying ‹on tick›, with the idea to never pay one's debt. – Gœthe said: *«He who always keeps striving forward, him we can redeem!»* – And one modern author wrote:

The Pupil must begin by giving —
not by taking!

錦繡中華之一頁　　裴明龍編

第八十章

小國寡民。使有什伯之器而不用；使民重死而不遠徙。
雖有舟輿，無所乘之，雖有甲兵，無所陳之。
使民復結繩而用之。
甘其食，美其服，安其居，樂其俗。鄰國相望，雞犬之聲相聞，
民至老死，不相往來。

80.

A little village: A solitary little handful of people … —
True, there are various workshops with artisans,
but they have no work to do.
True, again and again some people perish,
but they decline to emigrate.
Despite having boats and wagons, they go nowhere.
Despite having weapons and armors, they attack no place.
Even if these people had to endure twice their hardships:
they would withstand them:
Their nutrition is tasty, their clothing is clean —
their dwellings are cozy, and their nature is serene.

The village next to theirs: One sees each-other —
Poultry and dogs: one hears each-other —
People die very, very old — one does not visit each-other.

What a wonderful description of this little village! Conjured in so very few strokes of a spirited brush, it meets the reader's inner eye and feelings; – one might almost believe to hear its peaceful noises, inhale the colorful perfume of its mixed scents, and see the peaceful to-and-fro of its dwellers.

Maybe it is necessary to well know life on the countryside in order to get into the spirit of this unpretentious scenery. – Maybe also one needs to have seen a lot of misery in order to understand how humans can be happy in their desolation. At any rate, it is necessary to faithfully remain with the manuscript of our text, so as not to take this description as a caricature, but as a sympathetic sketch – an atmospheric picture in words.

Contentedness has since long been an exceptionality in our world; – and even a motive for mocking smiles. Who does not participate in the race for ‹success›, ‹well-being› and ‹happiness› – who does not strive to ‹expand›, «does not fill in» and soon will find himself alone – or rather: undisturbed. – Moderation gets no approval in today's society … – has this really always been so? – But what is the purpose of life?

Today's *Chinese commentators* of this chapter are divided: The ones recommend the silent modesty of the little village, where everybody is content in spite of most difficult conditions. These Chinese look upon the world-wide interlocking of world-powers and world-companies, with their formation of giant unions of states, as on a giant fraud by which a few privileged persons enjoy life at the costs of the ‹working populace›. – Others smile (same as *all* western translators do) because of the primitive little hamlet and the narrow view of its tenants. – The third ones, finally, think that it is precisely the people of the neighboring village who have lost contact with real life, and who through the great competition of the great world have forgotten the benefit of peaceful simplicity … –

The interpretation is quite interesting, following which the little village has *«returned to strings tied in knots, instead of writing»*. – Precise analysis of the sequence of glyphs instead results clearly in that there is said: *«Even if they were entangled in twice their troubles, these people would not want to emigrate»*. Only like this – and knowing real conditions and usages – this gross difference of understanding can be at least understood: *Qui-pu's* as they are known for Mexican Inca's of *Lao-Dse's* time, were never found in China; but at all times ornamental hitching of strings did, as a Chinese folklore in all layers of society – and it still exists. – However this may be: Everybody agrees that this handful of people in their solitary contentedness are leading a difficult but cheerful life.

Is not the same true for most people of today's humanity? – Even the most unsatisfied ones who daily and hourly complain about how badly they live, would not really want to change anything – nor would they want to switch lives with whom so ever … –

Who has chosen the *Path of DAO*; – who has abandoned a more or less typical life amidst modern careeristic society, choosing a life of orientation toward Gnosis, and accepting all consequences this entails, can easily become such a ‹solitary village› with very sparse contacts and exchange with others – with the ambitious go-ahead-people. The latter are so very different! They also are so terribly expansive, noisy, and in perpetual activity. Who is not on some business trip or military campaign does not count to them. – Peaceful are the others, serene and in a surrounding of reciprocal devotion: What one has, one takes care of. What one never had, one never misses. Don't we almost hear our villagers sing? – One needs neither descriptions nor justifications to understand why the two villages do not associate with each-other!

Now there might arise the question: *Does this mean that a Disciple on The Path of DAO* must automatically undergo material problems, a social off-side position in solitude – and be shunned by ‹good society› until being driven into early death?»

– No, that is not at all what it means: Many people who follow the Path of Gnosis with all its consequences, are well-esteemed in high-society and quite well off: Entrepreneurs, professors, artisans, clerks, teachers, sports athletes and artists – in short, it's a complete cross-section of world-population – in East and West, in North and South, in third-world countries as well as in modern metropoles; and many of then are very well to do. A Disciple of Gnosis lets life itself put him into life; – we may say: He and she let themselves be guided by *DAO*; for they have abandoned their pointed Ego-will: *«Lord, that your will, not my will be done: You tell me what I got to do!»* —

A pilgrim on The Path goes where The Path leads him to, finds his task, his subsistence, his contentment there where The Path puts him – and when he or she really let themselves be guided, they live in peace and happiness. This is no happiness out of some leaflet or TV commercial, but truly lived welfare, often full of joy and gratitude, permitting one also to restore others with the spiritual *‹Water of Life›*; – maybe by his sole presence – his lived *‹presence of Mind› – presence of Spirit. «Not he himself was The Light — but that he gave testimony for The Light!»* (Jo 1:12).

In order to be able to manifest itself throughout the whole World, the Gnosis needs *humans*. – Humans of flesh and blood who stand upright in this World, ‹like you ad me›; – Humans who, in their single orientation toward the One Path ask no-more: *«What shall we eat – what shall we drink?»* – but who really confess: «You tell me. Lord, what I am to do*; – lead me thereto where You want me to be!».*

And the Gnosis – DAO – Karma, the Law of Causes and Effects – will give them *what they need.*

«To know the World without stepping out through the door; – to know the ways of the Heavens without looking out of the window ... »

He who gives will be given!

德

錦繡中華之一頁　　　裴明龍編

第八十一章

信言不美，美言不信。
善者不辯，辯者不善。
知者不博，博者不知。
聖人不積，既以爲人己愈有，既以與人己愈多。
天之道，利而不害；聖人之道，爲而不爭。

81.

Trustworthy talk does not embellish —
Embellished talk cannot be trusted.
A virtuous man does not debate —
A man who debates is unsuitable.
Who has consciousness does not live in splendor
A self-serving person has no insight.
Who furthers the advantage of others,
has a better life himself.
The more he furthers others,
the more he receives back.

The DAO of Heaven – it is sharp, but without malice.
The DAO of the Wise —
it reaches its goal, but without fighting.

«True speech is not nice – nice speech is not true!» – How easy it could be indeed to just prolong the amazingly long queue of almost all prior translations of this N° 81 of the *Dao-De-Jing,* using exactly the same words to make of it a most enjoyable and tastily moralistic admonition! – But sane rational reflection stubbornly refuses to fall in with the *nice but untrustworthy words* of the renown version, and demands its rights.

Studying carefully each glyph in line 4 of this text, respecting pairs and even triplets of glyphs (here: 以为, 为人 and 以为人); – and if we remember that some glyphs – here as often – may just want to satisfy esthetic symmetries, while carrying multiple parallel significations, be it as substantives, verbs (active or passive), adjectives or adverbs – and they often really do so simultaneously – we receive a very suitable translation and interpretation relative to both inner conclusiveness of all statements and a global signification apt to fit into the general sense of the whole *Dao-De-Jing*. – By the way, *all actual Chinese commentators* who, moreover recommend themselves as *translators of antique Chinese*, reinforce above new version. – Yes, they even make some additional remarks in this same sense, and we will mention some of them, by-the-by.

The first argument: *trustworthy* or *true*?

If nice words were definitely *never to be true*, not only all the beautiful texts, speeches and quotations from and by the Wise of all times – from the Veda over Zerdusht, Pythagoras, Mani and Khalil Ghibrān unto the sentences by *Lao-Dse* himself – were *not true:* All nice compliments were false, and every truth an insult. A Chinese translator brings the key-word *Mantra* into play – this says enough. Another one writes: *«true words are not always friendly»*. This corresponds to the classical *«truthful speech not nice»*. Better even is this: *«To state a truth is not nice »*: The truth is, that to *pronounce an unpleasant truth* can also be *«not nice»* for who has to utter it. – An *entirely positive* statement regarding straightness and honesty of ‹the Wise› instead is our *«Trustworthy talk does not embellish»*, for, vice-versa, it is also valid to say: The ‹Wise› looks truth strait in the face – ‹unembellished›!

The second argument: *Quarrelling people*.

In order to know that a *quarrelsome person* is not good, not agreeable and obliging – in short: no virtuous neighbor, (all these are meanings of the same glyph 善), we don't need *Lao-Dse*. But that such a person is not (not yet) suited to be *«admitted to the Path of DAO»*, is easy to understand. – Meanwhile, how difficult can it be for someone to adopt a better attitude!

Suffice to think of the *world of thoughts* of a person: how untameably and chaotic it wants to behave; – How difficult it may be at times even for a pilgrim of many years on the Path of DAO, to silence anger, disdain – or even just a critical thought about some thing or person – let alone *not to allow it to surge at all*! Even a Disciple makes mistakes; and when he becomes aware of it … – he maybe gets angry about himself! – That's how difficult it is to completely leave behind anger, criticism and disappointment with all their consequences – even regarding oneself! – and never again to react on *any* provocation (instigation), ever!

Even to avoid all *useless discussions* can become an issue of fighting old habits. One Chinese commentator writes concerning this issue: «Do not blogg!»). – But the most difficult thing is to gain *the right inner distance* from the so called ‹10'000 things›. – And if some contradiction may arise by right and with good reasons, it may nevertheless never be accompanied by bad, aggressive feelings: The ‹wise› is impersonal in all instances!

The third argument: *Ignorant scholars*.

The inexactness of the statement that a scholarly person cannot have any inner knowledge (as indeed this text is normally rendered), is obvious for whoever is free of bias and dogmata. Where were Platon, Cato, Marsilius Ficinus, Spinoza, Newton, Heisenberg, Fulcanelli *e tutti quanti*, who only thanks to their deep and wide *scientific horizon* could fulfill their task in the world? – Every single high Initiate was a polyglot, and a scientist with it. – And the collect works of Shakespeare, Gœthe, Aristoteles, would be – looked from that strange point of view – *nowhere*!

The *Dao-De-Jing* however means to show us something quite different: The person knowable through self-initiation is not seeking for earthly glory, riches or magnificence that are *«eaten by rust and insects»*. If he is rich and potent, he nevertheless lives modestly. If he is not, he does not strive to become so.

Of the 43 meanings of the particle 博 regarding scholarly erudite persons, *five* indicate honors and riches, but *not one* means *«to know»*. And today's Chinese completely agree: *«The Wise does not heap up riches»*. Ambitious and greedy people they bluntly name *«dumb»*!

However, the Path of DAO is no scientific pick-nick! If it is true that scientific activities may lead to profound philosophical finds, it is nevertheless essential that the ‹Wise› put much most weight on *inner cognizance* (all the rest is just tools and adjuvants); – then, that he thinks with his *new way of thinking*, not mixing up one kind with the other: otherwise neither here nor there any solid knowledge can be acquired. Science as the new religion modern pseudo-scientists pretend it to be is but vanity. – Gnosis instead is *exact spiritual science – the rest is chimeric enthusiasm*!

However, in an earlier chapter relating the same question, there has been emphasized that someone who *knows* must *not expose his knowledge,* and, given he know illumination from his own experience, he does well to *do as if he did not know it* (N° 77). – The modern Chinese author moreover warns against people pretending to know what they have no real knowledge about: *«One is just to follow him for a while, ad one will see he is ignorant!»* – The actor unmasks himself …

The fourth argument: *Rewarded sponsors*.

Following the well-known Western translations, a person who bravely sponsors must thereby acquire great riches: All their donations there happen exclusively on a material level. But even if it can be said indeed that material donations may bring back material advantages to the giver, this cannot be the meaning of the present verse of the *Dao-De-Jing* – or else it would be the ordinary commercial *tit for a tat*: *«Give me first, and I shall give to you!»* – But *«The Wise does not calculate»*, says our N° 77; and in no way do we have here a question of material gain.

Rather, it means that, as soon as the Candidate's *New Soul* begins to speak up, so to speak, its ‹owner› is immediately summoned *to share* his small allowance with others. Doing so he will soon realize with great joy and gratitude that whenever he does so he sees his little fortune grow. The further he goes, the more he has to give; and the more he gives, the more *«comes back, multiplied»*. From this he will recognize the truth of the phrase already quoted earlier: *«Give, and it will be given to you ... – but the Disciple must begin by giving, not by taking!»*

One Chinese commentator very fittingly remarks: *«The more they (Initiates) can do for humanity, the more they rejoice. The more they can bequeath to others, the more they feel rich!»*

The fifth argument: *DAO of the Heavens and DAO of the Wise.*

The current translations are not quite wrong indeed when they assert: *« DAO of the Heavens benefits without doing harm»*; for, whatever Gnosis does, is well done. This cannot be otherwise, as DAO is the Good Law – the *harmony of the Universe itself*! – But to say that humans will never resent this ‹balancing dynamics› as a *«nuisance»* – never feeling pain by it ... – Whoever knows *The Path*, also knows how it really goes ...—

Yes, one needs a good portion of experience with Gnosis in order to *know deep inside* that, what ever happens *is good* and will bring its benefit, even when a narrow consciousness is not (yet) able to acknowledge it.

All translations up to now give way to the remark that whatever Man does *as a human* is always somehow flawed, and oft brings more nuisance than profit: This as well cannot be otherwise. – Therefore, the *Corpus Hermeticum* essentially says: *«Same as whatever the Al(-l-)one Good does, always cannot but be good because of its great perfection – so whatever Man does, always cannot but be flawed, due to man's great imperfection».*

And how does this look for ‹the Wise›?

He knows that whatever he does is imperfect, due to his own relative ignorance (see N° 71); – but he has learnt to live with that. What is essential for his judgment is hat whatever he does is done *in harmony with both* DAO and himself.: One with he Al(-l-) One, and One with himself. – To be *authentic* and in *autonomy*, in uninterrupted awareness and self-responsibility; – more no human can demand of himself. For, whatever is done that way, is also done *without strife*. – Not *«without effort»*, as several translators want; and neither *«without striving»*; – but certainly *without coercion, without a personal quarrel*!

Who stanchly remains *on The Path – oriented toward The Light, Truth, and Life* – who *learns to let go* of everything that could hamper his progress, practicing whatever can further his path, will ‹one day› – at the end of *his days* – see shine the golden pinnacles and the *«doors of nephrite»* of the new City – *his own* ‹New Jerusalem›. – Then he or she will have become *perfect*, for the joy of the ‹community of all those Saints› who excel every human church:

« … Who answers in self-forgetfulness
the call of times long ahead –
by the scent of the golden rose shall
from strength to strength be lead.
Oh do wake up! now is the time:
salvation and freedom wink!
Come, Brothers, Sisters, dare the deed!
The Sun is soon to sink!»

« ... Lightly is rocking red moon
the dewy arm of rustling reed ... »
(Ancient Chinese gouache)

NOTES

[1] The Sun-hero and half-god *Cuchullain* can be found among the Maya as *Quetzalcoatl* with the slightly different name *Cuculain* – i.e. the winged, or flying, snake – in China appearing correspondingly as *a flying, but scaly, «Chinese dragon»*. This kind of mythology seems to refer to an era *before Babylon* , while the qualifying word-ending «-atl» – dates back to Atlantis.

[2] *The Book of Jasher as referred to in Joshuah, 2 Samuel and Jesajah ... – faithfully translated from the original Hebrew into English. – Salt Lake City, Parr & Co., 1887.*

[3] See Zecharia Sitchin, *When Time began.* © 1993 ; – loc. cit. p. 179 ss.

[4] Introduction by Richard Wilhelm, with a foreword by C.G. Jung, rendered in English by Cary F. Baynes. HTML Edition by Dan Baruth.

[5] Understanding Reality: A Taoist Alchemical Classic. Publisher: UNIV OF HAWAII PR, 1987. – ISBN 13: 9780824811037 .

[5-A] See our previous book, *Compendium Creationis – the Symbolism of Aquarius Genesis Explained.* – ISBN 9783907 103 029.

[6] This edition was first printed in German, in 1986. – Another edition, translated and commented by *Mokusen Miyuki* appeared in 1984. If the edition by *R. Wilhelm* moderated the influence by *C.G. Jung*; the version by *Miyuki* instead *willingly enhances* this influence. The latter also includes glossaries with names and special expressions in Chinese, including their phonetic transcription and their ideograms.

Both indicated translations show typical and strong influences of a *subjective, hence infidel, reception*: Typical modern editors and translators are eager to introduce *‹completing›* or *‹correcting›* elements, absolute classifications and direct causalities. They experience the polyvalence of an expression as *antinomies* instead of *equivalent parallel layers*. Therefore, the precise original meaning of a text is victimized by ‹correct modern› syntax, vocabulary and intonation, where the lecture of various different versions (and preferably the Chinese original) should be read and meditated rather, in order to gain an individual *soul-experience* out of the original wording by the original author.

[7] *Secret of the Golden Flower*, loc. cit., p. 69 ss., where the influence of Buddhism onto Daoism – and their differences – are once more highlighted. Wilhelm also emphasized (loc. cit.) the similarities of Christianistic Gnosis and the Daoist understanding regarding the initiation of the process of generating the Light Circuit within a microcosm, from the first awakening of the divine seed unto rebirth from Water and Fire – *« ... to which the ‹Thought-Earth› (Spirit) must be added – as a mother-field or arable soil»*. The ‹light circulation› is also emphasized by Theosophists of the 16th and 17th century (Robert Fludd).

Moreover, he adds maxims like: *«The eye is the light of the body»*, and *«The Light is the Life of Humanity»* (comp. Joh. 1:4); along with expressions like *«mystic marriage»* and *«the Child»* (in Valentinian Gnosis: the ‹Fruit›). – See also N° 4. of the *Dao-De-Jing.*

The concept of *soil*, in Daoism used only as a mystical formula, appears in the Gospels as *physical* baptism, in Judaism as *ritual Mikweh*. – In the Rosicrucian concept of the 17th c.a.d., it comes again in a purely mystical sense – as part of the process of Rebirth – so called *Chymical Wedding of Christian Rosencreutz*: *«Be careful – diligently scrutinize yourself ... lest you will bath thoroughly, this Marriage will harm you!»*
Wilhelm additionally explains *«that the term Gold-Flower – Jin-Hua – also contains the meaning ‹Light›: «For, if one writes the two glyphs one below the other, so that they touch each other, then the lower part of the upper glyph and the upper part of the lower glyph will together give the glyph for Light (= guang). – Apparently, this secret glyph has been invented during a time of persecution...»*. This procedure reminds us of the symbol of the fish used by the first Christians. The origin of this «light-religion during the Tang Era (i.e. 618-907) Wilhelm sees it in *Persia* (meaning Zoroastrism). But this is also the time when first in Persia, then in Arabia, (Baghdad) *Sufism* came up, with *Harun ar-Rashid* and his son *Maimūn* as the founders of the esoteric school *‹Dar al-Hikmèt›*. In China, to this can be added a partly *Nestorian*, partly Manichean Cristian influence. Recent researchers went as far as to equate *Lü-Yen*, the founder of mentioned *Gin-Dan-Giau*, with *Adam*, the writer of the Nestorian commemorative tablet (Sianfu, 781), who signed as *Lü-Siu-Yen*. If so, the ‹Cave-Guest› would have been a Nestorian Christian; – hence the ‹Nestorian flowers on the Daoist dress of *Gin-Dau-Giau*›.

[7-A] In other words: The essence of whatever a creature may have done or said or even thought, remains eternally present in our space-time Universe.

[8] The indications given here are sufficient to locate the corresponding editions. However: all – indeed *all* these texts are unprecise, due to their often pathetic interpretations, with their fixation on European and American standards. The translation offered here unites in a synthesis the most faithful *choice out of all provable significations* of the Chinese pictograms. Even the smallest inserts are emphasized. On the other hand, the best choices in discarded solutions are explicitly mentioned within the commentary – and sometimes even quoted verbally.

[8-A] The two halfs of the present book quite pertinently begin each with a proper title leaf. Even here, the translation differentiates the commonly used main title for the whole book, and the less known sub-titles of the two halfs – according to the polyvalence of the Chinese glyphs. – The very beautiful *Hua-Hu*-Jing, which is ascribed to *Lao-Dse*, too, is not taken into consideration here.

[9] *Confessio Fraternitatis – Bekenntniß der Rosencreutzer-Bruderschaft*. – E.A. Kassel, W. Wessel, 1615 (all in German). – The *Confessio* is the second of the three renown Manifesto's issued from the classic Circle of Rosicrucians around the Lutheran pastor Johann Valentin Andreæ: *Fama Fraternitatis (Ruf der Rosenkreuzer Bruderschaft)*, *Confessio Fraternitatis* and *Chymische Hochzeit des Christian Rosencreutz* (*Chymical Wedding*). New text-editions of the three ‹Manifesto's› with esoteric commentaries

by Jan van Rijckenborgh have been published since 1966 at Rozekruis Pers in Haarlem, and have been translated in many languages.

10 G. Quispel, *Het Evangelie van Thomas – Uit het Koptisch vertaald en tœgelicht* ...– Amsterdam, In de Pelikaan, 2004; – a.a.O., Logion 2.

11 K. Jaspers, *Die großen Philosophen.* – München 1957, S. 908.

12 *Les Prophéties de l'Égypte Ancienne. – Textes traduits et commentés par A. Fermat et M. Lapidus* ... – Éditions La Maison de Vie, 1999.

13 *Ac quemadmodum cuncta educta ex uno fuere verbo Dei Unius: sic omnes quoque res perpetuo ex hoc unā re generantur dispositione Naturœ.* – Christian Adolf Balduin, *AURUM superior & inferior Aurœ superioris & inferioris HERMETICUM.* – Frankfurt & Leipzig, Geo. Hch. Fromann, 1675; – preserved in UB Basel <JrXI 16>.

14 Hamīd Muhammad al-Ghazālī, *Brief an den Jünger – Ayuha-'l-Walad.* – Ausgabe in Arabisch und Deutsch, mit einer kleinen Einführung in die Geschichte und Esoterik der Sufi-Philosophie samt einigen Anmerkungen zum Text. Nach der franz. Übersetzung von Tufiq as-Sabagh, und mit dem Vorwort von George H. Scherer. – Edition Oriflamme, Basel 2009. – And: The same in French and Arab. – ibidem, 2010.

14-A This last sequence is exactly identical with the last sequence of N° 12. – We most regret the impossibility to render adequately the wonderful play with assonances and resembling glyphs, beginning with *«Therefore ...»*, but it aids the certain understanding of the text (the translation renders here two meanings out of a choice, instead of only one):
是以大丈夫，處其厚，不居其薄。處其實，不居其華。– *chū-qi-hòu/ bu-jou-qi-báo. chū qíshí / bu jū-qi-huá.*

15 Fulcanelli: *Les Demeures Philosophales* – transl: *Dwellings of the Adepts – Hermetic Symbolism in the Concrete Reality of the Sacred Art of The Great Œuvre* (all in German. – This œuvre has been translated into several languages, the worst of them being the one into English, the best (operatively precise) of them being the one into German (two volumes in one; – Ppb., 624 pp.; – ISBN 3-9520787-7-8.

16 His most famous books are the *Currus Triumphalis Antimonii – Triumphwagen Antimonii,* and the even more famous *Vom Stain der Uhralten* ... samt den *Zwölff Schlüsseln der Philosophie* (Aurei Velleris Trißmosini Tractatus VIII ... Rorschach, ed. princeps 1600; beautifully illustrated since the second edition, ibidem (1602). – See note 39, and ‹Advertisements› S. 346 hereafter. The latter is known as *The Twelf Keys of Philosophy* ... —

17 His most important work besides his *Œdipus Ægyptiacus* is the *Mundus Subterraneus in XII libros digestus* ... – Amsterdam, Jansson Wæsberge & Sons, 1664, 1678, and more.

18 Due to the polyvalence of Chinese glyphs, this verse again proves very difficult for whoever wishes to quite understand and faithfully translate this text: It is so easy to write a sensible phrase – so easy to anticipate a significance that is reasonable as such, and then adapt ones phrase to what results from it. – Easy as well to weld the whole thing together as

a story for an ordinary life of ordinary people – or for high-strung mysticism. But it is quite difficult to find a solution offering a correct and sensible translation uniting both the level of ordinary life as well as that of *the Inner Path* into one harmonious whole, such as, without any doubt, *Lao-Dse* meant it to be. Both modern Chinese interpreters and Westerners offer but spicy interpolations linked to creatural life; – not a single one is spiritually enhanced as surely is intended also by the ‹travel report›. They all are doubtful about how this text is to be understood, and all of them offer similar unsatisfactory solutions. – Some understand the term 十有三 (i.e. *3 out of 10*) as equivalent to 十三, i.e. *thirteen* (10 [plus] 3, or 13), and then relate this to «13 members of the body»! But the glyph 有 means just *have*, *are, exist*, *there are* and such-like; – the complete phrase is thus, ‹literally›: *«Ten [and] there are 3»*.

[19] ‹Literally›: *«their inexperience, innocence, immaturity* (and suchlike) *is thick»*; – in other words: these people have not yet experienced enough *pain in this World.*

[20] Mk 16:16-18. – Translated directly from Greek of the ‹GRV› (i.e. the Gospel in 5 variants, combined into one text in Greek.

[21] *«He mitigates his acuity, solves the confusion, subdues his dazzling radiance, [and] becomes one with dust ...»* (*Dao-De-Jing*, N° 4).

[22] See our introduction at the beginning of the present book.

[23] R. Wilhelm & C.G. Jung, *Secret of the Golden Flower*, loc. cit.; – end of chapter 12 (see also in the present book, image on p. 16).

[24] See H.P. Blavatsky, *Secret Doctrine* – various instances – see index volume.

[25] Ibidem, see *Brahma*, *Prakriti*, *Logos*, *Purusha*, *Trinity* etc. – In all these instances one needs to make the difference between the Prime Ether (the *zero-element*, so to speak) and the *fifth element* – spiritual Fire-Ether.

[26] See H.P.B., loc. cit., – especially under *Fohat, cosmic ideation and ...*

[27] In place of the glyph 見 of the text *reproduced* here, and translated as *«to respect»*, the text used *for translating* has the glyph 见. The latter's significance is *humility, modest, esteem* and similar synonyma. This *ideogram* is particularly interesting because in fact it is a *pictogram*: We may see in it a *candelabrum* with its mechanism as it was still in common use during the 19th century, but here standing *«under the bushel»*. This part of the glyph is the same as the glyph for *portal, mouth, opening.*

[28] Regarding the numbers 1-2-3-4, see H.P.B., loc. cit., I, *Section III.*

[29] It is surprising, but helps to understand the text if we recognize in the left part of the glyph 救 (*rescue salvation, liberation, preserve*) the so-called ‹Christian› *Chrisma* (☧) that has its own *very ancient* history.

[30] Besides *«splendor»* (here: *splendor of the soul*), the glyph 明 also means *honor*. This passage therefore reminds us of the word by Paul: *«It is sowed in dishonesty, it is reawakened in glory; it is sowed in weakness, it is reawakened in strength;it is sowed a mortal body, it is reawakened a spiritual body»* (1 Cor. 15:43).

31 The expression *Endurá* was in use among the Brotherhood of the Cathars of the 12th century, in the meaning explained here. It is the Occitanian form of the Roman *endurar(e) – endure:* Earthly life seen as a chastisement.

32 Fulcanelli, (trad.) *The Mystery of the Cathedrals and the esoteric explanation of the hermetic symbols in the Great Œuvre. – With three forewords* ... (all in French; translated in numerous languages; the worst is the one into English, the best the one into German, as it is operatively correct. The latter accompanied by a bibliographic list showing the first editions of quoted analogous books in German of the 16th and 17th century. – Basel, Edition Oriflamme, 2004; –ISBN 395207827. – loc. cit. p. 221 ss. –

33 Sun-Dse, *The Art of War* (in different languages with different titles). – See note 44.

34 The indeed precise translation of the text, and parts of the commentaries was possible only hanks to the use of *numerous* Chinese internet pages, where this chapter is commented comprehensibly.

35 See Yuan Mei, R. Schwarz (trsl. /& ed.): *Chinese ghost stories* (in German). – Insel-Taschenbuch, 1997. – ISBN 978-3458336792.

Also is recommended the movie *A Touch of Zen* (2008), in German and Mandarin, subtitles in English), where the interpenetration of civil, governmental, Daoist and Buddhist establishment with the old tradition of Chinese spiritualism is beautifully presented – including an ironic smile from the Daoist point of view. – ISBN 4-260131126239.

36 As for the *RC-Manifesto's,* see precedent note N° 8 here-before.

37 This gives a total sum of nine spheres of initiation following hermetic tradition. – See Rœlof van den Brœk: *Hermes Trismegistus* ... – Amsterdam, In de Pelikaan, 2006; – loc. cit., chapter VI.

38 *Der Schlüssel zu den Zwölf Schlüsseln von Bruder Basilius Valentinus – La Clef des Douze Clefs de Frère Basile Valentin de l'Ordre de Saint Benoît.* – Worldwide only edition of this 18th century manuscript, previously owned by *Emile Nourry*: Transscript and translations by M. P. Steiner; –Introduction and notes by P. Martin. – Bilingual edition, including the edition of the *Twelf Keys* ... with its singularly instructive woodcuts of 1602, and more. Edition Oriflamme, Basel, 2006. ISBN 395207 8743.

38-A This remark was authored long before ‹Covid› and ‹gain of function› research with its utterly evil consequences (and no end of it in sight).

39 P. Martin, *Esoterische Symbolik heute, in Alltag, Sprache und Einweihung.* – Basel, Edition Oriflamme, 2010. (trad.: *Esoteric Symbolism today, in everyday's life, in languages and in initiations).*

40 *Skylla and Charybdis* are a pair of mythical figures in ancient Greek mythology. They play their most popular role in Homer's *Odysseia*: *Skylla* – a beautiful young lady was transformed by the envious gods while taking her bath in the sea. Thence her belly became a body with the heads and paws of *six dogs*, her bust instead became six snakes' throats with three rows of teeth in each jaw. She dwelled in a mountain, the peak of which touched the sky, and from her cave she seized and devoured marine ani-

mals and all travelers who came within her reach. – *Charybdis* instead had stolen the oxen of Heraklès and therefore by a lightening's ray of Zeus was transformed into a mælstrom of the sea, that devoured every ship coming into her reach. – These two monsters in the dangerous zone of he Detroit of Messina threatened the lives of shippers if they had been able to escape the magic of the Sirenes: Mermaiden who chanted so lovely on the beach of an island that mariners forgot all about helm and sails, thus being smashed to pieces on a rock … – *Odyssey, 12th Song*; – recounted by Gustav Schwab, *Sagen des klassischen Altertums*. – (edit. princ. of the full edition: Basel, Franckh, 1913 and later.

[41] Recommended edition in 12 volumes (in German), Ed. F.W. Hendel, 1926. Recommended edition in French: Transl. by Dr Mardruz.

[42] This is: http://en.wikipedia.org/wiki/Three_Treasures_(Taoism). – The page: http://www.tao-te-king.org/067.htm has many similarities with this, and another page allows many comparisons (including variants of other versions and poems taken into account here): http://goo.gl/MRp8S.

[43] Sun-Dse: , *The Art of War (Sun-Zi-Bing-Fa)*. – loc. cit.

As a time-frame, note: *Lao-Dse* lived «in the 6th century»; – *Sun-Dse* is said to have lived 544-496 – hence at the time of the Qi-Dynasty. The most famous general and Daoist philosopher who among other commented Sun-*Dse's Art of war* in a book of his own, was *Zhuge-Liang* (see note N° 47). The end of *Sun-Dse*'s life is not clear– as is the origin and disappearance of *Lao-Dse* (a pseudonym meaning just *Great Teacher*, or *Master*). It cannot be excluded that these two contemporaneous personalities are identical. Now this would be of no importance, had not several commentators stressed the close connection of the *Dao-De-Jing* with the *Sun-Dse-Bing-Fa*. – Equally, both authors' names allow for no conclusion regarding adherence to a specific clan, or family. Therefore it is equally unclear which of the two œuvres is older (if one is at all), and which author therefore might have been the Disciple of the other.

[44] Carl von Clausewitz (1780 -1831), famous German military theorist and general, wrote the book: *About War* ... (ed. princ. 1832 -1834). – *Complete edtiton:* three volumes in one, 1980, ISBN 3-427-82019-X.

[45] *Yin-Fu-Ging – The Classic of uniting the Yin.* – One commentator writes about this book that was penned in the 30th century b.C. (sic!): «*Yin-Fû-Ging, or The Classic of the harmony of visible and invisible things: In the Khien-lung catalogue of the imperial library, chapter. 146, paragraph III, this work has been placed at the top of all Daoist works, with three notes from Ho-shang Kung's commentary to the Dao-De Ging. From Lao-Dse's work one is lead along Daoist literature unto the year of 1626, when the catalogue of the so-called 1st Daoist Canon appeared. – Chapter 147 again names the Yin Fu Ging, along with 9 other works of the kind – the last of which is the commentary of Li-Kwang-Li, one of the first ministers and greatest erudite scholars at the time of Kien-lung's grand father known as Kang-Hsi, after the name of his kingdom.*» – The first of these notes states that the preface of an ancient copy names

as the author of this book *Hwang-Tî* (27th c. b C.), saying that it was commented by *Thai-Kung* (12th c.b.C.), by *Fan-Li* (5th c.b.C.), then in the hermitage of the Kwei valley (4th c.b.C.), then by *Kang-Liang* (✝ 189 b.C.), by *Ku-Ko-Liang* (181-234 b.C.) and by *Li-Khwan* of the Tang-Dynasty (ca. mid-8th c.b.C.) – Others even name the time of *Hwang-Ti* as the first apperance of this little Classic, not meaning that ruler himself however, but the latter's teacher, *Kwang-Käng-Dse*. – ({quoted internet page is gone}).

[46] A modern Chinese describes the curriculum of *‹Crouching Tiger› Zhuge-Liang* as the true *«heroic story of an early talent having achieved astonishing diplomatic and warlike deeds* – particularly the formation of the Three United Kingdoms at the turn of the 3rd c.b.C. He lived 181-243 a.D., that is at the end of the Han-Dynasty, and died 54 years old on a military expedition.

Zhuge-Liang moreover was an inventor – from the kite over a new crossbow onto an automatic machine for transporting cereals. At his death *«he bequeathed his* (popular until today) *work about military strategy in 24 tomes, and several hundred fruit trees, to his descendants. – He didn't heap up riches* (!) *and was the honored servant of his Lord, Lord Liu-Bei* (ruler of the largest of the three kingdoms)*»*.

(See http://history.cultural-china.com/en/183History5903.html)

[47] See Zechariah Sitchin (✝ 2011), *When Time began.* –

[48] The *Huainan-Dse* or *Huainan-zi* (i.e. *Master of Huainan*) is a Classic that was written under the directives of Liu An (180-122 b.C.), the Prince of Huainan. But it also shows influences from Confucianist and legalistic sources. It describes multiple subjects – among other, old myths, contemporary art of ruling a state, didactic historical anecdotes, astronomy, astrology, natural science, metaphysics, martial arts and music.

Tradition says that the *Huainan-Dse* has been composed by eight Daoist wise men. When these appeared at the court of *Liu An* – a center of sciences and arts – *Liu An* told them to demonstrate to him their new knowledge, whereupon the wise astonished him «with magic arts». Later, *Liu An* became their pupil. – The *Huainan-Dse* is said to be the protocol of the talks between *Liu-An* and the eight wise men.

This book contains 21 chapters, but only one treats the art of warfare; the others are all about the discovery of the World, about Nature, about Man and about DAO as such. Already the titles to the chapters are quite eloquent: *About True DAO; The Answers By DAO; About The Begin Of Reality; About The Underlying Spirit; About Fundamental Concadenation; About the Necessity Of Learning*, a.s.f.

[49] This makes allusion to a classic ballad in German, stressing in a poetic way that a man cannot consciously do any evil deed without *having a bad conscience*, that in some moment will betray him so that his deed will be disclosed and punished ... –

And the great German poet of the ‹Dada› movement – Christian Morgenstern – an initiated Anthroposophist and Rosicrucian who has left us with a bunch of excellent double-bottomed (half humorous, half profound) poems admonishes everybody to think well before talking, as every word we speak evaporates into the universal cosmic ‹atmosphere›, to stay there.

[50] All variants of texts and of known translations are taken from the internet page http://home.pages.at/onkellotus/TTK/_IndexTTK.php. – The three partly colored passages at the begin of the chapter are newly composed. – The Chinese ‹basic version› has been found at: http://www.chinapage.com/gnl.html.

[51] The two theosophists of the 17th century, J. Bœhme and J.G. Gichtel at times use the same language as the *Dao-De-Jing* in the 6th . c.b.C., – the same as the actual Gnosis uses since 1945. See also J.G. Gichtel and J.G. Graber, *Theosophia Practica.* – Most new editions follow the 3rd edition (Amsterdam 1736), with the classic images in color – especially: Basel, Edition Oriflamme, 2011; – loc. cit., with a comprehensive *introduction.*

[50-A] *Barrabas* might well be identical with *Barnabas*: The Acts name one Barnabas who accompanied Paul to Rome; but the Gospels here name one *Barrabas – or Bar-Abbas (Son of the Father)* – hence an *Heretic like Jesus* whom the Gospels report to have named himself a *Son of the Father*, and to have been crucified, viz. stoned for this (see our earlier book: *Interrogatio Iohannis* ... (ISBN 9783907 103067) with its accurate rendering of historical facts about the birth of Christendom. It is quite possible that *‹Barrabas› is in fact Paul's Barnabas*, thus another game-changer in Paul's (Luke's, Mark's – whose so ever) very inventive story in the NT.

[52] Yamamoto Tsunetomo: *Hagakuré –The Book of the Samurai.* – Tokyo, 1979.

[53] Yamamoto Tsunetomo, *Hagakuré* – loc. cit, see introduction.

Most people think that the art and path of the *Samurai*, (jap. *Bushi-Do*, from (*Bushi – the fighter; Do for Dao – path*) is completely Japanese. But this tradition, together with its codex and organization have come from China to Japan during the 7th century. Therefore, the Chinese Samurai of the Middle-Ages are close with Daoism, while the Japanese Samurai foster a Confucianistic tradition, suppressing for a long time the complete spiritual tradition of the sword fighters, preferring the death-defying – one almost might say death-maniac – heroism in the service of a feudal Lord. Today in Japan there exist both veins in parallel – but they still are divided, ideologically.

[53-A] Wolfram v. Eschenbach: *Parzifal.* – Best edition in both medieval German and translkation into modern German. – Reclam Verlag many editions.

[54] See note 15; – loc. cit. p. 96.

[55] Lk 3:5; 14:11.

[56] Eugen Herigel, *Zen in der Kunst des Bogenschießens.* – Curt Weller-Verlag, Konstanz, 1948, and later editions. –

E. Herigel was a professor of philosophy in Heidelberg, and a renown Zen archer, also see: http://www.ramakrishna.de/japan/zenbogen.php

[57] *Mundaka-Upanishad* 2.2.4

[58] Quoted in: Valentin Weigel, *Das Buch vom Gebet* (trsl. ‹*Book of praying*›). –Basel, Edition Oriflamme, 2006; introduction, p. 37 (all in German.

[59] Under the dominion of the Mongols – i.e. the ‹Qi-Dynasty› – the population had diminished by 40%. Little revolts generated the Great Peasants Revolution of the ‹*Red Turbans*› (red, as the color of renewal has an arch-old tradition!). Zhu-Yuan-Zhang became, first, a ‹band-leader›, then a general. When all leaders of the revolution's elder generation had died (the last of them in the presence of Zhu), and in rather dubious circumstances, the latter made himself the top leader and founded the Ming-Dynasty, as Emperor *Hongwu*. He chased the Mongols out of their capital *Dadu*, renaming the latter to become *Bei-Jing – but resided in Nan-Ging.*

[60] See E. Herigel, (trad.) *Zen in the art of cross-bow archery*, loc. cit.; – *The Zen experience of Eugen Herigel.*

整道德經

ADVERTISEMENTS

Fulcanelli: Mysterium der Kathedralen *und die esoterische Deutung der hermetischen Symbole des Großen Werks.* Vollständige deutsche Erstausgabe nach der dritten franz. Ausgabe (Paris 1964) mit drei Vorworten von E. Canseliet, F.C.H. Übersetzt und herausgegeben von M.P. Steiner. Mit 49 ganzseitigen Tafeln und 1 Frontispiz. – 348 SS.ISBN 3-9520787-2-7. – € 35.00

Fulcanelli: Wohnstätten der Adepten – *Die hermetische Symbolik in der konkreten Wirklichkeit der Heiligen Kunst des Großen Werks.* (Original-Titel: *Les Demeures Philosophales*). Vollständige deutsche Erstausgabe nach der 3. franz. Ausgabe (Paris 1964 / 1979) mit den drei Vorworten von Eugène Canseliet, F.C.H. Ins Deutsche gebracht und eingeleitet durch M.P. Steiner. Zeichnungen von Julien Champagne und spätere Photos sowie vier zusätzlichen ganzseitigen Tafeln. – 2 Bde. In 1 Bd.. – PB, 624 Ss. – ISBN 3-9520787-7-8 — € 50.00.

Ed. M.P. Steiner: ‹Interrogatio Johannis› (*The secret book of the Cathars* [John questions resuscitated Jesus]) – Translated from Latin, and for the first time with in-depth comments in English. –

Part II: The Secret Book of John (a Nag-Hammadi-Apokryphon), based mainly on teachings from Egypt, Persia and Arabia about Archons, and the Æonology of the first Gnostics. - A synoptic version harmonizing 1 French, 1 German and 2 English translations.

Introduction : The lions part of the book consists of historical analyses and research about true origins of Christendom, whereas official consensual doctrines are flawed and must be changed. This book leads to a new, sensible understanding of how, in our new Era, a **Live cosmic Christendom** can be understood and put into inspired daily practice. – PB, 284 pages, illustrated in color, with in-depth notes in fine: Documents, Book-references, mythologies, etymologies, onomatologuies etc. – ISBN 9783907103067. – **€ 27.00**

Valentin Weigel: Das Buch vom Gebet
Das *‹Gebetbüchlein›* von V. Weigel, dem ersten deutschen Theosophen, Vorläufer von Jacob Bœhme und J.G. Gichtel – in heutigem Deutsch herausgegeben nach dem Erstdruck von 1612. Ein Meilenstein der Geistesgeschichte, auf dem Weg zu freiem Denken und Glauben. – Mit einer Einführung und Anmerkungen von P. Martin. – Geb. m. S-Usl.; 152 Seiten, illustriert. – ISBN 3-9520787-5-1. – € 23.00 /.

J.G. Gichtel: Theosophia Practica – *Eröffnung und Anweisung der dreyen Principien und Welten im Menschen ...* — Nach der 3. Ausg., o.O. (Amst.?) 1736. – Mit den Farbtafeln des Originals sowie 5 weiteren Abbildungen. – Aus dem barokken Deutsch sanft in heutiges Deutsch gebracht und durch P. Martin mit einigen Anmerkungen und mit einer Einleitung versehen, die dieses Buch *zum ersten Mal bibliographisch vollständig und korrekt kommentiert*. – Ppb.; 172 Seiten; – ISBN: 978-3-9523616-0-3; – € 21.00.

Al-Ghazali: Lettre au Disciple («Ayuha-'l-Walad»).
Textes Arabe et français en parallèle, face à face. – D'après l'édition de Beyrouth (1959). – Traduction française par *Toufiq as-Sabagh*. – Préface de *G.H. Scherer* à l'édition princeps de 1951 avec la Vita de Al-Ghazali (1058-1111), et une introduction à l'histoire de l'Arabie Ancienne et du Soufisme. Le théologien et juriste académicien al-Ghazālī devint un Soufi, et sut harmoniser le Soufisme avec l'Islām. – La *Lettre au Disciple* propose une initiation au *Chemin Soufi*, elle est en même temps une introduction et un encouragement fiable et réaliste pour tout autre chemin spirituel. – Broch., 140 pp., 5 planches (dont 1 portrait de *Al-Ghazālī*), 1 carte géographique, et 4 vignettes. – ISBN 978-3-9520787-6-1 —

P Martin (Hrsg.): Die Raute und ihre Bedeutung in den Symbolsprachen.
Teil II: Runen und ihre Entsprechungen in den Hieroglyphen. — Eine vertiefte Einführung in die moderne Symbolik. Anhand der Glyphe des Rhombus (Raute) werden die vielen Bedeutungen dieses Symbols auf verschiedensten Ebenen entwickelt. – Teil II : Phonetische und geistige Entsprechungen von Runen-Namen und mittel-ägyptischen Hieroglyphen. Ein sehr spezieller Eingang ins Reich der Symbole. – PB, 96 Seiten, Illustriert. – ISBN 9783-907103-043. €/CHF 15.00

ADVERTISEMETS

Pierre Martin: Le Symbolisme ésotérique actuel sous l'aspect du langage et de la vie quotidiens, du Chemin gnostique et de l'Auto-initiation. Un livre copieusement illustré, voué au symbolisme ancien et moderne: Alchimie, mythologie, Hermétisme Héraldique – avec des exemples concrets pris du ***présent actuel de tout le monde***. Une introduction aux symboles élémentaires, leur omniprésence, leur effet magique inévitable ***dans la vie actuelle***, et à l'analyse autonome de presque tous les symboles. – Traduction Française, augmentée par rapport à l'édition originale. – Broch., 124 pp. – Avec un index bibliographique, un index des expressions spécifiques, et une table de référence des symboles les plus connus. ISBN 978-3-9520787-6-1.

M.P. Steiner (Hrsg.) :Popol Vuh – Das Heilige Buch der Maya und Inca, samt der Chronik der Quiché und den Annalen der Cakchiqueles. Ins Deutsche gebracht aus drei spanischen, einer französischen und zwei englischen Ausgaben. bietet dieses Buch einen tiefen Einblick in Mischkultur und intensives Zusammenleben der vielen Einwanderergruppen nach Yucatán im Laufe der ca. ***3000 Jahre vor der spanischen Invasion***: Der Text ist eingebettet in viele farbige Bilder jener Umwelt und in aktuelle Anmerkungen, die das Verständnis erleichtern und die damalige Atmosphäre fühlbar machen. ISBN 9783-907 103-074. 288 Ss., € 27.00.

P. Martin (ed. M.P. Steiner): Lodges, Orders And The Rosicross: Rosicrucianism in lodges, orders, and initiatic societies, since the beginning of the 16th century. – The innermost goal of all spiritual teachings and traditions is: knowledge by individual experience of the Cosmos, of human condition and of the Godhead Itself: Thence resulted the so-called Universal Doctrine embracing all bona-fide Brotherhoods, that in one word can be named Rosicrucianism. – This scrupulously documented and richly illustrated book shows how this inner knowledge came from the East and evolved during the last 500 years.

PB, 192 pp., 131 pictures, some of which full page; 66 portraits. – Print book ISBN 9783952426258, € 24. .00 — E-Book-Edition: ISBN 9783952426289.

Corpus Hermeticum, Lateinisch und Deutsch: Die lateinische Übersetzung aus dem Griechischen durch Marsilio Ficino (1468) nach dem Zweitdruck (Mainz, 1503), jetzt präzis ins Deutsche übersetzt. – Das Corpus Hermeticum – ein Text von poetischer Schönheit und höchster philosophischer Genauigkeit – spannt den Bogen von aristotelischer Elementenlehre bis zur Quantenphysik! – Facsimile des lat. Drucks und deutscher Text auf gegenüberliegenden Seiten. –Einführung, vertiefende Anmerkungen d. Hrsg., illustriert. – ISBN 0783952426241. –

M.P. Steiner (Hrsg.): Das Weisheitsbuch Jesus Sirach und Die Passion Jesu Christi in den Holzschnitt-Tafeln von Burkhard Mangold. (2014). – Bibliophiler Druck dieses *vorchristlichen Weisheitsbuchs*, mit den Holzschnitten des großen Basler Künstlers, ergänzt um die Serie der von ihm selbst handgedruckten, und colorierten Tafeln mit seinen Handnotizen. – Die Serie *Passion* ist die Krönung von Mangolds Holzschnitt-Kunst. – Einf.. d. Hrsg.. – Einige Farb-Repros seiner Werke. –Kart. m. S-Usl., Format 19.5 x 27.5, 186 Ss. – ISBN 9783952426227. – € 23.00.

M.P. Steiner (Hrsg.) : Jubiläums-Gesamtausgabe 400 Jahre Rosenkreuzer-Manifeste (1614, 1615, 1616). Zum ersten Mal alle drei Manifeste in einem Band, mit drei Zusatz-Kapiteln sowie 10 Sendschreiben an die, und Antworten aus der, RC-Bruderschaft (1612-1618). – Alles sanft in ein heutiges Deutsch gebracht, mit sprachlichen, historischen und philosophischen Anmerkungen. PB 288 Ss.. – Illustriert. – ISBN 9873524262-72. –

M.P. Steiner (ed.) compendium creationis: The Universal Symbolism of Aquarius Genesis – Explained by Pierre Martin. – With four additional texts: Why Eve was created – Cain and Abel today; Eve and Lilith: the Second Woman – About the Essence of Being:a Theory of Ideas. – A Genesis in 12 theses and 12 scholia in modern speech, adding to the known paradigmata of biblical and extra-biblical Geneseis the new paradigmata of the Aquarius Era, where Philosophy and Science complement each other. – With an introduction by M.P. Steiner. Largely illustrated and with notes to the scholia and pictures by P. Martin. –

PB, 244 pp., ISBN 9873-907-103029. € 22.00.

QUID IUVAT AETERNITAS
SINE AMORE PRO IN AMORE SACRA!

CPSIA information can be obtained
at www.ICGtesting.com
Printed in the USA
LVHW042009130123
736977LV00013B/850

9 783907 103104